A Most Promising Weed

This series of publications on Africa, Latin America, and Southeast Asia is designed to present significant research, translation, and opinion to area specialists and to a wide community of persons interested in world affairs. The editor seeks manuscripts of quality on any subject and can generally make a decision regarding publication within three months of receipt of the original work. Production methods generally permit a work to appear within one year of acceptance. The editor works closely with authors to produce a high quality book. The series appears in a paperback format and is distributed worldwide. For more information, contact the executive editor at Ohio University Press, Scott Quadrangle, University Terrace, Athens, Ohio 45701.

Executive editor: Gillian Berchowitz
AREA CONSULTANTS
Africa: Diane Ciekawy
Latin America: Thomas Walker
Southeast Asia: William H. Frederick

A Most Promising Weed
A History of Tobacco Farming and Labor in Colonial Zimbabwe, 1890–1945

Steven C. Rubert

Ohio University Center for International Studies
Monographs in International Studies
Africa Series No. 69
Athens

The books in the Center for International Studies Monograph Series
are printed on acid-free paper ∞™

03 02 01 00 99 98   5 4 3 2 1

All photographs are reproduced by courtesy of the National Archives of Zimbabwe.

Library of Congress Cataloging-in-Publication Data

Rubert, Steven C., 1947–
    A most promising weed : a history of tobacco farming and labor in
colonial Zimbabwe, 1890–1945 / Steven C. Rubert.
        p.   cm. — (Monographs in international studies. Africa series
: no. 69)
    Includes bibliographical references (p.   ) and index.
    ISBN 0-89680-203-5 (pbk. : alk. paper)
    1. Tobacco workers—Zimbabwe—History.   2. Tobacco industry
—Zimbabwe—History.   I. Title.   II. Series
HD8039.T62Z557   1998
    338.1'7371'096891—dc21   98-19136
                                                                  CIP

Contents

Illustrations

Maps

Photographs

Tables

Preface

In his seminal study of the lives of working people in England, E. P. Thompson admonished historians to rescue the "casualties of history . . . from the enormous condescension of posterity."[1] His work challenged historians to look at those ordinary people in societies around the world who daily labored to produce wealth from which they rarely benefited. Few historical studies of labor in colonial Africa published before the early 1990s took up this challenge. Even in those instances when labor was the primary focus of a study authors generally examined either colonial administrators' efforts to mobilize indigenous labor or the formation of labor organizations. Still, these works served an important purpose by helping to clarify questions concerning both the means by which European capitalism penetrated Africa and the new forms that capitalist relations took in Africa. Nevertheless, by choosing to focus on those processes they largely ignored the direct experiences of African peoples who spent parts, or in some cases the entirety, of their lives as domestic servants, miners, railway workers, or farm laborers.[2] Frederick Cooper succinctly analyzed this problem when he wrote that those scholars rarely asked "what people do when they work, why they do it, and how workers and managers alike try to shape the pace, intensity, and quality of what gets done."[3] Many earlier historians of Southern Rhodesia also regularly

ix

failed to mention the conditions of labor experienced by tens of thousands of African workers.[4] Notable exceptions to this tendency have been the works of Charles van Onselen and Ian Phimister.[5] Together, these two historians demonstrated that labor history can be more than a concern with numbers of laborers, where they originated, and what legal and extralegal mechanisms were utilized to get them to the mines. In particular, van Onselen's *Chibaro: African Mine Labour in Southern Rhodesia, 1900–1933* is acknowledged by Africanists as a landmark study that illuminated the lives of male mine laborers. The publication of that study so successfully stimulated additional research on the mining industry in Southern Rhodesia and southern Africa, if not all regions of Africa, that mine labor became one of the primary models for investigating the development of capitalist relations in Africa.

Indeed, until recently the influence of *Chibaro* on the writing of African labor history was so great that other forms of labor in the southern Africa region were often overlooked. One result of this exclusionary trend has been that the lives of thousands of African men, women, and children who lived and worked on European-owned commercial farms in Southern Rhodesia during the period from 1890 to 1945 have been virtually ignored. *Table* 1 provides an idea of just how many people's work experiences are being overlooked:

TABLE 1
African Wage Labor in Southern Rhodesia

Year	Mining	Work Other Than Mining
1914	35,946	45,0
1925	39,644	107,56
1930	45,226	111,561
1935	77,383	127,239
1939	83,590	158,56
1943	78,590	232,112

As these numbers indicate, a majority of African peoples who were employed for wages in Southern Rhodesia during the first half of the twentieth century were employed at jobs other than mining. A large percentage worked on European farms. Except for the few materials published by Phimister, and introductory comments in two other works, however, there has not been a comprehensive evaluation of the work experiences of farm laborers in Southern Rhodesia during the period preceding the end of World War II.[7]

This study begins filling that void by examining the work, living conditions, and socioeconomic relationships of African laborers on tobacco farms in Southern Rhodesia. Special attention is given to the Lomagundi and Mazoe districts of Mashonaland, two of the principal tobacco-producing areas in Southern Rhodesia.[8] Tobacco farms present a unique environment for a historical study of ordinary Africans who entered the wage economy. Labor on European-owned tobacco farms merits attention for several reasons. Tobacco was, and continues to be, a labor-intensive crop to grow. In addition, tobacco farmers generally employed their laborers throughout most of the year. This was contrary to other types of European farmers, such as maize growers, who often gave extended leaves to a majority of their laborers between the planting and harvesting periods.[9] Growing tobacco was so labor demanding because, in the words of the 1935 *Handbook for the Use of Prospective Settlers*, "tobacco requires intensive cultivation and careful handling from the time the crop is transplanted until the leaf is ready for market."[10] The commonly accepted belief was that in order to grow a marketable crop on an average tobacco farm (fifty to sixty acres) a work force of at least sixty laborers was necessary.

Furthermore, over the course of the first half of the twentieth century flue-cured tobacco developed into Southern Rhodesia's most important agricultural export commodity and

therefore the linchpin of the colonial government's European
settler policy. The importance of an African labor force to the
maintenance of that particular industry and policy was immeasurable. For example, tobacco farmers often based their
decisions concerning how many acres to plant in tobacco on
the availability of labor.

This study covers the years between 1890 and 1945, a period of significance for Zimbabwe and its tobacco industry. In
1890 the British South Africa Company's Pioneer Column occupied the territory of Mashonaland in the northeastern portion of what is now Zimbabwe. Immediately on their arrival in
Mashonaland a number of column members commented on
the potential the territory had for European farming, including specifically tobacco. A few early settler-farmers grew tobacco in the 1890s, but it was not until 1904 that the first
Virginia tobacco was flue-cured in the country. The study cul-
minates in 1945, the year in which Virginia flue-cured tobacco
surpassed gold as the territory's leading export. In addition,
by the end of World War II, G. Arrighi noted, "the structure
of the Rhodesian economy had altered radically."[11] This was
particularly true for the tobacco industry. Beginning almost
immediately at the end of the war, both the number of growers
and the areas under production greatly increased. Thus, while
much of the labor process remained the same, the entire scale
of the industry changed. Tobacco farmers ceased to be undercapitalized, barely surviving from season to season, and as a
group became successful and wealthy. Tobacco laborers were
no longer primarily migrants but rather became a permanent
labor force on tobacco farms.[12]

A principal concept underpinning this study is that "work"
is more than the exertion of physical activity by a person on
material objects such as land and tobacco plants. Anthropolo-
gist Henrietta Moore makes this clear when she states that
"work is not just a matter of what people do because any defi-

nition must also include the conditions under which that work is performed, and its perceived social value or worth within a given cultural context." A result of research grounded in this concept is a history that focuses on workers, how they lived and their experiences in the workplace.[13] To meet the challenge presented by this concept a number of retired or semi-retired tobacco farm laborers were interviewed. The remembrances of these African men and women supplemented the correspondence, district court records, and other materials in which African "voices" are found in the holdings of the National Archives of Zimbabwe (NAZ), which give a voice to African laborers. In addition, I also talked to retired European tobacco farmers.

Chapters One and Two provide a historical overview of the development of Virginia flue-cured tobacco farming and examples of state support for European farmers. The remaining six chapters make up the primary focus of this study. They examine the structure of European-owned tobacco farms, the work experiences of the African men and women, and the social relations that developed among the people who labored on those farms in the decades before 1945.

Chapter Three describes the capitalization and physical environment of tobacco farms in Southern Rhodesia, while Chapter Four examines the labor process on those farms. In particular, this chapter describes the work performed by African tobacco workers. The primary purpose is to create a vivid picture of the physical toil workers experienced day-after-day on Southern Rhodesian tobacco farms. Chapter Five examines the methods tobacco farmers used to instill work discipline, and Chapter Six looks at the physical organization of laborers' compounds and the social relations that existed in those compounds. Chapter Seven discusses the role of African women on tobacco farms, particularly the importance of women's labor, both paid and unpaid, to farmers and male

laborers. The chapter also briefly examines the labor of children on tobacco farms. Finally, Chapter Eight examines the
development of a moral economy on farms, and the ideas of
what both growers and laborers expected. In addition, the
skills and knowledge laborers brought to wage employment
on farms, and how those assets helped shape their actions toward farmers, are discussed.

Acknowledgments

This study could not have been accomplished without the support and encouragement of many friends and colleagues. First, I need to thank Christopher Ehret for his guidance throughout my years of graduate study at the University of California, Los Angeles. I also extend my thanks to Edward Alpers, Richard Sklar, Allen Green and Sidney Lemelle. In addition I owe a particular debt of gratitude to Leslie Bessant and Elizabeth Schmidt, both of whom I first met in Zimbabwe, for allowing me to use field interviews they conducted.

I owe special thanks to many people in Zimbabwe. I will always appreciate the opportunity given to me by the Department of History at the University of Zimbabwe (UZ). It was during my appointment as a Research Associate in 1984 and 1985 that the majority of research presented in this study was accomplished. In addition, I want to thank the Department of Economic History for its assistance during my second trip to Zimbabwe in 1996. Specifically, Victor Machingaidze and Joseph Mtisi of the UZ Economic History Department shared their considerable insights into the economic and labor history of Zimbabwe, and their collegiality and friendship. The staff of the National Archives of Zimbabwe (NAZ) were both gracious and energetic in their assistance. In particular I want to thank the members of the NAZ staff working in the Photographic Collection. Their help in locating the historical photographs used in this study was immeasurable. All the photographs are, of course, used with the permission of the NAZ.

Students from both the 1985 History and 1996 Economic History Honours Seminars constantly inspired me with their limitless enthusiasm for their country's history. In particular, I must extend my sincere appreciation and special thanks to Oliver Masakura. His help during my 1996 research trip was invaluable. I also wish to express my gratitude to the library staff at the Kutsaga Tobacco Research Station. Finally, I cannot give enough thanks to the men and women who took time to talk to me about their experiences on tobacco farms during the period covered by this study.

This study also benefited tremendously from the assistance given by O. W. Ambali and A. Askemu of the National Archives of Malawi. The staffs at the Public Records Office in London and the Arendt Tobacco Collection at the New York Public Library were very helpful. I am also extremely grateful to my colleagues in the History Department at Oregon State University for their encouragement. In particular, I want to mention Jonathan Katz, for making time in his busy schedule to read and comment on the manuscript, and to Paul Farber. No one could ask for a more supportive department chairman. In addition, my 1996 research trip was partially funded by grants from the O.S.U. Library Research Travel Grants program and the L. L. Stewart Faculty Development Fund, O.S.U. Foundation, Corvallis, Oregon. I am very appreciative of that support.

I have no doubts that the assistance provided by all of those named above has helped me to develop a greater understanding of the history of colonial Zimbabwe, and the history of labor on tobacco farms in particular. The limits of this study are, of course, my own responsibility.

1

A Most Promising Weed

Tobacco from its very beginning has been more than a
crop; it has been rather a crucible in which the diverse
ingredients were mingled which brought . . . Southern
Rhodesia into being.[1]

The impetus for the Pioneer Column's 1890 invasion of the
territory that is today Zimbabwe was the mistaken belief that
the area held untold mineral wealth. By 1893 the directors of
the British South Africa Company (BSAC) were aware that the
expected gold reefs did not exist. By 1907 the company's directors had officially countenanced that there would be no
"Second Rand" and shifted policy toward the promotion and
support of settler capitalist agriculture. A "white agricultural
policy" of encouraging European settlement was then formulated, with settler agriculture geared to creating a "greater economic self-sufficiency, cutting the import bill, and raising the
value of the land."[2]

Most of the men who joined the Pioneer Column did so in
the hopes of staking out rich gold claims in the area north of
the Limpopo River. Despite this preoccupation with staking
gold claims, a number of the column's members, particularly
those who had some experience farming in South Africa immediately appreciated the "fertile and well-watered" lands surrounding their final encampment at the base of a large, rocky

1

hill (*kopje*), a site which they named Fort Salisbury (present-day Harare). According to one of their contemporaries, a few of these Pioneer Column participants "saw themselves in imagination comfortably housed with wife and chubby children, surrounded by countless herds, and growing tobacco, rice, mealies, potatoes."[3]

From the very beginning of their occupation of northeastern Zimbabwe some Europeans recognized the area's potential to support European farming. By September 1892 there were nearly 300 registered farms in the territory, with at least a few of those early farmers toying with the idea of growing tobacco commercially.[4] From that initial recognition of "fertile, well-watered" lands in Mashonaland commercial agriculture developed slowly. By the mid 1940s, it would surpass gold mining as the colony's primary industry. By 1918, commercial agriculture was largely committed to the growing of flue-cured tobacco.

The first European reported to have grown tobacco in the colony was a Jesuit priest named Father Boos, who supposedly grew a small crop at the Chishawasha Mission farm east of Salisbury in 1893. The following year Dunbar Moodie, who had received a grant of 20,000 acres in the eastern districts of Mashonaland from Cecil Rhodes, sent Salisbury ten rolls of tobacco he had grown as an experiment. The first European farmer known to have actually sold tobacco as a commercial crop was Lionel Cripps, who later became the first speaker of the Southern Rhodesian Legislative Assembly. In 1895 Cripps sold a little over fifty-seven pounds of tobacco, at fifty-four pence per pound, in Umtali. The crop Cripps sold was not "Virginia leaf," the type of tobacco commonly used in the production of cigarettes, but a type grown locally by indigenous Africans which was air-cured and had "a very coarse, heavy, dark leaf," and was probably used as pipe tobacco.[5] An 1897 BSAC Directors' Report stated that tobacco "occurs in a wild

state, is grown universally by the natives, and has been produced of excellent quality by white farmers in several districts."[6]

H. W. Roberts, who wrote a series of articles on the Southern Rhodesian tobacco industry in the early 1950s, claimed
that "Virginia leaf" tobacco was first grown in Southern Rhodesia before 1900.[7] This type of tobacco took its name from
the fact that the seeds used came from the state of Virginia in
the United States. Nevertheless, the first Virginia tobacco to
be flue-cured, a process in which leaves were dried by slowly
heating for several days in a special curing barn, was evidently
grown during the 1903/04 growing season by E. H. South on
his farm of Warwickshire, east of Salisbury. George Odlum,
who had been sent to the United States in 1903 by the Agriculture Department to learn about growing Virginia tobacco,
reported that South had obtained several varieties of seed from
the Ragland Seed Farm of South Boston, Virginia. South then
followed suggestions on planting and growing tobacco published by Odlum in the *Rhodesia Agricultural Journal* in 1903,
and produced a crop of Virginia tobacco. When Odlum returned to Southern Rhodesia in 1904 he found that South's
crop was nearly ready for reaping, and over the following
weeks South and Odlum harvested and flue-cured the crop in
a barn made of poles, blankets, and grass. The director of the
Department of Agriculture, which had been established at the
turn of the century, proved prophetic when he reported that
the "culture of this class of tobacco will be greatly extended."[8]

The success of South's crop encouraged both government
officials and European settlers. Officials hoped that tobacco
represented the type of export crop on which they could sustain
white agricultural policy. The year following South's success
William H. Milton, the BSAC's administrator for Southern
Rhodesia, stated that he was very pleased with "the advance
made during the past year in the prospects of the Tobacco

industry," and that the country had proven "eminently suitable" for the growing of tobacco. He told farmers that the BSAC had invited a British tobacco processing company to the colony "with a view to providing the necessary facilities for dealing with this product." He also said that if that company proved unwilling to build grading and storage warehouses, BSAC was prepared to undertake the cost itself "in time to enable growers to take advantage of the next ensuing season."[9] In 1906, the agriculture department was optimistic to the point of announcing that the "future of the Rhodesian tobacco industry may now be regarded as assured," while three years later, a contemporary observer reported that "tobacco may already be considered an established industry."[10]

For the few settlers who grew tobacco (in 1904, there were about 100, out of a total European population of 23,606), the crop represented the possibility of quick riches that they believed could be made from growing one marketable crop for a

E. H. South at the entrance to Southern Rhodesia's first flue-curing tobacco barn, 1903.

few years.[11] This view was mirrored in a 1911 agriculture department report that stated "a great merit of tobacco is that with less capital than in other forms of farming, and in a comparatively short time after commencing operations, it is possible to secure a good return."[12]

This statement highlights one of the recurrent problems which plagued the European agricultural community for most of the period before 1945: speculation. Phimister accurately described the general situation when stating that in the "broadest outline, white agriculture comprised a mass of small, undercapitalized farmers around a core of big concerns." He went on to emphasize that the majority of the colony's early "farmers tended to rush from crop to different crop in search of elusive riches." This pattern plagued the agricultural sector and "imparted an extraordinary volatile element to the volume of production and aggravated the highly uneven productivity of the sector as a whole."[13] This tendency was particularly true for the tobacco industry, which was marked by cyclical periods of expansion, overproduction, and retrenchment. The initial period of expansion occurred between 1910 and 1914 and was largely the result of Southern Rhodesian tobacco being accepted into the South African market and being granted an exemption from customs duties in 1910. During the 1913/14 growing season tobacco acreage increased from roughly 1,700 acres to 5,627 acres.[14] Nevertheless, the year was marked by both massive overproduction and low-quality tobacco, and the selling price dropped below the costs of production for many farmers. The drop in price drove many tobacco farmers out of business, with total acreage decreasing to 1,310 acres during the 1915/16 season.[15]

Following World War I, the industry stabilized and slowly began to expand again. In 1917/18, tobacco farmers planted 2,434 acres and produced 415,210 pounds of Virginia flue-cured tobacco, and by the 1922/23 season 388 farmers grew

2,540,942 pounds of tobacco on a total of 7,758 acres. Those numbers increased to 5,313,168 pounds produced by 672 farmers on 13,160 acres during the 1925/26 growing season.[16] This period of expansion was largely due to the British government granting an imperial preference to Southern Rhodesian tobacco in 1919, and increasing that in 1925. The original preference waived one-sixth of the duty payable on tobacco, and the 1925 increase raised the total amount waived to 25 percent of the payable duty. In addition, no limit was set on the amount of tobacco that Southern Rhodesia could export to Britain. The imperial preference helped make Southern Rhodesian tobacco more competitive with tobacco grown in the United States, Britain's primary source of Virginia flue-cured tobacco during this period. Production was again stimulated in 1927 when the Imperial Tobacco Company built a plant in Salisbury to process tobacco for export.[17] The future was looking bright. It appeared to government officials and tobacco farmers alike that they had at last secured a market for all the tobacco they could produce. Their high level of optimism was underscored on 17 August 1927 when L. S. Amery, the British Secretary of State for Dominion Affairs, told Rhodesian tobacco growers at the opening of that year's Salisbury Agriculture Show that processing companies in Britain could "take six, or eight or ten times as much as you produce at this moment before our market is anything like filled up."[18]

Despite warnings that Amery's statement was overly sanguine scores of new tobacco farms were started. The 672 tobacco farmers of 1925/26 increased in the following season to 763, with total production increasing to over 18 million pounds. The year after that saw 987 growers produce over 24 million pounds of tobacco, even though the great majority were certainly aware that not all of the previous year's crop had been sold. Even as the 1927/28 crop was being harvested, it was apparent that overproduction would swamp the market and

TABLE 2

Southern Rhodesian Virginia Tobacco Yields, 1917–45 (in pounds)[19]

Year	Yields
1917	415,210
1918	1,179,932
1919	2,435,994
1920	3,192,662
1921	2,880,104
1922	2,540,942
1923	3,426,390
1924	1,987,382
1925	5,313,168
1926	18,631,069
1927	24,201,201
1928	6,704,936
1929	5,494,063
1930	3,268,926
1931	14,448,440
1932	13,777,286
1933	26,097,888
1934	20,472,648
1935	21,717,898
1936	21,300,000
1937	26,168,259
1938	22,500,000
1939	35,066,798
1940	35,582,549
1941	46,579,011
1942	30,338,798
1943	32,103,738
1944	47,523,663
1945	42,327,225

that prices would plummet. Once again, hundreds of tobacco farmers were forced into bankruptcy and at the beginning of the 1928/29 season there were only 272 registered growers, with overall production for that season dropping to less than 6 million pounds.[20] One farmer who survived that 1928 season remembered advertisements in the press which offered tobacco farms in exchanged for "a push-bicycle in fit condition to get . . . to the border." He added that "people were leaving the country wholesale."[21]

As a result of the 1928 crash, Southern Rhodesian government officials accepted the idea that tobacco growers would not regulate themselves. The government recognized that if the disastrous cycles of expansion and retrenchment were to be stopped it was absolutely necessary that it intervene and assume the responsibility for regulating the industry. To accomplish this, the government, over a period of eight years, passed a series of acts aimed at stabilizing production and marketing, and improving the product itself. The first of these acts, the 1930 Tobacco Sale and Export Control Act, created a Tobacco Control Board and compelled all tobacco growers to register with the board. In 1933, the Tobacco Levy Act placed a preset levy on all tobacco produced in the country, with the funds raised to be used to finance the Tobacco Control Board's activities. The Tobacco Reserve Pool Act of 1934 was designed to control both the quantity and, in particular, quality of tobacco production by requiring growers to place part of their crops in board-controlled pools. The act also authorized the board to inspect and grade all tobacco placed in the pools. If the quality of the crop did not meet the board's high standards, the tobacco was rejected and the grower could lose his registration, which meant he would not be allowed to sell his tobacco crop. In an attempt to improve overall quality, the 1935 Tobacco Research Act established the Tobacco Research

Board, which was entrusted with improving the tobacco produced in the colony.

Once these various acts were in place, the government formulated and passed the most important piece of legislation effecting the industry, the Tobacco Marketing Act of 1936. This act superseded the 1930 Sale and Export Control Act and replaced the Tobacco Control Board with the Tobacco Marketing Board. It also mandated the compulsory selling of all tobacco at Marketing Board operated auction floors. In addition, it compelled all growers to register with the board and empowered it to establish sales quotas for each registered farmer. The new Tobacco Marketing Board was also given the responsibility of searching out and establishing new overseas markets.[22]

This series of regulatory acts effectively ended the problem of speculative tobacco farming which had so strongly contributed to the roller coaster aspect of the industry before 1930. The next ten years witnessed a period in which production levels stabilized and overall tobacco quality improved.[23] In response to the legislative regularization of the industry, the number of growers slowly increasing from a low of 272 in 1929, to 419 in 1936, and 796 in 1945. In addition, total production increased from a low of almost 5 million pounds in 1930 to over 46 million pounds in the 1944/45 season. During this period tobacco accounted for the greatest percentage of the country's total agricultural exports, averaging approximately 45 percent for most of the 1930s.[24]

World War II had a sweeping impact on the tobacco growing industry of Southern Rhodesia. British manufacturers were largely cut off from the United States, their primary source of tobacco, and began to import more and more Southern Rhodesian tobacco. As a result, production increased rapidly, more than doubling from 1939 to 1945, and became the colony's top export in terms of value, the first product of any kind to surpass gold as Southern Rhodesia's leading export commodity.[25] The war also marked the end of the idea of people entering the industry for only a few years, possessing little knowledge and even less capital. As the *Rhodesia Herald* editorialized in December 1945: "The war mark[ed] definitely the end of one stage of Rhodesian farming and the beginning of another. Instead of the muddling of the past, there will have to be much more system and more individual knowledge. . . . there is no room for the squatter farmer who has low standards . . . and surprising ignorance."[26]

Lomagundi District—"The Land of Stumping"[27]

Lomagundi was a huge district before 1945, covering most of the northwestern half of Mashonaland Province. The majority of the district was part of the central plateau that separates the two great rivers of south-central Africa, the Zambezi and the Limpopo, and was crisscrossed with numerous rivers. This area was in the "high veld," averaging over 4,000 feet above sea level. The northern area of the district, along the Zambezi River, usually received less than 24 inches of rain annually, while its central core area, which extended northwest from Salisbury for nearly 150 kilometers, averaged between 32 and 40 inches annually.[28] Large areas in the southern half of the district were "of excellent alluvial soil, dark chocolate, red and black, interspersed with sandstone ridges, kopjes, and hills," and were generally considered excellent for growing Virginia flue-cured tobacco. Following the 1930 Land Apportionment Act, this southern part of Lomagundi was largely reserved for European settlement, while most of the northern half was designated for African reserves.[29]

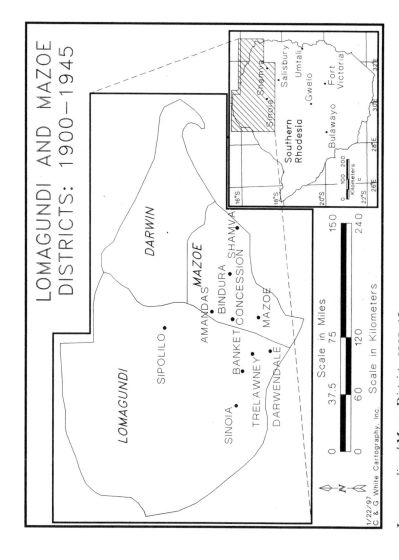

Lomagundi and Mazoe Districts, 1900–45

The first permanent European settlement in the district was established in 1895 approximately 115 kilometers northwest of Salisbury. The settlement, Sinoia (present-day Chinhoyi), eventually became the administrative center for the district. Most of the first Europeans in the district were transient prospectors. Nevertheless, the agricultural potential of the region was not lost on early government officials and in 1898 the area's first native commissioner noted that "agriculturally speaking, the district is an admirable one." He added that the "ground and climate admit the growing of two crops off the same land every year."[30] The district's first farm was developed at the Ayrshire Mine, near the hamlet of Banket, in the mid 1890s in order to grow maize for the mine's African labor force. In 1899, Cecil Rhodes granted Otto Christian Zimmerman (later know as O. C. Rawson) a land grant of 3,000 acres in the southern end of Lomagundi, and in the following year Zimmerman started the Darwendale Farm. After that the establishment of additional farms was slow and by 1904 there were only five active farmers in the district. Five years later, however, the native commissioner reported that "a large number of farms have been taken up by Europeans during the year."[31]

Two years after that, in 1911, the area's European population continued to increase following "a great influx" of settlers into the district. The district surgeon, however, estimated that the total European population of the district, some 700 in 1912, was made up primarily of miners and government officials. The district's European farming community increased more slowly, numbering only about 200 in 1914.[32] After the war that situation changed. The native commissioner's annual report of 1921 stated that "the farming community has spread very far afield during the year, land being taken up in all directions."[33] By 1926, there were 407 settlers in the district who listed their occupations in that year's census as "farmer," or as being otherwise employed in some aspect of farming.[34]

The settler farming population in the district continued to increase over the next few years, until the 1928 crash drove a large number of farmers out of business, with many abandoning the district altogether. From the early 1930s through the mid 1940s, the district once again experienced steady and increasing European occupation. Most of that growth occurred as a result of the expansion of the tobacco farming industry, with Lomagundi emerging as one of the top tobacco-producing districts in the colony between the mid 1920 and 1945.[35]

It is difficult to say when Virginia tobacco was first grown by Europeans in the district. When responding to the 1911 census, only ten farmers in the district stated that they grew tobacco.[36] The following year the department of agriculture noted that "tobacco is being more widely grown each year, and is gaining grown [sic] in . . . Lomagundi district."[37] In 1913 several farms listed for sale in the region around Sinoia were referred to as suitable for tobacco, and by the early 1920s tobacco began to be more extensively grown by established farmers in the area around Banket. The rising prices that followed the increase in the Imperial Preference stimulated settlement in the areas around both Banket and Darwendale, and led to the opening up of new farms in Trelawney (see map 1).[38]

The 1928 crash had a severe effect on the district, although a short-lived one in comparison to those in other districts of the colony. Despite government assistance, farmers in the district who had grown only tobacco found themselves in financial straits and many ended up losing their farms.[39] On the other hand, by 1931 a number of areas in the district began to show signs of recovery. The native commissioner reported that there seemed to be a greater demand for African laborers in November and December of that year "owing chiefly to a revival of activity in tobacco planting." The following year he stated that the previous year's indications of recovery were continuing, noting that this had been marked by "the return of a number of tobacco farmers to their farms." By the late 1930s, total acreage planted in tobacco was increasing above the 1927/28 levels, with the Banket to Sinoia region of the district being "largely devoted to tobacco farming."[40]

Mazoe District—"The Best Land in Rhodesia"[41]

Located directly north of Salisbury, Mazoe district was approximately one-third the size of Lomagundi, its neighbor to the west. The district was in a region that received 32–40 inches of rainfall annually, and rarely suffered prolonged dry spells. By the early 1920s Mazoe had also developed into one of Southern Rhodesia's top tobacco-producing areas, even though most of the district had heavy clay loam soils, which were not as productive for growing flue-cured tobacco as the sandy loams of Lomagundi.[42]

From the earliest European occupation of the region Mazoe attracted the interest of a number of Europeans, but like its neighboring district the great majority were transient pro-

TABLE 3
Tobacco Acreage, Lomagundi and Mazoe Districts, 1925–45[43]

	Lomagundi	Mazoe	Southern Rhodesia Total Production
1924–25	982	1,655	8,441
1929–30	2,645	2,849	10,468
1934–35	12,985	11,672	41,006
1939–40	17,064	12,107	59,957
1944–45	18,234	12,858	71,047

spectors. By the mid-1890s there were only a handful of European residents in the district and half of them were working at either the Alice or Jumbo mines north of Salisbury.[44] European activities in those early days were centered around the hamlet of Mazoe, where a small British South Africa Police (BSAP) outpost and the local native commissioner's station were located.[45]

Although some farms had been staked out in Mazoe district prior to 1900, this was apparently done more with an eye to securing land that could be prospected at a later time than to establishing working farms. The first European attempt at farming in the district was by a group of ten settlers, who took up six separate farms in the vicinity of "Moore's Concession," north of Mazoe, in 1901. The ten settlers included three sets of brothers: Gilmoor, Charles, and E. R. Southey; Edgar, Noel and H. H. Marriott; and S. and W. Biggs. The two remaining individuals, R. C. Firth and A. R. Morkel, were in partnership with the Biggs brothers.[46] In 1903 the district's native commissioner stated that farming in Mazoe was continuing "to make headway," and in 1907 the minute book of the Mazoe Farmers' Association noted that there were "over fifty bona fide farmers" in the district.[47]

Virginia tobacco apparently began to be introduced into Mazoe sometime around the turn of the century. The earliest report of growing tobacco in the district comes from L. H. Gann, who mentions that a Dr. Sketchley in the Mazoe Valley, grew a small crop of tobacco in the 1890s.[48] In 1925, Morkel stated that of the ten 1901 settlers, R. C. Firth was the only one interested in growing tobacco. He went on to note that by 1904 "tobacco, under the able advice of Mr. G. M. Odlum, came and stayed. Barns were erected, and a promising side line helped the needy farmer to augment his hitherto scant income."[49] In 1907, H. H. Marriott, a Mazoe resident, won a

£75 prize at the Salisbury Agriculture Show for his "bright leaf of the Virginia type." In the following year, R. Gavin of Mazoe was awarded the same amount for growing the "best crop of leaf grown from American seed, weighing 5,000 pounds and over."[50] In April 1908, the Mazoe native commissioner claimed that nearly "thirty-three percent of the farmers have grown tobacco in this district during this season." He also stated that the general belief held by all farmers in the district was that "the crop is one of the most remunerative which can be grown." In his annual report written later in the year, however, he reported that "tobacco seems to have been put on one side for the present," the farmers having voluntarily reduced production as a result of a dispute with tobacco buyers. At that time, such buyers often bought tobacco directly from the farmers, and the Mazoe growers seem to have believed that the buyers had too much control over the market.[51]

Sources from the next decade point to a slow but steady expansion of farming in Mazoe district, but do not specifically mention tobacco growing. It can be assumed, however, that tobacco production picked up to some degree during the 1910–14 boom period and that farmers who were growing tobacco as their primary crop suffered financially from the 1914 crash. As with other tobacco growing districts, there was probably not much expansion of tobacco acreage during World War I. By 1920, however, the Mazoe native commissioner commented that "tobacco is being more extensively grown."[52] In May of that year the *Rhodesia Herald* reported that the Mazoe Farmers' Association had requested that the government tobacco expert schedule a visit to the district because "many farmers in the Mazoe district were growing tobacco . . . for the first time."[53] If he did visit, his journey from Salisbury over pothole-ridden dirt roads was not in vain for at the end of the 1922/23 growing season Mazoe ranked as the top Virginia leaf producing district in the colony, and it remained one of the top four producing districts until the 1928 crash.[54] A primary reason for the district's rise to prominence in the early 1920s was the expansion of tobacco farming into the Umvukwes region of northwestern Mazoe. The Umvukwes were "pre-eminently suited for producing the finest quality tobacco," John Macdonald claimed in the *Rhodesia Herald*, adding that it "would be folly to dream of touching any other" crop in that locality.[55]

Tobacco farmers in Mazoe district suffered the same consequences as their colleagues in other tobacco-growing districts

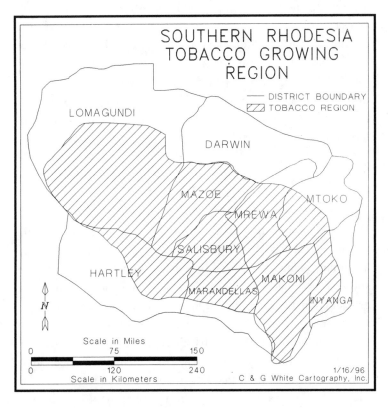

Southern Rhodesia's Tobacco Growing Region

following the 1928 tobacco market crash. Some were driven into bankruptcy while those who were able to keep their farms were forced to drastically reduce their tobacco production, which then remained at a low level for about five years. In 1930 the district commissioner reported that tobacco farmers had "reduced [their] labourers to the lowest possible minimum, in fact at times one is forced to the opinion that the farms cannot be worked satisfactorily."[56] By the time of the 1933 annual report, however, the native commissioner noted with some optimism that the total acreage under tobacco was beginning to increase. By the end of the 1934/35 growing season, the district had regained its position as one of the top tobacco producing areas and maintained a steady level of production of high-quality tobacco throughout the remainder of that decade. "Of course, when the war came in 1939/40," commented H. J. Quinton, who began growing tobacco on his uncle's farm in the Umvukwes during the 1920s, "expansion of the tobacco industry started in real earnest and never really looked back."[57]

Labor Supplies

During this brief introduction to the development of Virginia flue-cured tobacco farming in Southern Rhodesia, reference to a primary element required by settler farmers if they were to succeed as tobacco growers has not been mentioned. That crucial element was the need for African labor. Tobacco farmers in Southern Rhodesia benefited from their location at the northern end of southern Africa's regional economic system. This was particularly true for tobacco farmers in the Lomagundi and Mazoe districts. For example, there were two primary labor migration routes from the north and they passed through the tobacco growing regions of Lomagundi and

Mazoe. The first, which eventually funneled labor migrants
through Lomagundi, ran from northern Nyasaland to Fort
Jameson in Northern Rhodesia, then south toward Salisbury.
The second originated in southern Nyasaland, then went
south through the province of Tete in northwestern Mozambique, then southwest to Mtoko and on to Salisbury.[58] Therefore, partly as a result of their location, and partly owing to
the reluctance of the local Shona peoples to work on European-owned farms, the majority of "voluntary" labor in the
two districts was comprised of Africans from Nyasaland and

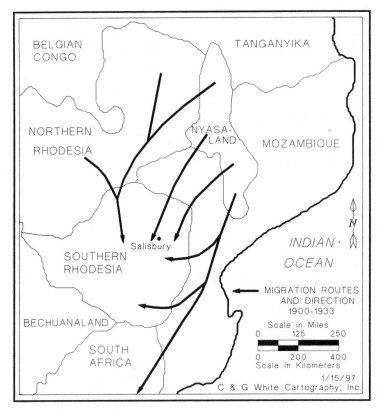

Labor Migration Routes

Mozambique. Farms in the two districts also attracted migrants by providing them with an opportunity to replenish supplies and earn cash that was necessary for them to continue south.[59]

As early as 1899 a Mazoe native commissioner reported to his superiors that a "great number of Portuguese natives have passed through" the district, although due to the scarcity of farms in the district at that time, his observation could only portend the possibility of adequate supplies of labor for farmers in future years. That same year the native commissioner for Lomagundi reported large numbers of northern Africans passing through that district in search of work.[60] Nevertheless, it was not until the end of the next decade that annual reports from the two districts began to mention laborers working on farms. The Mazoe native commissioner commented in 1908 that "up to November and December there was a fair supply of labour . . . both on farms and mines. Nearly all the labour is from the North."[61] The following year, the Lomagundi native commissioner's annual report not only mentioned farm labor for the first time but also noted that the "supply of Nyasaland farm labourers is . . . an especial boon to this district."[62]

2

Salisbury Lends a Hand

That our Government has been alive to the importance of
fostering the farming industry by all the means in its
power and . . . to the limit of its financial resources has
never been seriously in doubt.[1]

In addition to suitable soil and barns, the culture of tobacco demands technical knowledge, experience, dogged
application and some capital.[2]

"Dogged application" to a chosen task is, of course, determined by an individual's character and cannot be dispensed by
any government. Technical knowledge, capital, and even some
degree of experience, on the other hand, can be provided. In
the case of Southern Rhodesia, if the white agricultural policy
was to succeed it was necessary for the state to assist settler
farmers with financial and technical assistance programs.
These programs covered such diverse activities as reimburs-
ing farmers for cartridges used during hunts to rid farms of
baboons, digging boreholes, purchasing capital goods, establishing an agricultural college to provide "a sound agricultural education to the sons of settlers, and to others who may

desire to become settlers in the country," and publishing journals like the *Native Affairs Department Annual* and the *Rhodesia Agricultural Journal.* The *Native Affairs Department Annual* disseminated a variety of information concerning local African peoples, including items "employers needed to know . . . so that they could get the best value out of African labour," while the *Rhodesia Agricultural Journal* informed farmers about government-sponsored agronomic experiments, new farming practices and the most up-to-date farming equipment.[3]

As members of the Southern Rhodesian European farming community, tobacco farmers benefited from these and other government-sponsored programs throughout the period from 1890 to 1945. They were, in addition, the primary beneficiaries of a number of programs promulgated by the state to support the tobacco industry specifically. Three such programs were the payment of African laborers' wages following the 1928 crash of the tobacco market; crop experimentation; and the Southern Rhodesia Free Migrant Labour Transport Service, better known to African laborers by the Nyanja word for "free"—*Ulere.*[4]

State-Sponsored Financial Assistance Programs

> The object of agricultural credit is to enable farmers to
> borrow the necessary funds for their work on easy terms
> of repayment. . . . From the national point of view the
> object is to stimulate the occupation, cultivation, and im-
> provement of agricultural land.[5]

Financial assistance to settlers for the specific purpose of establishing and developing farms in Southern Rhodesia began with BSAC's decision in 1907 to institute the white agriculture policy. In 1908, BSAC established the Estates Department to provide crown lands to prospective settlers and to assist their migration to the territory. The 1925 Empire Settlement Scheme later extended this practice by subsidizing the passage expenses of new settlers' from Great Britain, paying already established farmers to train recent arrivals, providing low interest loans to purchase land, and advancing operating capital for improvements to farm infrastructure. In 1929 the settler government initiated the Contributory Purchase Scheme to help settlers buy farms on privately owned lands. This scheme "gave settlers with limited capital an alternative to Crown land farms, and contributed to bringing some of the 'idle' privately-held land into production."[6]

One of the primary agencies for financial assistance to farmers during this period was the Land Bank, which was first established in 1912 with an operating capital of £250,000. It was authorized to make loans of up to £2,000 at 6 percent interest. Loans could be used to purchase land or buy capital equipment and had to be repaid within ten years, with payments due at six-month intervals. Mr. M. Olive, the bank's first manager, stated that the goal of the bank was "to help the [European] farming community . . . to acquire or improve their holdings."[7] In addition to this somewhat altruistic reason, the BSAC had other reasons for providing financial assistance to prospective European farmers. For example, the company profited directly through sales of land and increased revenues from both customs duties and railway fees, since it owned all the rail lines over which supplies and increased agricultural exports had to travel.[8]

In 1924, the newly established settler government took over the responsibility for supporting settlers. In part it accomplished this by creating the Land and Agriculture Bank of Southern Rhodesia (which was also commonly known as the Land Bank). The new bank was initially capitalized at £300,000, but that amount grew rapidly to £970,000 by 1930, and provided farmers with shorter term loans than the original bank. One advantage for farmers was that loans could be secured with more "shaky" collateral, usually the next year's crop, as compared to the BSAC's Land Bank, which only accepted capital property as collateral. As a result of the more relaxed procedures, the new bank provided both a greater number and a higher total value amount of loans than the earlier Land Bank.[9]

Loans from both banks were available to any farmer in Southern Rhodesia that met minimum requirements, irrespective of which crop they specialized in growing, but two additional programs were developed for the direct assistance of tobacco growers following the 1928 collapse of the tobacco market. The first program was designed to help tobacco farmers "tide over the difficult period" and to eventually "continue production on a smaller scale with caution." Many members of the Legislative Assembly supported this bill because they believed that the survival of tobacco farming was at stake and that it was "a matter of National Importance" to secure financial relief for tobacco growers. In March 1928, O. C. DuPont, secretary to the minister of Agriculture and Lands, made clear that "the State was ready to take some, even great, risk in giving this assistance" to growers.[10]

Four months later the assembly authorized the treasury department to begin paying advances to tobacco farmers through the auspices of the Land Bank. Advances of 5p per pound of cured tobacco were paid to farmers for tobacco delivered to the Rhodesia Tobacco Warehouse in Salisbury. The advances were meant to allow farmers to pay merchants' bills, mortgage payments, and other operating expenses until their tobacco had been sold, whereupon the advances would be subtracted from the final sale price, with the difference paid to the farmer. Under this legislation, payments were also made to the Rhodesia Tobacco Warehouse for expenses it incurred in erecting additional storage facilities and attempting to market the surplus tobacco. Over the next two years the warehouse sold most of the surplus tobacco, although largely at prices below the cost of production. The eventual cost of this government largesse was estimated at £708,317, of which £194,500 was eventually written off as an "irrecoverable" loss.[11]

The second financial program specifically designed for the benefit of tobacco growers was promulgated in late 1928 and addressed a growing concern over the impact of unpaid wages owed to tobacco farm laborers. This program was in some ways a response to the first, as tobacco farmers ostensibly used most of their advances to pay at least portions of their debts to European creditors. As a result, a large number of growers then had insufficient funds remaining to pay their African laborers' wages.[12]

Farmers and state officials alike feared that if laborers were not paid, those farmers still operating would be unable to convince laborers to stay for the upcoming 1928/29 season. This concern was noted when the Amandas assistant native commissioner reported that "the problem in regard to Native wages in the Umvukwe area . . . is rapidly becoming worse and it would appear necessary to take some action to ensure some, at least, of the money owed being paid to the native labourers in that area before they leave their employers."[13] Other government officials agreed and argued that without government assistance tobacco farmers like R. J. Searle faced legal action by his unpaid workers. As the nonpayment of contracted wages was a legal debt, the workers would win and a judgment for the full amount (nearly £114) could force Searle to be "sold up, his home broken up and he will have to leave the Colony."[14]

Government officials were willing to pay these outstanding wages for two principle reasons. First, it was feared that the prospect of attracting sufficient labor in the future would be greatly harmed, thereby endangering the future of the tobacco industry. That would have directly threatened individual tobacco farmers as well as the state's policy of maintaining a European community based on commercial agriculture, which was increasingly pinned to tobacco.[15] Second, government officials were equally concerned that there might be additional repercussions that could affect all employers in the country. Sir Ernest Montague, a member of the Legislative Assembly, said that if "the native labour is not paid . . . it may result in a national catastrophe. If boys come down to this country and their money is not forthcoming, it affects the whole country, and the country gets a bad name. The boys go back to their homes and say that they have not been paid . . . and they do not differentiate between the tobacco growers or the mealie growers or any other form of industry."[16] These concerns were apparently well founded. In an account from September 1928, a farm worker from Nyasaland, speaking for a group of fellow northern workers, told the Mazoe native commissioner: "We have asked for our wages many times, we are told to wait. We have waited, and we have got nothing. . . . What is the good of waiting for something that never comes? We want to go to our homes, as we cannot get our money and we shall never come back here to work."[17]

In response to these conditions, Premier H. U. Moffat agreed in November 1928 that the Southern Rhodesian government would advance "the amounts to enable the wages of the employees to be paid in cases where no funds are available and after careful enquiry into each case."[18] The money was provided directly from Treasury funds and was administered by the office of the Chief Native Commissioner. Although the initial program was to pay only those wages earned prior to August 31, 1928, the government kept it going at reduced levels until the outbreak of World War II. It did so in an attempt to maintain the country's "good name" among foreign laborers.[19]

"Nothing Can Be Fully Determined Without Experiments"[20]

[I]mprovements will be made through the medium of plant breeding and improved methods of curing, and experiments in these directions call for skilled control and the expenditure of considerable money and thus are not within the reach of the planter.[21]

Throughout the period 1890–1945 tobacco growers continually called on the colonial state to provide them with technical assistance to improve the quality and quantity of the tobacco they grew. In 1910, for example, the newly formed Rhodesia Tobacco Planters' Association asked that the Agriculture Department provide an expert adviser who would travel to the country's tobacco growing areas to deliver lectures to farmers' associations covering the latest knowledge on tobacco growing, and visit individual farmers to answer specific questions regarding growing tobacco on their farms.[22] In 1922, Trevor Fletcher, president of the Rhodesia Tobacco Co-operative Society, expressed the desires of many tobacco farmers when he called for the government to establish an experimental farm. According to a *Rhodesia Herald* article, the farm would examine problems such as how the "altitude of the country and the dry climate" affected the tobacco crop and what new varieties were suited to the colony.[23] By the mid 1930s, farmers wanted the government to sponsor experiments for the "alteration of the leaf so that it more nearly approximates the American."[24]

These statements were founded in the belief that a local variety, similar in taste to American-grown tobacco, could capture a greater share of the British market from the United States, Britain's top supplier. Tobacco farmers also hoped that new higher yielding varieties could be developed so that production could be increased without clearing new lands. They could then expand overall production and increase their profits, without drastically increasing costs. The colonial state responded positively to these requests from tobacco farmers, with leaders of both the BSAC administration and the settler government willingly supporting technical assistance projects as part of their general support for programs that fortified the white agricultural policy. They also funded programs that provided training for newly arrived immigrants so that they had a rudimentary knowledge of farming in Southern Rhodesia before they took up their own farms.

Tobacco research programs went through three phases from the 1890s to 1945. Prior to 1907, the BSAC's support consisted of sending an agriculture department official, George Odlum, to the United States and Turkey to learn about methods for growing tobacco. He published what he had learned in articles in the *Rhodesia Agricultural Journal* and in a book, *The Culture of Tobacco*, published by the BSAC in 1905 and provided to prospective settlers. Although Odlum spoke to meetings of farmers and frequently visited individual farmers, his actual work was confined to making suggestions and occasionally assisting with work on farms growing tobacco. During this first phase, the Agriculture Department conducted field research on tobacco and other crops at a small research station north of Salisbury. This early research, however, was limited and not very systematic.[25]

The second phase of tobacco research occurred between 1907 and the mid 1920s. Research programs in this period tended to focus on questions of which varieties produced the highest yields under local growing conditions, how to produce quality local seed, the eradication of insect pests, and the most efficient methods for flue-curing tobacco.[26] The country's first systematic tobacco research took place during the beginning of the period at the BSAC's Central Land Settlement Farm. The farm was located near Marandellas, southeast of Salisbury, and was managed by H. K. Scorror. In addition to tobacco research Scorror also experimented with citrus fruit and cattle breeding, and helped train newly arrived settlers. His tobacco experiments tended to focus on soil types, the use of manure, optimum spacing of seedlings, and curing. By 1910, these experiments had been so successful that the BSAC decided to expand the farm's tobacco acreage and grow it, and other crops, commercially. With the implementation of that decision the farm ceased to be a training and research center and became a working farm.[27]

With the closing of the Marandellas farm as a research station the agriculture department began to supervise a program in which individual tobacco farmers ran experiments on their farms. Their work focused almost exclusively on the use of fertilizers, and how to eradicate insects and plant diseases. In 1912, the department appointed J. W. Lewis to assist the farmers with these experiments, and, in 1913, compiled its findings in *A Handbook of Tobacco Culture for the Planters of Southern Rhodesia.*[28] Lewis was succeeded by H. W. Taylor in 1918, who bore the new title of tobacco and cotton expert. Taylor served in that position until 1925, when he was succeeded by D. D. Brown (who served until 1950).

Under Taylor the BSAC established a new agricultural research center in 1922 at the Virginia Farm in Mazoe district. The majority of experiments conducted at the farm were concerned with improving the yield and quality of tobacco plants. Two years later, the new settler government opened an additional research station in Salisbury. The Hillside Tobacco Experimental Station there was the first center exclusively for tobacco research. In its first year of operation 28 plots, covering 15 acres, were cultivated. The following year there were 96 plots on 40 acres. During those first two years, "special

attention" was given to "problems connected with tobacco
rotations, green manuring and the use of fertilizers; also to variety trials and method of planting and 'topping' tests."[29] This
systematic, scientific research marked the third phase of gov-
ernment-supported tobacco cultivation in Southern Rhodesia.
By the early 1930s, while earlier questions remained important, researchers began to focus more on improving plant
qualities such as taste, aroma, burning capability, and other
leaf characteristics so that the tobacco produced conformed
more closely to the general standards required by British to-
bacco-manufacturing companies.[30] In the years that followed,
the government opened two additional tobacco research stations, at Marandellas in 1929 (closed in 1931 for financial reasons), and at Trelawney in 1934. As mentioned previously, in
1935 the Tobacco Research Act placed all tobacco research
under the direction of the Tobacco Research Advisory Board.
It was empowered to direct the operations of the country's tobacco research stations and place tobacco research on a "more
satisfactory basis, enabling it to be conducted in such a manner as to be of maximum benefit to the industry." This aim
was accomplished primarily by expanding the research station
at Trelawney.[31]

The Ulere Motor Transport System

> The Government's most significant contribution lay in the
> provision of assistance to facilitate the passage of "inde-
> pendent" migrants from the north . . . to provide suffi-
> cient unskilled labour for the colony's expanding economic
> enterprises.[32]

The *Ulere* motor transport system was unique in that it was
the first state-sponsored motor vehicle transportation system
to operate between the territories of the two Rhodesias and

Nyasaland. It was also part of a long series of attempts by the state to address a complaint heard from most employers in Southern Rhodesia: the shortage of labor. In 1899, for example, the native commissioner of Lomagundi reported that local European employers were finding it "difficult to get boys to work for more than one or two months at a time, which is unfortunate."[33] In a 1911 letter to the editor of the *Rhodesia Herald*, a Mazoe district farmer described the labor shortages facing local farmers as "one of our institutions."[34] Fourteen years later the Rhodesia Agricultural Union referred to the labor shortages faced by farmers as "hardy annuals."[35] In 1943, the chairman of the Rhodesia Tobacco Association "thought it was time that the Government [be] forced . . . to take more active steps in regard to the labour supply for the future."[36] The state's financial assistance and research programs meant nothing to farmers if they lacked the laborers to transplant, cultivate, and perform numerous other tasks required to produce a tobacco crop.

Tobacco farmers were, of course, not the only group of employers faced with the problem of procuring adequate labor supplies. Therefore, it was necessary for the Southern Rhodesian state to support a variety of labor-procuring programs in attempts to meet the demands of all the country's employers. Van Onselen has detailed the creation and operation of the Rhodesia Native Labour Bureau (RNLB) in its various incarnations. Although the RNLB was initially meant to provide labor primarily for the mining industry, it also provided recruited *chibaro* workers to farmers, eventually providing more laborers to farmers than to any other single group of employers.[37] In addition to the RNLB, Southern Rhodesia also entered into several agreements between 1913 and 1935 with the Portuguese authorities in neighboring Mozambique, attempting to guarantee that labor from that territory went only to the farms and mines of Southern Rhodesia.[38] Beginning in 1925 the Southern Rhodesian state also began maintaining a network of food depots along the labor routes that ran from the Nyasaland border (it was against Nyasaland law to recruit or assist migrants in any way inside that country) to Southern Rhodesia and operated several ferries along the Zambezi River. These outposts were established with the specific purpose of assisting Nyasaland, Northern Rhodesian, and Mozambican migrants on their journeys south in search of employment in the colony.[39]

In further attempts to encourage voluntary migration from the north, the government also attempted to regulate the activities of recruiters. This was done because government officials believed that if northern laborers were lied to, cheated, or physically mistreated by recruiters, whether private or employed by a government-sponsored agency like the RNLB, the northerners would ultimately hold the government responsible. Officials feared that this, and rumors initiated by such incidents, would "impair the reputation of the Colony as a satisfactory field of employment" and would result in large numbers of additional migrants refusing to come to the country in search of work.[40]

In perhaps its most aggressive attempt to encourage northern labor migration, the Southern Rhodesian government inaugurated the *Ulere* system in 1936. This free transport system was established as a result of the "Salisbury Agreement" on migrant labor, signed by representatives of the governments of Southern Rhodesia, Northern Rhodesia, and Nyasaland on August 21, 1936. The agreement was based on the principle "that the labour requirements of the three Territories should have first call upon their available supplies," and that only those laborers in excess of local requirements should be allowed to migrate to other areas of employment, and then only within the three territories. The unspoken correlative to this was that the three governments, each for their own reasons, hoped to be able to control, if not abolish altogether, the "evil" of "clandestine emigration" southward.[41] Officials from each of the colonies felt that this voluntary, uncontrolled movement southward (to South Africa from Southern Rhodesia, and to South Africa and Southern Rhodesia from north of the Zambezi River) both threatened local capitalist development by denying local employers cheap labor, and represented a drain on state revenues through the loss of taxes. This was a somewhat less important concern for Southern Rhodesia than for the governments of the two northern territories who viewed it as "a cause of considerable anxiety." Unlike South Africa and Southern Rhodesia, the Northern Rhodesian and Nyasaland economies had not yet begun to show signs of recovering from the impact of the worldwide depression of the 1930s.[42]

Under the terms of the agreement, Northern Rhodesia and Nyasaland officials agreed to allow "free" labor migration from those territories after migrants had obtained a valid identity certificate, known as a "passport" or *situpa*. For its part, Southern Rhodesia promised to allow entrance into the country only to those migrants who possessed the necessary legal documentation and to return all others to their respective home areas. They also agreed to repatriate both taxes and a percentage of migrants' wages to their home districts, maintain rest camps and food depots, ascertain to the best of their ability the numbers of workers needed (so that the northern governments would have a better idea of how many certificates to issue), and acknowledge that it was "desirable that rapid and cheap transport should be provided for [the] movement of labourers within the three Territories."[43]

The meetings that culminated in the agreement were initiated by Prime Minister Godfrey Huggins of Southern Rhodesia in response to the changing socioeconomic conditions in that country, and in particular to the needs of the recovering tobacco industry. By the mid 1930s, tobacco farming was one of the few sectors of the economy that was showing relatively strong signs of recovering from the depression. Representatives of the tobacco industry, as well as government officials, believed that it was necessary to procure additional labor supplies in order to sustain that recovery.[44] The tobacco farmers had been mired in a financial crisis since suffering the traumatic drop in production after the 1927/28 season, a crisis exacerbated by the early years of the worldwide depression. By 1931, however, a number of tobacco growing regions in Mashonaland had begun to show signs of recovery. The native commissioner of Lomagundi, for example, reported that there seemed to be a greater demand for African laborers in November and December 1931 "owing chiefly to a revival of activity in tobacco planting." The following year the same official stated that the previous year's indications of recovery were continuing, noting that this had been marked by "the return of a number of tobacco farmers to their farms" and a corresponding increase in the demand for African laborers. By the late 1930s total acreage planted in tobacco in Lomagundi was rapidly increasing, with the central part of the district, which encompassed the farming areas surrounding the towns of Banket and Sinoia, being "largely devoted to tobacco farming." Tobacco production for the country as a whole mirrored the developments experienced in Lomagundi district, increasing from 5.5 million pounds in 1930 to an average of over 20 million pounds a year by the end of the decade.[45]

Although actual field operations of the *Ulere* system began in 1938, the genesis of the idea for such a system went back to at least 1928 and the recommendations of a Southern Rhodesian government committee of inquiry into farm-labor conditions. Although the committee examined both the working and living conditions existing on farms throughout the colony, it eventually exceeded its terms of appointment and suggested ways of improving those conditions, including addressing ways to provide more laborers to farms. As part of their recommendations the members of the committee noted that for some time a number of private recruiting agents had used motor lorries to transport their recruits to Southern Rhodesia and had attained "excellent results" in increasing the number of workers they brought south. The committee suggested that these results were due to "the mere fact [that] getting a motor ride is in itself a great attraction to the raw native." They also stated their belief "that were rapid Government [motor] transport facilities with cheap fares provided from the remote districts and labour Ports of Entry, not only would the number of native labourers be increased but such services would quickly become payable concerns."[46]

The committee's recommendations were echoed in 1930 when A. L. Holland, the Southern Rhodesian supervisor of government labor route ferries and rest facilities, wrote that the number of Nyasalanders migrating south "would naturally increase if motor transport was available."[47] In late 1932 the Rhodesia Tobacco Association (RTA) picked up the idea and began to lobby government officials in an effort to gain support for the establishment of a motor transport system. During their annual meeting that year, the executive committee of the association passed a resolution which asked that "some system of transport by lorries should be arranged."[48] Later that year, during a meeting with the colonial secretary in London, an RTA delegation estimated that it took one to two months for northern migrants to walk to the tobacco farms of Mashonaland. They also mentioned that private recruiters charged excessive fares for a return trip to the north. They argued that the combination of these two things acted as deterrents to Nyasalanders attempting to seek employment in Southern Rhodesia and stated that "the economic loss involved amounts to about £70,000 per annum on a conservative basis."[49]

In addition to the argument concerning financial loss, both RTA representatives and government officials also expressed their concern, heavily cloaked in paternalistic language, for the physical well-being of the migrants. They claimed that a fast, inexpensive motor transport system would alleviate the dangers northern migrants faced while trekking south in search of work. Supporters of the idea argued that in addition to greatly decreasing the physical toll exacted by "a month's walk through the difficult and unhealthy country on both sides of the Zambezi," a motor transport system would also provide migrants with protection from wild animals, from "picking up diseases in the villages in route," and from highway bandits and "immoral temptations" they might encounter along the labor routes.[50] The *Bulawayo Chronicle* astutely summarized both the desire to have laborers who would be physically ready to work immediately upon arrival in the country and the paternalistic concern for the migrants when it editorialized in early 1938 that northerners would arrive "fresher and ready to commence work without much delay" once the free transport system was fully operational.[51]

When the idea of a state-sponsored motor transport system finally came to fruition with the signing of the Salisbury Agreement, Southern Rhodesian government officials declared that the new program was to operate along the same lines as earlier programs, i.e., to assist northern migrants on their journeys south without directing them specifically to any single group of employers. Once they arrived at one of the ports of entry at Mtoko or Mrewa, about 120 kilometers and 70 kilometers northeast of Salisbury respectively, they were to be let "off to spread out through [the] country as a whole." In reality, because the initial routes passed through Mashonaland districts, including Lomagundi and Mazoe, a large number of migrants took jobs on the tobacco farms in those districts and

did not continue on to other areas of wage employment further south.[52]

The actual carrying of passengers began in May 1938 with
three routes. The first went from Fort Jameson, in Northern
Rhodesia, to Mrewa. The second funneled laborers from Feira,
on the Mozambique border, to Mount Darwin (110 kilometers
north of Salisbury). The third went from Chirundu, on the
Northern Rhodesian border (north of present-day Kariba), to
Sinoia.[53] These routes were chosen for two primary reasons.
They all shadowed traditional pedestrian routes used by
northern migrants, and once inside the country they linked up
with the local Rhodesian Motor Service, which had been created in 1927 as "a precondition for [the] further development"
of new European farming regions.[54] In 1941 an additional
route was opened from Kazangula (at the western tip of the
country) to the railhead at Victoria Falls. In the following
years several additional routes were added. By 1938 *Ulere* lorries and buses were providing transport into Southern Rhodesia for 20,426 migrants, and by 1945 the annual total had
reached 38,190.[55]

Transport into the country was free and included rations
and overnight boarding at rest camps along the routes. Fares
for return passages were initially set at ten shillings, but by
the 1940s they had been tied to a graduated scale, increments
of which were determined by the length of time a migrant had
worked inside Southern Rhodesia. Those who had worked in
South Africa were charged more. Migrants were limited to 25
pounds of baggage on their southward journey, but were allowed up to an additional 50 pounds when they returned
home. The amount and type of baggage they carried north
also helped to determine the cost of their return passage. For
example, migrants departing from Mount Darwin were
charged 5 shillings for their return ticket (20 shillings if they

had worked in South Africa) and were allowed to carry up to 70 pounds of baggage at no additional charge. If they wanted to include a bicycle as part of their luggage, however, an extra charge of 2/6 was added to the cost of the ticket.[56]

A unique element of the *Ulere* system was that in conjunction with providing free transport into the country for "voluntary" migrant workers, almost all of whom were men, *Ulere* agents also encouraged the wives and children of recruited male workers to accompany the men south. These dependents were promised that they could return home free of charge at any time after the man they had come with had completed at least six months employment in Southern Rhodesia. This practice was encouraged by *Ulere* agents, government officials, and farmers alike and was based on the belief, held by most European employers in Southern Rhodesia, that northern workers who were accompanied by their families remained in employment for longer periods of time than other men. The common addendum to this for many farmers and government officials was that workers "improved with experience," and as their efficiency improved, fewer laborers were required and the farmers' cost of production was cut, with a corresponding

TABLE 4

Ulere *Motor Transport System, 1938–45*[57]

Year	Bringing People In	Taking People Out
1938	20,426	5,970
1939	23,542	11,290
1940	24,347	16,896
1941	39,396	16,185
1942	33,335	19,351
1943	34,842	17,572
1944	40,804	19,103
1945	38,190	21,660

increase in profits.[58] Nyasaland officials generally approved of this aspect of the *Ulere* system because it addressed the issue of "the decay of village life," which they argued was caused by the migration of adult males. In early 1944, Major F. T. Stephens, a Nyasaland labor official, stated that this problem was ameliorated when male migrants were able to take their families south with them. Rather than "breaking up home life," Nyasalanders were "contented" when they had their families with them and were allowed to "settle down . . . have their little gardens . . . [and receive] a ration for the wife and children."[59]

As for the migrants, they were somewhat hesitant to take advantage of the *Ulere* system during the first several months it was in operation, but by August 1938 it was fairly clear that they had changed their minds. In that month the *Rhodesia Herald* reported that migrant workers were quickly growing accustomed to the new service and no longer considered walking any further south than to one of the pick-up points, where they would then wait "as long as a week to secure a seat in the bus."[60] In November 1938, the Lomagundi native commissioner reported that as a result of the new motor transport service "many of the tobacco growers have been obtaining their labour direct from Nyasaland."[61]

Although the *Ulere* transport system quickly gained a degree of popularity with northern migrants and government officials from all three colonies, it had its detractors. Once the relatively large number of people taking advantage of the new system became known, at least one Nyasaland official objected to the service on the grounds "that it would denude Nyasaland of labour."[62] By early 1939 the Rhodesia Tobacco Association, which had strongly lobbied for the creation of the program in the beginning, began to criticize the government for not doing enough to keep northerners who used the system's lorries and buses from proceeding further south into South

Africa. Farmers from a number of areas, particularly in the northern districts of Mashonaland, echoed that complaint and claimed that prior to the inauguration of the *Ulere* system they had never been short of labor, but that after it started they never had enough. In 1938, Edward Noakes, a member of parliament as well as being active in the Rhodesia Tobacco Association, told his colleagues in parliament that farmers in Mazoe were experiencing labor shortages because *Ulere* lorries had caused northern migrants to switch "from the old channels by which they came" into the colony. Noakes argued that by delivering the northern migrants in a much more fit condition, the *Ulere* system was facilitating their further movement into South Africa, an area of employment which offered wage rates Southern Rhodesian employers could not equal.[63] Later that year a tobacco farmer from Inyazure, southeast of Salisbury, claimed that when it came to securing adequate supplies of labor for local farms the "lorry system has taken the district off the face of the map." Two years later a government compound inspector reported that employers in Mrewa and Marandellas, southeast of Salisbury, were "upset" with the *Ulere* service because it had resulted in a "decline in labour supplies in their areas."[64]

Nevertheless, at least some of the criticism of the *Ulere* system was not directed at the overall system itself, but rather at the choice of particular routes and placement of food depots and overnight rest camps. For example, in October 1938 the chief native commissioner noted that tobacco farmers from the area of Concession, one hundred kilometers north of Salisbury, had been complaining that they lacked sufficient supplies of labor because they were being bypassed by *Ulere* lorries.[65] Major Wane, Concession area native commissioner, replied that the problem could be rectified by putting "on a lorry service from Sipililo via Banket to Concession . . . this [route] has not been explored as far as lorry facilities are concerned."[66] In the same month, Shamva's assistant native commissioner argued that were Shamva to become a terminus of the transport scheme, then "Natives registered here would have to pass along occupied farms . . . with the very great likelihood they might take up employment en route."[67]

This brief examination of three government sponsored assistance programs has provided examples of the Southern Rhodesian state's attempts to secure the success of its white agricultural policy. Crop experimentation was required if white farmers were going to develop and produce varieties of tobacco that could be grown under local conditions and were at the same time acceptable to British buyers. Greater yields per acre and improved taste and aroma meant nothing, however, if European farmers lacked labor to transplant, cultivate, harvest, and grade the tobacco crops. The payment of tobacco laborers wages in 1928 and the creation of the *Ulere* transport system were attempts by the state to secure "a sufficiency of labour" to do those jobs.

Together they demonstrate a coherent policy. The *Ulere* transport system was an indication that crop experimentation and other earlier efforts of the state to support European commercial farming had borne fruit and that by the late 1930s capitalist agriculture in Southern Rhodesia had reached a new level of historical development. By encouraging wives and children to accompany laborers for the first time, the Southern Rhodesian state was recognizing that the tobacco industry had reached a point were it could begin to sustain a more permanent, stable labor force.[68]

3

Farms and Farmers

The vast majority of tobacco farms in Southern Rhodesia during the period 1890–1945 were located in the provinces of Mashonaland and Manicaland. A 1959 agricultural survey of the country classified over two-thirds of Lomagundi and nearly one-half of Mazoe, both in Mashonaland, as regions of "intensive crop production," with tobacco being the primary cash crop.[1] This survey merely provided statistical support to what most people involved in tobacco production had known for nearly sixty years. Between them, the two districts spanned ecological regions that were ideal for tobacco production, with the areas of greatest production between 3,500 feet and 5,500 feet in altitude, having sandy, well-drained soil, and receiving average annual rainfall of 32–40 inches. In short, the districts were ideally suited as areas in which to establish a tobacco farm.

There was no "typical" tobacco farm in Southern Rhodesia, as farms varied greatly in both total size and acreage planted in tobacco. In addition, on many farms tobacco was the only cash crop grown, although additional crops like maize, "monkey nuts" (groundnuts), beans, pumpkins, and other vegetables were grown as rations for the African laborers or as green manure crops. Tobacco growers not only grew crops, but also kept oxen for plowing and pulling transport wagons, and sometimes maintained small dairy herds as a source of extra income. Two farms, nearly 50 kilometers apart, provide good examples of the differences that could exist between tobacco farms. In October 1926, W. E. Meade, editor of the *Rhodesia Agricultural Journal*, visited the Great "B" farm, owned by "one of the most successful tobacco growers in the Colony," A. C. Henderson, and located about 24 kilometers north of Salisbury, in Mazoe district. The Great "B" farm had 7,000 total acres and during the 1925/26 growing season Henderson planted 300 acres in tobacco and employed 220 African laborers, as well as two European assistants during the planting season, and a third hired for the curing season. The farm had 14 tobacco barns, although each was somewhat larger than the average flue-curing barn, so Henderson actually had barns with a capacity equal to 18 normal-sized barns. In contrast, four months later, Meade visited a second tobacco farm, one which he described as a "farm in the making." This farm, totaling 1,555 acres in size, was located about 24 kilometers south of Salisbury and had first been occupied in September 1926. In the five months that the new settler and his family had been on the farm, they had supervised the clearing of 34 acres. The grower had planted 12 acres in tobacco, an additional 17 acres of maize, 4 acres of groundnuts, and an acre of beans and potatoes. The grower worked with his 17 year-old son and employed 22 African laborers. The farm's first flue-curing barn was in the process of being built at the time of Meade's visit. These two farms represent the extremes of tobacco farms, although the second was more similar in overall size to tobacco farms in the Lomagundi and Mazoe districts, where farms varied from about 1,000 acres to 3,000 acres.[2]

Although the total farm size was large, nowhere near that total acreage was used. The exact acreage planted in tobacco on any given farm is difficult to determine. Sources giving accurate accounts of acres planted are rare, as farmers in this period were notorious for not keeping records of any kind and most government reports were based on estimates. Fortunately, some farmers did keep private records and a few reports based on on-site inspections of farms by government officials do exist. Between the 1932/33 and 1944/45 seasons, Mpandaguta Farm, near Banket, planted an average of nearly 94 acres of tobacco annually. The largest crop during that period was 114 acres, while the smallest was 52.[3] A report by Compound Inspector D. C. Parkhurst for November 1940, provides an additional indication of tobacco acreage planted by growers. After reports of labor shortages in the area around Norton, southwest of Salisbury, the local native commissioner requested that Parkhurst visit the area and submit a special report. He visited 38 farms in the area, 13 of which he defined as principally tobacco farms. He found that for the 1938/39 season, the farms averaged almost 85 acres of tobacco, the largest planting being 150 acres and the smallest 35 acres. One additional farm began growing tobacco during the 1939/40 season, and the average for the fourteen farms was nearly 96 acres during that second year, with the largest being 250 acres and the smallest 20 acres. One of the tobacco farms visited by Parkhurst was owned by E. D. Palmer, and Parkhurst reported that Palmer had planted 46 acres of tobacco in 1939 and 34 acres in 1940.[4] When interviewed in the 1980s, Palmer stated that the overall size of his farm was 3,200 acres, and that was average for tobacco farms in the Norton area.[5] Generally speaking, the averages noted above for acres in tobacco were only obtained after several years of residence on a farm. Experienced growers and government publications alike consistently indicated that new growers would be well advised to plant no more than 30 acres of tobacco in their first year of growing. Then, as they gained experience in growing and curing tobacco and in "handling" labor, they could clear new land, build additional flue-curing barns and make other capital improvements to the farms.[6]

Tobacco farmers in Lomagundi and Mazoe explained the disproportionate ratio between the overall size of farms and the actual acreage planted in tobacco by pointing to the necessity of acquiring sufficient land that would be both adequate for tobacco farming and for making the farm a self-sufficient enterprise. This line of reasoning was rooted in the soils of the two districts and the farming technologies of the period. Together they required farmers growing tobacco to rotate their tobacco fields at least every two years. This biennial rotation pattern was necessary because tobacco leached nutrients out of the soil very quickly. Even with the use of fertilizers, which were only sparingly used until after 1945, there was a noticeable drop off in production with a second-year crop. In effect, on an average tobacco farm a first-year crop produced a good quantity of quality tobacco, while a second year on that same land would produce a crop somewhat smaller in quantity and coarser in quality.

In addition to needing adequate fallow lands to offset the effects of a tobacco crop to the soil, farmers also required acreage to make the farm self-sufficient in other crops to feed the farm's labor force and draft animals. When interviewed in 1984, H. J. Quinton gave an example of the formula tobacco growers used to determine the total size of a farm: "You put down 150 [acres] this year and then you let that 150 lie for three years. . . . So your arable land ha[d] to be measured for your tobacco by three times 150. Now, to feed your staff you would want 200 acres of maize, at least. In the early days, of course, we had to feed our bullocks, so you'd need 500 acres of mealies; [and] you need[ed] an enormous amount of grass."[7] In Lomagundi district when a new settler wanted to become a tobacco grower, it was considered necessary to have a minimum of 400 acres of land suitable for tobacco, plus land for food crops and grazing. To John Scott, who worked as a government land inspector and surveyor in the 1920s and 1930s, it "was looking for that minimum that controlled the size of the farm." He explained that some "parcels would have a hell of a lot of rocky kopjes. So to get these 400 acres you'd have to peg out a 4,000 acre property." On the other hand, at another site a surveyor might see a property "with 400 acres absolutely the cat's meat, [with] 900 acres you've got proper composition" for a self-sufficient tobacco farm.[8]

When inspecting land earmarked for European settlement, a number of considerations were kept in mind in trying to determine the suitability of an area to become a tobacco farm. Proximity of a water supply for seed beds and tobacco fields was always a principle consideration. The prevalence of nematodes or insects detrimental to tobacco plants greatly increased the acreage required. The system of field rotation generally used in a district could also determine the total acreage of a farm. The rotation pattern in the Lomagundi area was two years of tobacco, then one year of maize, followed by a green manure crop, and a year, or often two, lying fallow. Utilizing this pattern, the grower could reuse his tobacco lands every six to seven years.[9] The accepted rotation pattern for Mazoe was generally one to two years shorter, with two years of tobacco, one year of maize and usually a year of a green manure crop, followed by the land lying fallow for a year.[10]

In addition to the ecological factors that went into influencing the acreage a grower might plant in tobacco, there were two other major considerations. First was the desire of farmers, like other European settlers in Southern Rhodesia, to attain and then maintain a preconceived standard of living. A result of this way of thinking was that many farmers accepted the idea that a given acreage, different on each farm, had to be harvested in order to reach the income level that would provide the desired standard of living. This idea often influenced the total acreage planted in tobacco and is a factor that cannot be ignored when attempting to understand how farmers decided on the number of acres to plant in tobacco.[11] The second non-ecological factor was the availability of labor. It was generally accepted that a tobacco grower required a minimum of one laborer for every acre of tobacco planted.[12] E. D. Palmer explained that the availability of labor was a "realistic" consideration in determining how many acres to plant, saying that a farmer "had a basic figure. [I]f at the time of planting I found there was going to be a severe labour shortage, I'd probably cut out ten acres."[13] Reports from the agriculture department throughout the period indicate that actual shortages, or even the fear of possible shortages, in the availability of labor could effect the acreage farmers planted. For example, the Agriculture Department Annual Report of 1907 stated that tobacco growers "urgently" required additional labor and that the shortage had already "had the effect of deterring many farmers from planting more than a very limited acreage."[14] In some cases, however, farmers would go ahead and plant the acreage they had projected as the amount necessary to provide adequate financial returns, then hope that the labor needed to manage the fields would materialize later.[15]

Tobacco Farm, 1926

Taken together, the factors mentioned helped to establish the perceived value of a given farm. As with property values anywhere, a variety of market and non-market factors also entered into determining the particular value of the farms. It is possible to provide a few specific examples of the cost of individual farms in the Lomagundi and Mazoe districts during successive decades. An advertisement in the January 4, 1907 edition of the *Rhodesia Herald* asked £300 for a 3,500 acre farm in Mazoe. A month later, a 2,000-acre developed farm, with "380 acres of mealies, 20 acres of tobacco . . . [and] erecting two barns and a packing house," near present-day Concession in Mazoe was selling for £400. In 1912, a Mazoe farm of about 3,360 acres was described thus: "river frontage, heavily wooded, brick house—two rooms and a kitchen— barns, 250 acres under cultivation—65 acres gave 600 bags of mealies, and 39 acres gave 22,200 lbs. of tobacco." The asking price for the farm was £3,500. In 1921, advertisements in the *Rhodesia Herald* asked £8,000 for a 1,623-acre tobacco farm with "300 acres irrigated, and barns" in Concession, £2,000 for 2,790 acres near Banket, and £5,200 for a 6,120 acre farm with "many improvements" in Sinoia. In September 1936, a land inspector visited a farm near Shamva that had a total acreage of 4,820 acres, possessed suitable soils for tobacco, maize, and other crops, and had a homestead, poultry houses and a cattle dip. The inspector considered it "a good farm suitable for any type of farming, as it has a variety of soils." He valued the land at £2,000, and the buildings and equipment at £500 2/10s.[16]

The last example cited shows that capital improvements increased a farm's total valuation, but so could non-material economic factors. Commander R. M. G. Knight was a retired naval officer who came to Southern Rhodesia in the early 1920s. Judged by the standards of the day, he was eccentric, egotistical, and argumentative. His complaining became legendary in the district, with individual complaints ranging from the lack of cheap labor to trespassing across his farm by local Africans and European neighbors alike. According to a government memorandum, he had "no farming experience" and was "a victim of his own lack of knowledge of the elementary principles on which successful farming must be based." In 1925 he bought the 4,400 acres Between Rivers Farm, located fourteen kilometers outside Banket in the Lomagundi district, and began to raise tobacco and dairy cattle. At the time he purchased Between Rivers, the farm was valued at £2,177 by J. F. Templeton, the Land Bank's land inspector for the Banket area. Over the next eighteen months, he had several buildings constructed on the farm, probably a number of flue-curing tobacco barns and a grading shed. The addition of these buildings increased the value of his farm by an additional £525.[17] During that same eighteen-month period market factors also increased land value as Great Britain announced an increase in the imperial preference on tobacco. As might be expected, the announcement drove up the price of land in the country, particularly in the major tobacco growing districts. It appears from correspondence that, based solely on the knowledge of the new preference and its effect on land pricing, Templeton believed he had cause to increase his valuation of the Between Rivers Farm by an additional £573. Therefore, in eighteen months, as a combined result of the capital improvements Knight made to the farm, and the increased appraisal of the land based on the change in the imperial preference the valuation of Between Rivers Farm was raised by £1,098.

Virgin farms gained added value when occupied and worked by European settlers. Then, improvements had to be made to the farms, including building modest homesteads for the farmers and their families, bringing additional acreage under cultivation through the clearing of virgin land, and the erection of buildings necessary for the type of farming the new

Old-style farm house

farmers were planning to undertake. For tobacco farmers that usually meant building flue-curing barns and grading and bulking sheds, and purchasing equipment such as plows, ridgers, and hoes.

As with the cost of land the money spent on these improvements varied throughout the period, with the exact cost to an individual farmer depending on factors such as whether the farmer was buying virgin land or a farm with some improvements, and whether the farm came with some equipment. If prospective farmers planned to farm tobacco as the primary crop, the minimal equipment they would have had to buy or build also depended on how many acres were to be planted in the first year.

The first and most important buildings constructed on any tobacco farm were the special flue-curing barns. The term "flue-curing" refers to the process of slowly removing moisture from tobacco leaves after they had been picked, and was adopted from the American tobacco industry. In the first years of growing tobacco in the country, a single barn may have been used to cure up to 15 acres of tobacco, but by the early 1920s the number of barns a tobacco grower needed for flue-curing was figured on the ratio of one barn for every 10 acres of tobacco.[18] The first known flue-curing barn in Southern Rhodesia was built in 1903 by E. H. South and had pole and dagga walls and an iron roof. George Odlum later described that barn as not being exactly air tight: the "roof dripped moisture so it was hastily covered with grass" and air "leakage threatened premature drying."[19]

The colony's first part-brick flue-curing barn was constructed by Dr. Charles Jarron Sketchley in 1908, on a farm in the southeast corner of Lomagundi district. Over the next several years a number of barn designs were experimented with, and by the beginning of World War I the building of tobacco barns had become standardized. From then on barns were built to fairly standard dimensions and were often constructed in pairs with a common interior wall. Barns generally had six ventilators, one door, and two furnaces, separate but immediately adjacent to the barn. The furnaces were stoked with wood from one side and from the other side a flue, a tin tube, from each of the furnaces joined into a single, larger flue which went into the barn. This larger flue was positioned in the center of the barn and was half buried in the packed earthen floor. The hot air passing through the flue heated the air inside the barn, curing the tobacco over a five-day period.[20]

Barns were always built with materials that were almost exclusively taken from or made on the farm. Their foundations were cleaned stones set in and covered with cement mortar. A one-inch thick layer of cement, the principal ingredient in tobacco farm construction bought off the farm, was then laid along the top of the foundation to provide a flat course on which to construct the walls. This cement also acted as a barrier to dampness and ants, two scourges of tobacco growers. The walls were built from farm-made bricks set in lime mortar,

Southern Rhodesia's first brick flue-curing barn, built by Dr. Charles Jarron Sketchley, Darwendale, 1908

Portelet Tobacco Estate, tobacco barns, 1926

with the exterior walls being nearly 20 feet high, 32 feet long, and 14 inches thick, with interior walls that were about 9 inches thick. Barns were topped with a roof of galvanized iron, the second item that farmers had to purchase. By the 1920s, agriculture department tobacco experts were recommending that barns have rain gutters and down spout "running at least four feet from the barn," but this advice was slow in being adopted by most tobacco farmers. The farmer and his African labor force generally did all the work on a barn, a practice meant to keep the expense of erecting a barn to a minimum. As might be imagined, barns were the largest buildings on a to-bacco farm and the few available expense estimates show that next to the land itself, barns were the tobacco grower's most expensive capital outlay.[21]

Flue-curing barns were not, of course, the only items a new farmer needed in order to improve a farm. According to hand-books made available to prospective settlers, in addition to three barns like the one described above, the capital equipment necessary to start farming thirty acres of tobacco included bulking and grading sheds, a disc plow, a tooth harrow, two cultivators, a wagon, three baling presses, three hand rakes, six watering cans, and ten hoes. Spans of oxen and "other buildings and equipment," presumably items such as chicken coops, storage sheds and grain bins were not included in the lists, as "they are necessary on any farm."[22] Additional items necessary on a working tobacco farm, but also not included on the lists, were materials like tobacco seed, fertilizer, and a steam boiler. As with many commonly used material goods, records of the exact contemporary costs of many of these items are not known, but sources such as advertisements in the *Rhodesia Herald* and the *Rhodesia Agricultural Journal* pro-vide some representative prices. For example, a three-blade disc plow imported into the region in 1916 would have cost a farmer about £30. In the following year tobacco fertilizer cost

£17 a ton if paid for in cash, while buying it on credit added £1–3 per ton to the price. Pickheads sold at 1s./6d., shovels at 2s./3d. and mattocks for 2s./6d. in 1924, while in 1926 tobacco seed was advertised at 5s./6d. per ounce.[23]

Isolated prices for land and capital goods mean little by themselves. They only begin to take on significance when placed in the context of the actual cost of operating a tobacco farm. At a 1924 Shamva Farmers' Association meeting, members estimated that a farm could be started on virgin crown lands for an outlay of about £1,000 in the first year. This included £100 for necessary buildings and £750 for living expenses, stock, and African laborers' wages and rations. The £1,000 did not include any payments for land as the farmers believed that farmland "should be absolutely free for the first five years" as long as the farmer lived on and was making improvements to the farm.[24] In 1927, the assistant director of the Lands Department, a Mr. Jennings, estimated that starting a tobacco farm on virgin lands would require an initial investment of between £1,500 and £2,000. If a person bought a developed farm, Jennings estimated that an additional £1,000 would be required, presumably to cover the cost of those improvements already made on the farm.[25] Exactly what could the new tobacco grower expect to receive for that investment? In response to Jennings' estimates, Southern Rhodesia's London-based land settlement officer provided the following estimates for costs that were likely to be incurred when starting a farm in which the new settler planned on growing ten acres of tobacco in the first year:

Small house/huts for a single man	£ 50
1 Tobacco Barn & lean-to packing shed	125
1 Grading shed	150
Implements, tools & such like	150
1 Span of bullocks	100
Native wages & food	180

1 Boiler 100
1 Wagon 130
Misc., including fertilizer, limbo, etc. 80
Living expenses at £7.10/- per mensem 90

TOTAL: £1,155

Add to that a small acreage of maize costing £50 and the cost of the first year's working will be £1,205.

A new settler would not necessarily have needed to have the entire amount in hand in order to begin farming. In the situation just mentioned, the new settler would have been expected to personally advance £880 of the total, with the balance being met through government-provided loans. Money for improvements to the farm in following years would have been available through additional loans from the Land and Agriculture Bank.[26]

The disdain most farmers had for maintaining farm records makes it difficult to know how close these estimates came to actual costs. Fortunately, exceptions like the anonymous settler "who took up land in Mashonaland in 1926" exist. The *Rhodesia Agricultural Journal* published extracts from the unnamed farmer's ledgers providing costs for a producing tobacco farm in the 1927/28 season. The farmer grew 55 acres of tobacco that season, with expenditures on:

Native labour, average 50 boys, wages and rations . . £ 517. 6. 3
Cost of erecting five tobacco barns (own labour) 454. 2. 3
Cost of erecting one grading shed (own labour) 162. 4. 6
Cost of implements & accessories 298. 0. 0
Cost of 30 oxen 158. 0. 0
Fertiliser & seed 111. 3. 5
Part cost of wagon 75. 0. 0
Cost of stumping 55 acres 63. 5. 0
Material for grading & baling 39. 0. 8

TOTAL . . . . £1,878. 2. 1[27]

A second important source that provides detailed production costs for the late 1930s exists in the records of Charles William Cartwright of Waltondale Farm in Marandellas district. Cartwright immigrated to Southern Rhodesia and began farming in the early 1930s and from the very beginning of his career as a farmer kept monthly ledgers detailing his operating expenses. After raising chickens for several years he first grew tobacco in 1936, and his ledgers provide a clear example of the expenses other farmers growing tobacco could have expected to incur.[28]

Prices for land and related investments in equipment provided above give an idea of the capital required by settlers taking up tobacco farms in Southern Rhodesia before 1945. Settler handbooks issued periodically between 1924 and 1935 indicate that there was little change in either the capital required or in the capital equipment needed to start up a flue-cured tobacco farm during that period. In general, this situation meant that farmers had little control over the fixed capital elements of their production costs. As the farm operating expenses detailed by both the 1926 Mashonaland settler and in Cartwright's ledgers indicate, however, the largest single annual expense on farms was not for land payments or capital equipment, but for labor. These examples suggest that about 30

TABLE 5
Waltondale Farm Operating Expenses, 1939/40

Farm Expenses	£	s	d
70% car expenses	111	13	7
General expenses	219	12	1
Rations	83	8	3 *
Fowls	22	6	3
Railage	41	11	10
Implements, repairs	41	4	2
Stationary	6	2	10

TABLE 5 (*Continued*)

Farm Expenses	£	s	d	
Tobacco expenses	168	15	1	
Tobacco fertilizers	186	18	1	
Cattle expenses	3	16	0	
Engine and mill	17	19	1	
Piping	2	0	0	
Seed	16	13	6	
Wages	418	14	9 *	
Interest	70	4	3	
Sub-total				£1,410 19 9
Farm Capital Expenses				
Balance on Ford	168	13	0	
Implements, Large	206	12	6	
Implements, small	11	7	6	
Building (incl. wages)	49	2	5 *	
Payment—Farm purchase	400	0	0	
Piping	24	2	2	
Cattle purchases	288	7	6	
Wages, improvements	30	0	0 *	
Sub-total				1,118 5 1
Personal Family Expenses				
Living	195	14	1	
Dks Tobacco	105	4	6	
Clothes	83	3	1	
Doctor & chemist	17	5	9	
Sports	12	17	0	
Electric lights, new installation, repairs	58	0	4	
House (furniture, etc.)	75	13	0	
Schooling	139	18	9	
Personal	179	0	4	
30% car expenses	44	6	4	
Sub-total				911 15 2
Total Farm Expenses				£3,441 0 0

* Expenses directly attributable to African Labor.

percent of the total annual operating expenses of a tobacco farm went to pay the wages and costs of rations for the farm's African labor force.[29] Within this 30 percent farmers could attempt to reduce their operating costs. When labor was abundant they cited economic laws of supply and demand and cut wages. At those times when labor was scarce, they pointed to the costs of land and capital equipment as proof that they could not possibly pay an additional shilling to laborers. They used the cost of capital equipment, items they had little control over, to justify low wages, bad accommodations and inadequate rations for their African laborers. Van Onselen's observations concerning mine owners' attempting to control their labor costs also apply to the colony's tobacco farmers. Just as much as gold miners, tobacco farmers "appreciated that the need to reduce costs . . . meant curtailing expenditure on, among other things, food, accommodation . . . [health care] and compensation for injury. Cost minimisation was in short not only to reflect itself in the compounds, but to govern the living conditions" of African workers.[30]

The cost of taking up a tobacco farm in Southern Rhodesia during the years between 1890 and 1945 constituted a considerable financial outlay. Although some of those expenses could be ameliorated through European farmers' access to government-sponsored loans, others could not. The largest of these was the wage bill for African laborers. In addition to being expensive, African labor was, next to the purchase of the land itself, arguably the most important factor in establishing a tobacco farm. After all, African laborers were not only needed to clear new fields, they also built the farmer's homestead and the new curing barns, used the farm's capital equipment and, most importantly, tended the crops. All of these had to be accomplished if a farmer was to prove that he was making improvements to the farm, and thereby qualify for continuing assistance.

4

Making the Grade

The 1924 *Handbook for the Use of Prospective Settlers on the Land* described the parameters for growing Virginia flue-cured tobacco as "intensive cultivation and careful handling from the time the crop is transplanted until the leaf is ready for market."[1] H. J. Quinton reiterated the point sixty years later by stating that he "always had sufficient work to keep [laborers] going, all year around."[2] Although most tobacco growers required labor throughout the year, there were also those who would "call them up and sign them off," terminating their employment after tobacco grading, the generally accepted end of the growing season, had been finished. In other cases, growers found a middle ground and only signed off those laborers who expressed a desire to leave when the grading had been completed.[3]

The number of months tobacco growers required African labor was primarily determined by the natural time-table of growing and curing tobacco. From about 1900 through the 1930s, tobacco growers required the services of their laborers for at least eight to nine months, from September to late April, and often into May. This requirement changed somewhat in the mid-to-late 1930s, as both total acreage and yields per acre began to increase and the tobacco growing season was extended by one to two months. In addition to the actual growing season, however, most tobacco farmers throughout the period also cleared new lands to increase their acreage for the next year's tobacco crop, or to meet the need to rotate the tobacco crop to fresh land. Clearing was usually done during the winter months of June through August, and along with other labor requirements, such as stockpiling firewood for the next season's curing, extended the period a tobacco grower needed to employ African labor to the entire year. This chapter provides a detailed look at those tasks, and a brief perusal of the material and organic tools used on tobacco farms between 1890 and 1945.

Farm Equipment

Major equipment like plows, harrowers, and ridgers were expensive and most tobacco growers could not afford to buy the latest models. When individual growers wanted to expand production they tried to increase the use of the equipment and oxen that they already owned, and the labor they employed, rather than build or purchase new ones. The largest and most expensive instruments of labor used on tobacco farms were the flue-curing barns, but after the barns the harrowers, ridgers, and plows used to prepare cleared fields for tobacco seedlings were the most expensive equipment on the farm. Although a few tobacco farmers were using tractors by the early 1920s, the vast majority of farmers during the 1890 to 1945 period used oxen for plowing, hauling, and general transport, while most fieldwork tasks were done by laborers using rudimentary hand-held tools. These included short-handled hoes, known as *badzas*, for cultivating, and "planting pegs," short wooden poles with iron points used to make holes in which to transplant tobacco seedlings to the fields. In addition, during the earliest stage of the tobacco-growing process, the growing of plants from seed, hessian cloth and hand-held watering cans were the most important items.

Fertilizers were always used in the seedbeds and after the early 1920s, increasingly in the fields during transplanting of tobacco seedlings. They had not been extensively used before that time for two basic reasons. First, most tobacco growers were planting tobacco in newly cleared, virgin lands and the contemporary wisdom was that fertilizers did not substantially improve the harvest. The second reason was that fertilizer was expensive. Only in the early 1920s were farmers in areas where tobacco had been grown for a decade or more compelled to enhance soils with fertilizers in order to obtain good yields.[4]

Of the relatively few technological innovations in tobacco growing that occurred before 1945, most happened in two areas of production. The first involved improvements in the tobacco itself, with researchers attempting to increase yields, fight plant diseases and control insects (see Chapter Two). The second involved changes that affected labor tasks and were generally labor saving, at least from the point of view of the tobacco farmers. They accelerated the pace of tasks involved in the reaping and tying of tobacco, and thereby increased the overall amount of work required. For example, two separate innovations reduced the time it took to transport reaped tobacco leaves from the fields to the barns. During the earliest days of tobacco growing in the country, and lasting in a few areas until the early 1930s, reaped tobacco leaves were placed into baskets as they were picked by the laborers. When a laborer had filled a basket it was placed on sleds called *sandangas*, made by placing large tree branches into a "V" shape, with wooden planks laid across the top. When a *sandanga* had been loaded with a number of baskets it was pulled by oxen to the barns where it was off-loaded. This method was slow, labor intensive, and limited the amount of tobacco that could be reaped quickly. The practice changed when farmers adopted wheeled, flatbed wagons sometime prior to World War I.[5]

A further innovation in equipment used for reaping tobacco was the development of the *mujita*, a container described by one farmer as looking like "a bed without legs." *Mujitas* were made by attaching wooden poles to the bottom planks of a crate and then wrapping the poles with hessian cloth. Before *mujitas*, when flatbed wagons were used almost exclusively, reaped tobacco was handed to laborers on the wagons who then placed the tobacco leaves in two-by-four feet wooden crates. There were a number of these crates on a wagon, and when filled the wagon was pulled by oxen to the barns. The filled crates were extremely heavy and in order to safely off-load them a minimum of four laborers was needed. The crates were then carried into tying sheds where they were emptied and the tobacco was tied. Although more efficient than the *sandangas*, this practice was also relatively slow and labor intensive.

The development of *mujitas* greatly improved this situation. When placed in a *mujita* leaves were packed "loose, to a certain height, [with] hessian over [the top] to prevent sun scorch." A single *mujita* held nearly twice the amount carried in a single 2′ x 4′ crate, and a flatbed wagon usually carried two *mujitas*. While nearly as heavy as a wooden crate and still requiring at least four laborers to off-load them, they did have the advantage of holding nearly double the amount of tobacco carried by a wagon. Some tobacco farmers attempted to solve the problem of the weight of the *mujitas*, and thereby speed up the process by digging out the floors of their tying sheds. The wagons carrying *mujitas* could then be driven directly into the

Sandanga, sledge made from triangle of three logs

sheds, where laborers employed in tying could reach straight into them without having to first off-load the *mujitas.*[6] The invention of *mujitas* meant that more tobacco could be harvested at one time and barns could be filled more quickly, which meant some reallocation of labor. For example, for those farmers who dug out the floors of their tying sheds, the laborers formerly required to off-load the heavy crates and *mujitas* could be shifted to other tasks, such as reaping or tying tobacco as it was brought in from the fields.

Another labor-saving innovation, the invention of the two-string tying pole, occurred sometime in the 1930s. When tobacco was brought in from the fields it was tied into "hands of tobacco." A "hand" was three leaves tied together at the thick end of the stem. About thirty hands were then tied onto a pole, then the pole was placed in the barn so that the tobacco could be cured. Before the mid 1930s these tying poles had a single string, which was used to secure the hands to the pole by placing alternating, reverse loops around the butts of the tobacco hands and then tying the string at the end of the pole.

Tying tobacco

With the introduction of the two-string tying pole, the strings were crisscrossed at the butt end of each hand and then pulled tight and secured, thereby holding the thirty hands in place. This method of tying was somewhat quicker than the one-string method, which meant that barns could be filled a bit faster. The new device also reduced the number of laborers needed to "tie a barn," because fewer laborers could tie an equivalent number of hands in the same amount of time as used in the older method. The real time saving came, however, when the hands were untied. Before the use of the two-string system it usually took several hours to safely untie a barn so that the tobacco could be bulked and graded. After the introduction of the two-string tying pole, a barn could often be completely cleared and untied in an hour to an hour-and-a-half.[7]

Though simple, these innovations reduced the time required to both fill and empty tobacco barns, and also reduced the overall number of laborers needed to complete these tasks. The farmers saved money, but for workers these innovations meant an increased level of work as tobacco farmers required them to pick and tie a greater quantity of tobacco each day.

An additional innovation in the cultivation process enhanced the potential profitability of tobacco farming by decreasing the impact of late rains, and therefore increasing the acres that could be planted in seasons with below average rainfall levels. In the first two to three decades of the century, tobacco was planted with the first rains, which usually occurred in late October or early November. Late rains could limit the total acreage planted and this could ultimately mean a financial loss. Beginning in the mid 1920s, some growers tried to combat the problem by developing a system where tobacco seedlings were transplanted and watered by hand. It was usually tried on a limited scale of five to ten acres and required a specially constructed water cart which had a number of hoses attached. A 1926 article in the *Rhodesia Herald* reported that "there is no reason why this should not become a regular practice for a first planting if it is found that the leaf produced is equal in quality to that grown under natural conditions."[8] It apparently produced good quality leaf because the same practice, with improved water carts, was still being used on many tobacco farms as late as the 1980s.

As mentioned earlier, most tobacco farmers in this period used oxen to pull plows, farm wagons, and *mujitas*. Although there were steam-driven tractors in the country from the 1890s, most farmers could not afford them, and gasoline-powered tractors only began to be used sparingly in the 1920s. The same unnamed *Rhodesia Herald* correspondent who observed watering practices also stated that the first tractor in the Umvukwes region was being tested by a Mr. Andrews. The reporter commented that when the tractor had been driven from the nearest railhead at Concession, about forty kilometers south of the Umvukwes, it operated at a speed of about three miles an hour, "which is not bad going considering the

Cart used for water planting

depth of dust on the 'improved' portion of the road."[9] In addition to the initial buying price, the primary problem with the new tractors was that the gasoline needed to keep the tractors running was difficult to procure and relatively expensive. Even when a farmer could afford the gasoline, it often took at least a full day to fetch it from the nearest rail depot, where it had to be shipped from Salisbury. The irony is that it often took ox-drawn wagons two to three days to pick up the gasoline sufficient for a week's plowing.[10]

Farm Labor

The work tasks involved in growing tobacco changed even less than the technology during the period before 1945. The descriptions of seasonal tasks as detailed by George Odlum in 1905, E. A. Nobbs in a 1913 government handbook for newly established growers, by D. D. Brown in 1929, and those by an observer of tobacco farming in the late 1940s, are all basically interchangeable.[11] Based on these sources, the labor required on an average tobacco farm can be divided into four basic periods: (1) limited labor was required for seedbed work and general field preparation from late August to early November; (2) from November to January, there was a heavy demand for labor to transplant seedlings to the fields and for cultivation and weeding; (3) from February to April, large numbers of laborers were required for the reaping, curing and early grading of the crop; and (4) from early May to as late as July, depending on the acres a farmer had planted, there was a reduced demand for labor to finish grading the last of the year's crop.

Most farmers hoped to have their basic labor force, those workers needed for transplanting and subsequent tasks, hired by the beginning of the season in September. That basic labor force was based on an accepted ratio of one laborer required for every acre to be planted in tobacco. Most farmers felt that they could fill their needs for extra labor, universally referred to as "casuals," that might be required later in the season with the wives and children of their male employees, and with migrants from neighboring territories whom they expected to show up asking for work late in the season.

In years when the rains were late, or failed altogether, tobacco farmers were forced to greatly limit the size of their tobacco crop. When this occurred they did not usually summarily dismiss their labor force and hope for improved conditions the following year. Rather, they retained as many as they felt they could afford and tried to use the time to make improvements to their farms. For example, in the midst of drought conditions during the 1922/23 season the Secretary of the Agriculture Department reported that "the normal work being largely in abeyance, the opportunity was largely taken of making bricks, building houses, sheds . . . and stock yards, constructing roads, dams . . . silos, fencing, sinking wells, clearing scrub, and in other ways preparing for the better seasons which are confidently awaited."[12] In addition, tobacco farmers also employed a few laborers during the months of June, July, and August to prepare fields for the coming season. These tasks generally needed to be completed in preparation for transplanting, which was the start of actual field work and the first task requiring a relatively large number of laborers.[13]

The most important tasks that African laborers did during the off-season months were the stumping and clearing of virgin lands and the stockpiling of supplies of firewood for the coming season. On newly occupied farms these tasks obviously had to be completed as quickly as possible so that the new farmer could begin production. On farms already occupied and where the farmer required additional lands to either expand or rotate production, these tasks were usually scheduled to begin at the end of the tobacco season, so the new fields would be ready for the start of the next season. Stumping and clearing of virgin lands was probably the most strenuous work performed on a tobacco farm for it meant cutting down trees with hand saws and axes. Felled trees that were too large to be dragged out of the fields by spans of oxen then had to be cut into manageable pieces. In addition, thick brush needed to be cleared and wood and brush that could not be used as firewood in the barns, or as building materials on the farm, had to be manually removed from the fields and burnt. It was not burnt in the fields because farmers in that period believed that low tobacco production would result if ash mixed with the virgin soils. After trees and brush had been cleared laborers then used picks and *badzas* to dig out the larger roots and big rocks found in the fields.[14]

The pace at which stumping and clearing of virgin lands proceeded differed according to whether the lands were covered by sparse brush or were heavily wooded. The former could be cleared at a pace of about four-tenths of an acre a day, while the best a farmer could hope for on the latter was between a quarter to a fifth of an acre per day. The cost per acre of stumping and clearing virgin lands is difficult to pinpoint, but in the mid-1920s it averaged between £1 to £1/15s per acre in the Mazoe district. Once a farmer had become established and had a bit more operating capital available, these costs could be reduced to some extent by hiring specialized gangs of African laborers, usually with six to ten members, who independently contracted with farmers to stump and clear land for a specific price per acre, the only task they did on the farm.[15]

The other field tasks that had to be completed prior to the first rains in preparation for the transplanting of tobacco seedlings were the initial plowing, harrowing and ridging of the fields. The completed ridges were broad at the base, flat on top, several inches in height, ran the length of the fields and were usually spaced three feet apart. When the rains came laborers transplanted seedlings into these, using farm-made spacing chains to ensure that the seedlings were properly spaced along the ridges. The practice of ridging was nearly universal by the 1920s, but before that time many farmers transplanted seedlings into individual dirt mounds three feet apart from any neighboring plants. This earlier practice was extremely labor intensive and slow. Whether placing seedlings in mounds or ridges, the goal was to facilitate accomplishing later tasks. Also of importance was that the plants be somewhat elevated, so as the plant matured the heavier, lower leaves did not lie on the ground and were not destroyed, causing financial loss to the farmer. Plowing, harrowing and ridging could be time consuming, depending on the type of soil being worked and whether or not the work was being done on virgin fields. A span of sixteen oxen could usually be relied on to plow about two acres a day in fields of soft, sand soil which had been previously used for crops. If the soils were heavier, like those in the southeastern parts of Lomagundi, then two acres a day was exceptional. In recently stumped fields, two acres a day was still the goal, but this was rarely achieved as the equipment often snagged on roots that had not been dug out when the land was cleared.[16]

The labor required for field preparation would have varied from farm to farm, depending on the number of acres a farmer wanted to plant and the number of oxen spans a farmer owned. For each span of oxen, a farmer employed a driver and a juvenile "lead boy" who led the span from the front and attempted to keep the span moving in a straight line. Because of the skill involved in driving a span of oxen, drivers were, next to "boss boys" and the farmer's household domestics, the highest paid employees on a tobacco farm. The job of leading the span, on the other hand, was one of the lowest paying, even though pushing and pulling a span of oxen could be an exhausting day's work. In addition to the drivers and juvenile leads, a small number of laborers were also required to mark the ridges for future transplanting. On those farms that used fertilizers a group of laborers would follow those marking the spacing and apply a small amount of fertilizer, about a cupful, around the marked spot and then cover it with the mound of dirt.[17] Regardless of which method was used, tobacco farmers hoped to have field preparations completed by the coming of the first rains so that their entire labor force was available to transplant seedlings.

While some workers were preparing the fields, a small numbers of other laborers were required for the preparation and care of seedbeds, one of the most important jobs in the entire growing season.[18] Tobacco seeds are much too delicate and small to be planted individually, with approximately 300,000 seeds per ounce (albeit up to 75 percent could be sterile). Because of their size, tobacco seeds carry a very limited natural reserve of food, which means that after initial germination young seedlings must draw nutriment entirely from the soil, thus the need for properly prepared and fertilized seedbeds.

Breaking virgin soil for tobacco, mid 1920s

Plowing

Harrowing tobacco lands, 1912

The total number of seedbeds a tobacco farmer needed to sow depended on the number of acres to be planted. The accepted ratio during the period before 1945 was one seedbed for every two-and-one-half acres. Nevertheless, farmers were always strongly advised to have at least twice the number actually required in order to be prepared for late rains, hail damage, eelworm and other pests destructive to young plants, and other unforeseen circumstances.

Growers generally started their seedbeds about 60 days before the first rains were expected. Additional seedbeds were then prepared over the next several weeks so that growers always had a supply of mature seedlings, 6–8 inches high, available for transplanting. Individual seedbeds were generally 3–5 feet wide by 75–100 feet long, and while the total number of laborers that worked on them was relatively small, a rather large number of separate steps were needed to prepare them properly.

Seedbeds were always located near a source of water, usually a river or stream but often a *vlei*, and the first step after clearing the site and marking the proper dimensions was to enclose the seedbeds by bordering them with bricks. Beds were then saturated and the soil was sterilized by super-heating the top three to four inches by placing sticks across the bricks, piling brush on top of the sticks, and then burning the brush. The goal was to kill pests and organisms in the soil that might damage young seedlings. After raking off ash and unburnt pieces of brush and wood, laborers hoed the seedbeds to break up any clods of dirt. About one-half teaspoon of seed was then placed into a hand-held five-gallon watering can containing a mixture of water and water-soluble fertilizer. This mixture was then sprinkled over the length of the seedbed. In order to keep the seeds slightly wet to facilitate germination, the seedbed was then covered with a layer of combed grass and a light muslin cloth to prevent rapid evaporation. The cloth, held six inches above the soil by sticks, created a greenhouse effect. The combed grass was usually removed within a few days of when the new seedlings began to show through the soil's surface. When the seedlings were about an inch tall, laborers thinned the seedlings so that those that remained had approximately one square inch each in which to develop further. When the seedlings were about six to seven weeks old, and had reached a height of about six inches, the muslin was removed each morning so that the young plants could "harden" to direct sunlight, and replaced each evening to protect them from night pests like moths. By about the ninth week after sowing, the seedlings were ready for transplanting. To ensure that the seedbeds were properly maintained farmers generally permanently assigned a number of laborers to the seedbeds until transplanting was completed for the season.

Due to the lack of irrigation systems during this period and the uncertainty of how long the early rains might continue, it was imperative for tobacco growers to plant as many acres as possible as quickly as possible once the rains began, making the transplanting of seedlings to the fields one of the most

Tobacco seed beds near Sinoia, 1912

intense periods of work in the entire season. For the workers this often meant working from sunrise to sunset, much of that time in the rain, and in some instances working the entire time without rest breaks or time off to eat.[19] In order to make the process go as quickly as possible, the work force was divided into two groups. The smaller of the two groups went to the seedbeds where, along with the laborers regularly assigned there, they soaked the seedbeds so that seedlings would not be damaged when pulled from the soil. Each young plant was then quickly examined to determine if it was diseased; if it was, it was discarded. The seedlings were then carefully placed in boxes and carried to the fields where the second group was working. Whether planted into mounds or ridges, the process followed was basically the same as described in a 1913 handbook for new tobacco growers: "The plants are dropped along the rows at regular intervals. . . . There follows a [laborer], who, with a round stick about six inches in length, makes a hole, and then inserts the plant into the hole, and, while holding it firmly with one hand, presses the earth firmly round the roots with the stick. The surface of the soil is then rapidly smoothed over, and left in as loose a condition as possible."[20]

This routine could be modified two ways. First, some farmers used a system in which laborers placed a small amount of fertilizer directly into the hole, prior to the seedlings being planted. In that system, one laborer usually made the hole and sprinkled in some fertilizer, then a second laborer placed the seedling into the hole and tamped the soil around the root. The second alternative method occurred at those times when transplanting had not been completed during the first rains and the soil had dried out a bit, or when the rains were overly late and growers felt they could not wait any longer to begin planting out the tobacco. In that situation, a laborer would either follow the laborer making the hole and pour a small amount of water from a hand-held watering can into the hole before the planter planted the seedling; or conversely, the laborer would follow the planter pouring water into a second, smaller hole made by the planter next to the seedling.[21]

The next phase of the labor process, cultivation, began as soon as the plants had become established and working around them would not disturb their growth. Most tobacco farmers believed that cultivation, which involved breaking up and loosening the soil around the base of the plant, facilitated the access of water and air to the root system and stimulated the growth of the plant and that it could not "be repeated too often."[22] Although the process could be accomplished by using oxen and a plow, most tobacco farmers employed their African workers, using *badzas*, to cultivate, particularly in the weeks following transplanting when the plants were still young. In addition to working the soil, another task was sometimes included during cultivation. This occurred when a section of a planting was damaged by hail or some other natural calamity. If the plants were not destroyed entirely, laborers were sent through the devastated fields where they cut off the damaged

Pulling tobacco seedlings for planting, mid 1920s

Transplanting tobacco into fields, 1912

stems and leaves, leaving the lower part of the main stem from which a new shoot, a "ratoon," would appear. This process was referred to as "ratooning."[23] Preparing seedbeds, planting with short sticks, and cultivating with *badzas* was extremely tiring work for laborers. For workers these tasks meant spending the entire working day, often ten to twelve hours or more, bent over at the waist with arms stretched downward, slowly moving backwards as they reached between and around each plant to loosen soil and remove weeds.[24]

The next three tasks in the tobacco production process, "priming," "topping," and "suckering," were less physically strenuous than transplanting and cultivating, but were necessary to ensure healthy plants that would produce quality leaves that yielded good texture and color. The goal was to develop those leaves which came off the plant's stem beginning at a height of about one foot above the ground. This required limiting the development of leaves lying in the dirt, as well as late developing shoots and the blossoms of most plants. These three tasks were performed in the same sequence on all tobacco farms, although the exact timing of when to do them differed from farm to farm. Regarding the actual allocation of the labor to the tasks, a 1929 article by D. D. Brown suggested that growers split their work force during priming, topping, and suckering, using one group on healthy plants, and a second group on diseased plants. This approach was viewed as a means of ensuring that laborers did not inadvertently infect healthy plants after having worked with one that was diseased.[25]

Priming began when the plants were about a foot tall, and required laborers to pinch off the plants' lowest leaves close to the stem. For most tobacco plants it was repeated several times, until the plant was several feet tall and ready to be "topped." Ultimately, priming left the plant's stalk bare for at least its first twelve inches, with the remaining leaves hanging clear of the ground. Laborers carried the primed leaves out of the fields, where they were destroyed. The only exception to this regimen was when some growers cured the last priming. These leaves were usually extremely dusty and dirty from having lain on the ground and their curing and grading was a "ghastly" task, often resulting in laborers coming down with respiratory infections caused by the excessive dust.[26]

"Topping" was the process in which the plant's blossom and several top small leaves were removed. With a large crop, topping usually began when about half of the plants were in flower. The remainder of the crop was then topped as individual plants flowered. Laborers would go through the crop, gently bending the tops of each flowering plant to one side and pinching off the small top leaves and flower. Once priming and topping had been completed, individual plants retained six to sixteen leaves of, farmers hoped, high quality tobacco. In other words, the two processes combined to produce "a great change in the plant by increasing the surface and thickening the leaf," accompanied by "an increase of . . . protein compounds and nicotine in the leaf, as well as hastening the process of ripening."[27] In the early years of tobacco farming, growers apparently overlapped topping with the last priming, but by the late 1920s the two processes required separate passes through the crop.[28] Suckering began almost immediately after topping was completed. The process entailed the removal of "suckers," new shoots that rapidly appeared after the blossom had been removed, and had to be repeated about once a week until the plants were reaped. Suckering was a fairly simple task and many farmers employed the children of their adult laborers to do it, thereby freeing the parents for jobs elsewhere on the farm.

The major alternate task to the three just described was the growing of seed. During this period many farmers grew seed both for their own use and for sale to other growers, particularly first-time growers. In order to procure pure seed that had not been cross-pollinated, farmers selected plants they believed would produce good seed and workers placed paper or muslin bags over the buds as soon as they appeared. Obviously these plants were not topped, although they were primed and suckered. When the seed heads had ripened satisfactorily, they were cut off in the bags and safely stored away.[29]

The last three primary tasks of the tobacco production process were reaping, curing, and grading. These tasks placed the greatest demands on laborers of the entire growing season. Reaping combined a series of tasks that brought leaves from the fields to the barns. The first of these was the actual picking of leaves from the tobacco plant. Tobacco growers claimed that they produced high quality tobacco partly because the leaves were hand picked.[30] The usual practice was for those laborers who could be trusted to pick ripe leaves to go through the fields picking only the two lowest leaves on each plant, leaving those higher on the plant time to continue to mature. The quantity of leaves picked in a day was determined by the number of barns that could be filled that day, with this routine repeated daily until all the tobacco plants on a farm had been picked. As with the daily picking quotas, the timing of the passes through the fields largely depended on the availability of barns.

After picking the ripe leaves the reapers handed the leaves to a "waiter," usually a juvenile boy. When the waiter's arms were full, he took the leaves to the nearest *mujita*-loaded wagon. At season's end, once the reaping of all suitable leaves had been completed, laborers went through the fields one last time to cut the remaining stalks just below ground level. These were then carried out of the main tobacco fields and burnt in the expectation of preventing any tobacco diseases from somehow remaining in the fields and infecting a subsequent crop.[31]

When the *mujitas* in the fields had been filled, they were

Harvesting tobacco, 1905

taken to the farm's tying shed, usually adjacent to the curing barns. The tobacco leaves were then first tied into hands and then onto four-foot-long sticks. This process was often facilitated by first mounting the tying sticks onto a piece of equipment called a "horse," a wooden plank laid on the floor that had upright forked sticks secured to each end. Laborers tied between fifteen and twenty hands of tobacco along each side of the stick, and as each stick was finished it was given to one of several juvenile waiters who took it to the barn that was being filled. In some cases, usually at the end of a day when it was becoming too dark to work, tied sticks were kept overnight in the tying shed and the barn was filled the next morning. At the barn, sticks were handed to a worker who placed them onto the barn's interior scaffolding, called "laths," from the top down, and when full the barn's doors were shut and the curing process began. Between twenty and thirty laborers could fill a barn in a single day, and laborers often worked seven days a week during this period of the season. Those days began with reaping at sunrise and often ended at nine or ten o'clock at night for periods lasting up to two-and-a-half months.[32]

Curing, the process by which tobacco leaves were heated in order to remove all the moisture in them, was totally controlled by the grower, with many farmers "sleeping at the barns." After the drying process had been accomplished and the barn allowed to cool for twenty-four hours, the cured tobacco leaves were usually too brittle to be handled without breaking. Therefore, in order to slightly moisten and soften the tobacco so that it could be safely removed for grading, a limited amount of cool steam was introduced into the barns by means of a perforated pipe which ran along the flues.[33] Although growers controlled the curing process, they assigned one important task to African laborers: the stoking of the barns' furnaces. On most farms two workers, alternating day and night shifts, were assigned to keep the furnaces burning as needed. If a farm had ten barns, only three or four would have required stoking at any one time, for as some were curing tobacco, the others were either being filled or emptied. The assigned laborer would shuttle between the furnaces that required attention adding firewood, or coal on some farms by the end of the period, when necessary.[34]

When emptying the barns, laborers carried the sticks to the bulking sheds, located close to the barns, where the tobacco was untied and placed in large piles, called "bulks," until it could be graded. The bulking sheds were made of the same materials as the barns and had darkened windows that allowed air in but prevented sunlight from shinning directly onto the cured tobacco. To prevent mold from developing, the tobacco was bulked on raised platforms, and workers were required to regularly turn the bulks so that there was a free circulation of air around the entire bulk.

Workers bringing tied tobacco to barns, mid 1920s

Grading, where each leaf had to be inspected and separated into class, type, and grade, was the last task of the tobacco season. All tobacco with the same qualities was packed into a three feet-by-two feet-by-two feet (3′ x 2′ x 2′) bale. A full bale weighed up to 240 pounds and was wrapped in waterproof paper and then hessian. The process sounds simple, but laborers had to quickly develop a knowledge of different textures, aromas and color variations to be able to grade tobacco properly, for even in the highly competitive labor market of Southern Rhodesia they could be fired on the spot for misgrading. Farmers kept a very close watch on the grading process because poorly graded tobacco, various grades in the same bale being the most common problem, cost the farmer money as the entire bale sold at the price of the lowest grade.

Like reaping, laborers were often required to work sixteen hour days for a month or more at a stretch during grading. In addition, it was perhaps the most unhealthy period of the season for many tobacco workers. Grading tobacco was a dusty job under the best of conditions, and during this period it was

Rough grading

Grading and baling tobacco, mid 1920s

rarely done in the best of conditions. Grading sheds were usually small, cramped, poorly ventilated places, with workers required to stand in one spot for several hours on end. As a result, many laborers contracted minor respiratory ailments, usually colds, although it was not uncommon for large numbers of tobacco workers to develop pneumonia.[35] In 1928, for example, the government's Public Health department reported that tobacco grading was "considered by some to be a fruitful agent in the increase of the pneumonia rate, and there is no doubt that both natives and Europeans alike who are engaged in [it] . . . have suffered . . . to a greater extent than other forms of labour."[36]

Tobacco had not always been graded on the farms. In the years before World War I, it was almost exclusively graded at a few large government-operated warehouses located throughout the tobacco-growing districts, with the most important warehouses for farmers in Lomagundi and Mazoe districts located at Darwendale and Salisbury, respectively. During this early period, tobacco growers cured and bulked their tobacco, but almost all of them then delivered it to the nearest warehouse to be graded, baled, and sold. The warehouses performed these services for a fee which was deducted from the final price received for the crop. This practice was prevalent at the beginning of the period because most growers and government agricultural officials considered grading to be too complicated to be successfully accomplished on the farms. In 1914, G. S. Money, a tobacco farmer, wrote to the editor of the *Rhodesia Herald* stating that grading was "quite a separate and complete undertaking. It is not, therefore, possible, however expert he may be, for the grower to do his own grading."[37]

By 1918, however, tobacco growers had begun to overcome this attitude. By grading tobacco on their farms they could sell directly to buyers, retain the fees they had been paying the warehouses, and increase their profit margins. In 1920, the

Agriculture Department indicated that it strongly supported the idea that more and more grading should be done on the farms and in its annual report commented that one quarter of all tobacco farmers were grading on their farms.[38] In 1922, department officials, while continuing to support grading on the farms, warned growers that "in many cases tobacco had to be re-worked [at the warehouses] owing to the faulty conditions," such as insufficient conditioning of leaves and irregular baling.[39] By 1923, most tobacco farmers were forced to make the transition to grading their own tobacco as the agriculture department notified farmers that the tobacco warehouses would no longer accept ungraded tobacco. Nevertheless, not all growers, particularly those new to the industry, graded their own tobacco even then; instead they used privately owned commercial grading warehouses which were being established throughout the tobacco growing districts.[40]

With the great increase in production in the 1926/27 and 1927/28 growing seasons, the Agriculture Department began virtually beseeching growers to grade their own tobacco. In the 1926 Annual Report, the department's secretary stated that "the question of grading is a matter for which farmers must make satisfactory provision. . . . Growers must either do their own grading or co-operate and provide for district grading."[41] The following year, a government report on agricultural conditions in the country emphasized that it had "become imperative that a greater proportion of the leaf should be graded on the farm."[42] By the early 1930s, the Agriculture Department's campaign had succeeded. By that time, most tobacco growers had made the transition to doing their own grading on the farms. This final transition to farm grading was partially stimulated by the depression which followed the 1927/28 season. Those tobacco farmers who were able to keep their farms and continued to grow tobacco adopted farm grading as a means of reducing their production cost. They were able to accomplish this reduction because with so many farmers going bankrupt, there was an overabundance of laborers, often in desperate need of employment in order to feed themselves. As a result, workers were generally forced to accept heavy wage cuts, making it less expensive for growers to hire additional laborers to grade on the farms.

The corollary to grading being done on the farms was that tobacco growers increasingly devalued the skill and knowledge necessary to do grading. Farmers might have pointed out that certain individual laborers were better at grading than others, but they would not have repeated Money's insinuation that it required an expert to grade tobacco correctly. On the contrary, by the early 1930s grading was considered by most tobacco growers as one of the ordinary tasks that every member of their labor force was expected to either know how to do when hired, or at the very least be able to learn within a few days.

After grading, the only remaining tasks were directly related to transporting the tobacco crop to Salisbury. The first of these was for workers to wrap the bales of cured tobacco in waterproof paper; workers then sewed strips of hessian cloth around the bales. The bales were then loaded onto transport wagons and shipped to Salisbury for sale.

The tasks that have been detailed to this point were specifically related to the production of tobacco. Even on those farms where tobacco was the only commercial crop grown, however, there were other tasks that required labor during the tobacco season. For example, all tobacco farmers rationed their laborers with maize that was grown on the farms. In addition, "depending entirely on the season and the labor available to do the field work" many farmers also put in other rations crops such as groundnuts and beans. Work on the maize crop was generally perceived by the farmers as part of the regular labor requirements on their farms, but rather amazingly work on the other ration crops was not viewed in the same way. Work on those crops was often not considered by farmers to be "part and parcel of the farming system as such," but rather as extra work put in on crops when the "occasion was right, the land available and the labour available."[43] This dichotomy only makes sense when it is understood that tobacco farmers of the period generally defined "acceptable work" as only that work which affected the production of the tobacco crop, the crop that generated income for the farmer. Therefore, assigning part of the labor force to plant, cultivate and harvest maize, the staple of farm workers' rations, was considered "part and parcel" of the required work because it was necessary to feed laborers so that they were capable of working on the tobacco crop. Any use of labor that took laborers away from that crop was considered gratuitous.

In addition to the laborers who worked on the tobacco crop a further group of "essential" laborers worked on every farm. These were the cooks and domestic servants who worked in the farmers' homes, and the "garden boys" who tilled the homestead garden and grew fresh produce for the grower's personal requirements. In addition, most tobacco growers also employed "crop guards," whose duties included protecting the farms' tobacco and ration crops from both animal and human marauders. These workers and the tasks they did were, apparently, also considered part and parcel of the farming system.[44]

The work performed by African laborers on tobacco farms was central to the tobacco-growing process. Without the skills and knowledge required to work tobacco which African workers possessed before starting work, or learned quickly thereafter, the government's financial support and experimental crop programs would not have made any difference. In short, European farmers would not have been able to remain on the land. They would not have been able to make the grade.

Sewing canvas around bales of cured tobacco, 1912

Dispatching bales of tobacco to Salisbury, mid 1920s

5

Labor and Discipline

Tobacco farmers before 1945 generally believed that if a farm's soil fertility was good, the rains were timely and sufficient, and the workers completed their tasks properly, then that farm's owner stood a good chance of having a successful year. Underlying these factors was a cornucopia of human relationships between African laborers and European tobacco growers which more often than not really determined whether or not a tobacco farmer was successful. Because of this tobacco farmers developed a number of methods to try to control laborers and, as a result, created on many farms what one contemporary observer called "a system of benevolent paternal autocracy."[1] These methods sought to regulate both the quantity and quality of daily work and insure that laborers stayed on until the end of the season.

Daily Work Discipline

In 1934, Rawdon Hoare, a tobacco and maize farmer in Mazoe, presented a view of an African laborer's typical work day:

Just before the sun steals over the valley, the simbre or bell warns the natives of the beginning of another day. A curious collection struggle out from the pole and dagga huts, some wrapped in blankets, some in coats, but all shivering . . . . They seldom eat until mid-day, when there is an hour and a half's rest. On many occasions when natives are given definite contract work they will not return to the compound for food until round three o'clock in the afternoon. . . . At sunset, the day ends and the quiet of the veld is broken by singing and chattering natives, wending their way to the compound in gay anticipation of their evening meal.[2]

The method of work that Hoare refers to as "contract work" was more commonly called "piece-work" or "task-work" by farmers and government officials. African laborers called it *mgwaza*. This type of work, and the more directly supervised "gang labor," were the two primary means by which farmers attempted to discipline their laborers' daily endeavors. In actuality, both methods were used on tobacco farms in the course of a growing season, with the decision on when to use which method principally determined by the requirements of the work and by the personal preferences of the individual farmer. With that said, *mgwaza* was generally used for stumping, collecting of firewood, and most prominently during the period of cultivation. In addition, some tobacco growers also used it during the tying and untying of tobacco toward the end of the season. Gang labor, on the other hand, was almost exclusively used for the transplanting of tobacco seedlings, for the priming, topping, and suckering of maturing plants, and during reaping and grading. This was because these tasks generally required intensive labor at specific times during the tobacco growing season.[3] For example, some farmers used a system for grading in which a gang of laborers was required to grade the contents of a single curing barn, 900 to 1,000 pounds of tobacco, each day during the grading season. When using gangs of laborers farmers were most concerned that tasks be completed satisfactorily, and less with how long that might take.[+]

As for *mgwaza*, tobacco farmers sometimes assigned it the previous night, often staking out rows with the names of individual laborers, so that workers "knew when they got up in the morning exactly what they had to do." Other farmers took their laborers to the fields each morning and after assessing the situation, assigned that day's work. Although the amount of assigned work could vary, most farmers tried to allot enough work to keep each worker busy for seven to eight hours. How to determine the amount of work that could be accomplished in those seven to eight hours was another, more puzzling question. In the late 1920s, for example, a Lomagundi farmer was reported to have worked in the fields alongside his workers to better "gauge the limits of the daily task." Richard Colbourne, who worked on his father's tobacco farm near Banket in the 1930s and later took it over himself, believed that "a task finished on Monday finished an hour or two later than on Saturday," when laborers wanted to finish quickly because the

Planting tobacco, 1912

time from then until Monday morning was their own time. Therefore, each work day a farmer should "assess what they [could] do on a Saturday, because you [knew] they [could] do it."[5]

Regardless of how the amount of work was determined the decision to assign *mgwaza* instead of gang labor was rooted in a farmer's belief that it was more efficient in regulating laborers' daily work. In 1934, for example, L. W. Morgan, who grew tobacco on the farm Blauw Vlei, near Sinoia, argued that the "only farmer who might make a success of farming is the one who aims at and succeeds in getting the most out of his natives . . . and I maintain that this is not practicable unless it is done as task work, for it is not possible to continually be with the natives."[6] E. D. Palmer, who began tobacco farming in the mid 1920s, agreed and assigned *mgwaza* whenever possible because he felt it was "the most efficient," even though "it took a lot of supervision, probably more so than the other method because you had to go back and check every labourer." On the other hand, Michael Howell, a close friend of Palmer's, disagreed. With "piece work, the smart alecks would be finished by half-past-nine or something like that. It was impossible to see what was happening because you've got one finishing at half-past-nine and some of them going up to four. . . . It was a hopeless business."[7]

Regardless of which type of daily work discipline tobacco farmers used, they all required a means to record a day's work. They eventually adopted the "ticket system" used on the mines in Southern Rhodesia, in which each worker was given a ticket, usually with the numbers one to thirty printed on it, and as each day's assigned task was judged to have been successfully completed, a line was drawn through the next succeeding number. When all the numbers had been lined through the laborer was paid. This system was officially sanctioned for use on farms by a 1909 amendment to the Masters and Servants Act of 1901. Under the terms of that act, individual Africans were allowed to legally contract, either orally or in writing, with farmers for any length of time from one month to one year.[8] Although legal from the turn of the century, the adoption of the ticket system was relatively slow. During the earliest years of tobacco farming in Southern Rhodesia farm workers generally contracted for a single calendar month at a time. Around 1910, however, this practice began to be replaced on farms by the ticket system, which normally took anywhere from 35 to 45 days to complete. In 1924, a speaker addressing the Shamva Farmers' Association suggested that whenever 30 or more laborers were employed, farmers should adopt the use of the ticket system "so that the labourer gets his work recorded and credit for it, and yet the employer gets a record as to whether he is getting satisfaction for the wages he is paying out."[9] By 1931, the chief native commissioner could state that "every employer and every [African] employee in this country understands the ticket system," and then added that "by long usage it has become customary."[10]

The possibilities for abusing the ticket system were even greater for farmers than van Onselen argues was the case for mine owners and managers.[11] Mines were subject to inspection by government compound inspectors, but farmers in Southern Rhodesia before the early 1940s did not have to worry about government inspection, except in rare cases when treatment of laborers was, even by contemporary standards, extremely bad. In addition, it is apparent that a large number of farmers believed that it was to their advantage to "lay on the tasks," because if the assigned amount of work took a number of days to complete, then they had effectively extended their laborers contracts without having to pay additional wages. For many farmers, however, the practice of laying on tasks did not go far enough and they further increased the level of exploitation by refusing to mark laborers' tickets, claiming that they had not completed that day's assigned task. A good example of the "improper marking of tickets" came to light in 1929 when a public prosecutor reported that several laborers on a farm in the Amandas region of Mazoe "had only completed one or two tickets in six months" due to the farmer consistently refusing to mark tickets after declaring that assigned work had not been properly completed.[12] Farmers also refused to mark the tickets of laborers they accused of committing infractions of farm rules. The 1928 Native Labour Committee reported that a "large majority of farmers" failed to mark laborers' tickets "for all sorts of petty offenses," with "disobedience, neglect of duty and absence without leave being the commonest." Of course, all of these "offenses" were subjectively judged by the farmers themselves.[13] Although the failure to complete a task was at the top of the list of offenses farmers cited when docking pay, stealing from the farmer was second. The list becomes more difficult to delineate after these two because, depending on individual farmers, any act could be classified as an offense and punished. C. W. Cartwright's ledgers provide a number of examples. For example, a field laborer named Homman had his ticket docked one day after being found with "no shoes." In May 1937, Freddie and Tawasa each had three days docked off their tickets "for running away," while in the following month two workers were docked six days each, Tayengwa "for going off" and Jacob "for not returning after leave." In February 1939, Musora's ticket was not marked for an entire month after "losing three cows," and Shoni met the same fate "for not reporting same"; nine months later Shoni lost another week after "losing oxen."[14]

In conjunction with not marking tickets, farmers often made laborers make up time they were accused of missing or wasting. Missed work usually meant being late for roll call or not showing up for work at all, while wasting time was usually defined as working slower than other members of a gang or resting while others were working. Offenders sometimes had to make-up this time by working late on Saturday afternoons, a time farm workers traditionally considered free time. This form of punishment was more than merely an attempt to discipline farm laborers to a standard work day and pace of work by making them make up "lost" time. It also incorporated an element of personal ridicule and sought to humiliate individual workers by forcing them to continue to work "in full view of the remainder [of laborers] gaily going home." By belittling laborers in front of their co-workers, some farmers obviously hoped to limit tardiness and "loafing."[15]

Unfortunately, farmers did not always stop at humiliation, but resorted to physical violence in their attempts to instill daily work discipline. Throughout the period, many farmers justified the use of physical violence as a way of educating laborers to the work of the farm. In many cases these farmers saw caning, whipping, or "clouting" as essentially beneficial. In 1909, a farmer argued that "where there is no fear of the master there is no work done."[16] Rawdon Hoare agreed that "a good clout over the head frequently has excellent results," but warned that "thrashing in the proper sense of the word is a mistake and only ends in the lowering of the white man's prestige."[17] Despite Hoare's admonition to his fellow farmers, there are ample examples which indicate that "a good clout" often encompassed a high degree of violence toward farm laborers. In 1912, a plow driver stopped work when his span of oxen encountered a large rock just below the soil's surface. After being told to continue plowing by his employer the plow was broken on another rock. The farmer then tied the driver to a nearby tree and hit him nearly twenty times on the back with a thick stick. Ten years later Nicholas von Biljon beat a laborer after accusing him of tying broken leaves into a hand of tobacco and then placing them in a barn to be cured. The district's medical officer testified that the laborer's left leg would take several months to heal.[18] Though these cases involved field laborers, they were not the only farm employees who faced the dangers of being beaten. For example, W. W. Tucker was fined £2 in January 1912, after he "boxed the ears" of a household servant. Jeannie Boggie reported that she once hit a young male employee with "a home-made brush made from the stalks of some weed" for failing to properly wash his hands before separating milk.[19]

In other cases the physical mistreatment of farm workers went tragically beyond hitting, whipping, and "a good clout." In 1915, for example, a Sinoia farmer named Archibald Steel got into an argument early one morning with a former employee he found still living in the farm compound. Steel later claimed that the man threatened him with an ax handle and Steel hit the man with a *sjambok*, an animal hide whip, then went to the farm homestead to get a rifle. When he returned to the compound the man had run off, but Steel became even angrier because the other laborers had not gone to the fields. He fired his rifle in an attempt to hurry them out to the fields. He had not looked in the direction he had fired his rifle and as a result shot a laborer from a neighboring farm, who was visiting his brother on Steel's farm, in the head. The man died five days later. Steel was found not guilty of culpable homicide when the local magistrate ruled that the shooting had been an accident.[20] According to witnesses in another case, Bindura farmer U. H. Lloyd beat one of his workers with a belt on the buttocks and repeatedly kicked the man "violently with great force." The laborer had been assigned to look after the farm's pigs, and when they got loose and spilt several tins of fresh milk, Lloyd went after the man with the purpose of beating him to set an example to the other laborers. The wounds he inflicted were so severe that they did not heal and the man died when they became infected. Lloyd was found guilty of "assault with the intent to do grievous bodily damage" and fined £3 or seven days hard labor.[21]

These cases make two points. The first is that a large number of farm workers had very good cause to develop a "fear of the master." Second, many farmers placed little value on the lives of their African employees. It is also apparent from the not guilty verdicts and minimal fines handed out in those cases when farmers were found guilty that many government officials acquiesced in this view.

Reproducing of a Seasonal Labor Force

In 1910, the Director of Agriculture reported that offering higher wages for agricultural work "seldom attracts boys not otherwise seeking employment."[22] In the late 1930s, Mazoe District's native commissioner opined that "the feeding of labourers and care of the sick are greater inducements than wages" when trying to attract northern migrants to work on farms.[23] Over forty years later two retired farmers, both of whom had grown tobacco before 1945, still disagreed on this issue, one claiming that "money was paramount," while the other believed that "the food was probably more important than the money."[24]

The centrality of wages, rations, and medical care as inducements necessary to attract and maintain a work force for the length of a tobacco-growing season would seem to be obvious. As the above statements suggest, however, the three items were at the center of a debate that raged among farmers and government officials throughout the period from 1890 to 1945. The premise of that debate was that rationing and rudimentary medical care were sufficient to induce people to offer themselves as farm workers, even when wages were lower than those offered in other types of employment. Some farmers went so far as to argue that by supplying rations and medical care they could even reduce the general agricultural wage rate without adversely affecting their labor supplies.

Wages

Time and again farmers were admonished by government officials that in order to attract sufficient numbers of laborers they needed to increase the level of wages they paid. In 1911, the BSAC's secretary to the administrator told farmers that their efforts to re-engage laborers would "be useless and an unnecessary expense unless farm wages were appreciably increased." In 1925 the assistant native commissioner in Shamva repeated the warning to local farmers that "the ruling [wage] rate will have to be raised if an adequate supply of labour is to be assured." A decade later, Chief Native Commissioner C. L. Carbutt reported that farmers would not be facing a shortage of workers for the approaching tobacco harvest if only they offered "a rather higher wage for this class of unskilled labour."[25] Farmers generally disagreed, instead arguing that "the more pay you give the native the more he extends his period of repose . . . his period of hibernation . . . if he is paid less he will work for longer periods."[26] In late 1926, a mini-debate erupted in the pages of the *Rhodesia Herald* over this issue. It centered on a proposal that the problem of wages and labor supplies could be resolved if the government would support efforts to establish a "standardized" wage for farm labor. Although there were several supporters of the proposal the majority of letters and articles agreed with the Ayrshire-Sipolilo Farmers' Association that implementing such a thing would be "impossible, even if desirable." Some even argued that such a wage would be unfair to laborers, noting "that some natives were really worth high wages, whereas others were next to useless."[27]

TABLE 6
Agricultural Wages, 1900–42 (30-day Work Ticket)[28]

Year	Throughout Zimbabwe	Mazoe	Lomagundi
1900	8/ to 15/		
	5/*		
1903	10/ to 20/		
1908	6/8 to 15/		
1910	11/ to 13/6		
1911	10/ to 15/		
1913	20/		
	20/**		
1914	18/**		
1915	18/**	10/	
1916	5/ to 15/	10/	
	18/**		
1917	15/	10/	
	18/**		
1918	20/	10/	
	18/**		
1919	18/	7/6	8/ to 10/
	18/**		
1920	12/6		10/
	18/**		
1921	18/**		15/
1922	5/ (minimum)		
1923	17/6 to 20/		
1925	10/ to 19/6		
1926	10/ to 21/4	17/6	20/
1928		15/ to 17/6	5/ to 25/
		12/6 to 20/	
		5/ to 12/6*	
1929		12/6 to 22/6‡	
		5/‡	
1930	15/		

TABLE 6 (*Continued*)

Year	Throughout Zimbabwe	Mazoe	Lomagundi
1931	10/	8/ to 10/	
1932	10/ to 12/ 7/*	10/ to 12/	
1933	9/ to 15/ 5/*	10/ to 12/ 5/*	10/ to 15/
1934	12/6to 20/§ 20/ to £5#	8/6	10/ to 15/
1935	10/ to 15/		10/ to 15/
1936	7/6to 15/ 5/ to 7/ (Wankie)		8/ to 15/
1937			8/ to 15/
1938	12/6		
1940	15/ to 20/	15/	15/ to 20/
1941	17/6(men)	15/ to 17/6 (men) 15/ (women)	15/ to 20/ 15/ (women)
1942	15/ to 17/6		15/ to 17/6

* juveniles
** wages paid to laborers recruited by the Rhodesia Native Labour Bureau
† Twelve month contracts only
‡ adult wage before 1928 "bust," adult wage after "bust"
§ "unskilled"—probably general field labor
# "skilled"—probably drivers
General Notes: Unless otherwise noted, the wages given are for adult male field laborers. The wages for "boss boys" and/or "skilled" laborers, like drivers, would be higher, by as much as 150 percent. Also, from at least the late 1920s, wages on tobacco farms were generally, although not always, a bit higher than on farms specializing in other cash crops, like maize or cotton.

It would therefore appear that the majority of farmers were opposed to an officially established wage. Nevertheless, farmers were not so much opposed to a fixed wage as fearful that it might be fixed at a higher level than they were willing to pay. This interpretation seems appropriate because farmers operated like other employers of labor and attempted to fix workers' wages at the lowest level they thought they could pay and still attract adequate numbers of laborers. Also, they already practiced a de facto system of fixing wages. This was accomplished by setting wage rates at the district level through the collusion of the district's farmers. An examination of farm labor wages in Lomagundi establishes this point. Between August 1933 and December 1935, wages on farms in that district were fixed at 10–15 shillings per 30-day work ticket. Yet on a number of occasions during that time the local native commissioner reported variously that labor supplies, particularly on local tobacco farms, were "inadequate," that there was "a very general shortage of agricultural labor," and that the "shortage of agricultural labourers in the Sinoia area continues to cause concern." These reported shortages existed despite "a fairly steady stream of boys passing in and through the District seeking work."[29] In several reports, the native commissioner repeatedly pointed-out that farmers were the cause of their own problems, because there was "a natural tendency for the work seekers to travel as far as possible before engaging in the hope of finding an employer who will give a higher wage."[30]

Farm wages paid to adult male laborers in Lomagundi and Mazoe before 1945 ranged from a low of 5/– to a high of 25/– per 30-day ticket during the expansion years prior to the 1928 depression. Nevertheless, the average for the two districts for the period 1890–1945 would have been between 12/6 to 15/– per 30-day ticket. Still, knowing the actual wages is only pertinent when they can be compared with the prices of goods those wages could purchase. There are, fortunately, a few sources which allow some comparisons to be made. In 1919 shirts sold for about 4/– each, khaki trousers cost 15/–, and a khaki coat went also for 15/–. Two years later, lightweight blankets measuring 64 by 68 inches sold for 5/9. By 1932, the cost of the same type of blankets had risen to 10/–.[32] In June 1940, the assistant native commissioner in Bindura compiled a list of "those goods considered as essential" by local African

TABLE 7
Prices for Trade Goods in Bindura[31]

Article	June 1940	Late 1930s
Blankets	From 3/ to 12/ each	2/ to 10/
Shorts	2/ to 3/	2/ to 2/6
Trousers	6/ to 10/	4/ to 7/6
Shirts	2/6 to 7/	2/ to 5/
Vests	6d to 1/	6d to 1/
Dresses	3/ to 5/	2/6 to 4/
Mufflers	3d to 6d	3d to 6d
Print [cloth]	1/ per yd.	1/ per yd.
Calico	6d per yd.	6d per yd.
Hats	2/6 to 6/	2/ to 5/
Tennis shoes	2/6 per pair	2/ per pair
Overcoats	10/ to £1	10/ to £1
Jackets	7/6 to 12/6	same
Plates	3d to 6d	3d to 6d
Pots	11d to 1/	7d to 8d
Mugs	6d to 9d	3d to 6d
Dishes	3/ to 5/	4/ to 6/
Beads	3d per bunch	3d per bunch
Sacks (2nd hand)*	9d	4d
Salt*	10–12 1 lb. bag for 1/	14–15 1 lb. bag 1/
Sugar	3 1/2d per lb.	3d per lb.
Mealie Meal	5 lbs. for 6d	5 lbs. for 6d
Plows (approx.)	£2 to £2–5/	35/
Paraffin	6d per bottle	6d per bottle
Peanut Oil (beer bottle)	3d	3d
Soap	3d, 6d, 1/	3d, 6d, 1/
Bicycles	£3–15/ to £5	£3 to £4–5/
Matches	3d (4 packets)	3d (4 packets)

* Standardized by Legislation

workers. The list gave both the 1940 prices and the prewar prices of the late 1930s, which he estimated were 15 percent lower. C. W. Cartwright's farm ledgers also provide a comparative look at wages and the cost of trade goods, in this case bought by Cartwright for his workers. Cartwright charged 5/ for a blanket, 10/ for a coat, 2/ for a shirt, and 2/6 for a pair of work shoes. During the period covered by the ledgers, he paid his adult field laborers an average of 10/ to 15/ per ticket.[33] The information provided by Cartwright and the Bindura assistant native commissioner indicate that it could cost a general field laborer as much as one-quarter of his wages from a completed ticket to purchase work shoes or a shirt; one-half to two-thirds of a ticket to get a blanket; and at least one full ticket, representing a minimum of five to six weeks' work, to buy one pair of khaki trousers or a khaki coat.

This raises the question of whether wages maintained their real value between 1890 and 1945. Sources indicate that farm wages decreased dramatically in real value during the period. In 1921, the government's Cost of Living Committee estimated that farm workers' wages had increased about 21 percent since 1914, equaling the rise in domestics' wages and greater than that received by mine workers (13 percent). Nevertheless, the committee members also stated that the prices of trade goods commonly bought by African farm laborers had increased by much greater percentages. They specifically noted that the price of blankets was up 145 percent, *limbo* (a popular blue cotton cloth) was up 212 percent, shirts were up 150 percent, and foodstuffs were up 115 percent.[34] These estimates suggest that the ability of farm workers to buy common trade goods had been greatly reduced between 1914 and 1921. Moreover, farm workers' purchasing power was probably lower than the committee estimated. Additional evidence also raises questions as to whether African farm laborers' wages really did increase over those seven years. A little over a half decade after the Cost of Living Committee's report, the 1928 Native Labour Committee flatly asserted that "native farm labourers' wages have not greatly increased since 1913/14."[35]

Although there were no additional official inquiries into farm laborers' wages later in the period, other sources demonstrate that the committee's 1928 statement could also have been made through the remainder of the period. Tobacco farm wages decreased precipitously following the collapse of the tobacco market following the 1927/28 season, and during the early and middle 1930s there was a "violent depression of wages" on many farms whenever there was a period of surplus labor.[36] According to one former laborer: "You aimed at doing something after work, but the money was always short. . . . You had to spend the whole year if you were aiming at buying anything. You really needed to be a miser and deny yourself."[37]

Rations

Regarding the feeding of farm laborers, the 1928 Native Labour Committee commented that there should be "no doubt that the provision of a proper and sufficient scale of rations by the employer is one of the most important factors in obtaining and retaining a sufficient and efficient supply of labour."[38] Unfortunately for most farm workers the committee's advice was rarely followed. Farmers' basic defensive argument was the equivalent of the "board-and-lodging myth" presented by Van Onselen in his study on mine labor. Although admitting that wages were "deplorably low," they argued that wages were not the only issue because "we fed them."[39]

The question concerning real wages can also be asked about the quantity and quality of rations issued to farm workers during this period. Unlike the rations provided on mines, rations given out to the vast majority of farm laborers were not officially regulated before 1935. The one exception would have been those farm laborers recruited through the RNLB. Those laborers contracts stipulated that standard rations, similar to those given to mine workers, be provided, but it was rare when that level was met on farms. Farmers were able to avoid the RNLB regulations because their farms were rarely visited by RNLB inspectors. In 1935, the government attempted to change this and officially regulate all contracted farm laborers' rations by enacting Government Notice 573. That proclamation established new regulations concerning the treatment of mine laborers and for the first time also stipulated that the same rations should be provided to those laborers on farms who had been contracted through labor agents. Government officials clearly hoped that those regulations would then act as a guideline for rationing those laborers who had voluntarily signed on at the farms. Nevertheless, if farmers knew about the scale of rations set down by the new government notice, something many denied, they ignored it. In 1940, a compound inspector reported that he had "not yet met a farmer who realized that he had committed himself to the issue of rations on this scale.[40]

On the vast majority of tobacco farms rations were issued once a week, usually on a Monday. Mealie meal (finely ground maize), generally provided on a scale of two pounds per day per laborer, was the staple of a farm laborer's diet and was the one ration item provided consistently throughout the period. The other items most likely to also be issued regularly were salt and groundnuts or vegetables. Although exact conditions differed on each farm, ration scales being somewhat better on larger farms and on almost all tobacco farms after the mid 1930s, it can be fairly stated that other items such as beans, sweet potatoes, fruit, *matembas* (dried fish), and particularly fresh meat were issued much less regularly. As one contemporary observer noted in 1938, a farm worker's rations consisted

of "as much mealie meal as he can consume. . . . [It is] the
exception rather than the rule for farm labourers to receive an
issue of meat and salt, except when one of the farmers' oxen
die."[41]

Because of the low scale of rations provided by most farmers, the majority of farm workers were forced to supplement
their diets with additional food procured from a number of
sources. Those laborers who had some money could buy mealie
meal from farm stores and sometimes from African peasant
farmers in nearby reserves or, occasionally, from the wives of
fellow workers. More commonly, workers supplemented their
rations by cultivating small garden plots. This option was
open mainly to laborers who were married or lived with a
woman. Single men generally did not have sufficient time to
care for garden plots, particularly during the planting, reaping
and grading phases of the season. Wives of workers, however,
though often employed as part time casual laborers during
these same periods, still tended their plots a few hours a day
and grew small crops of maize, *rapoko* (finger millet), groundnuts, and sometimes sweet potatoes and other vegetables.

Laborers also supplemented their rations through hunting
or trapping small game, although this was only legal if they
had received their employer's permission. Laborers also gath-
ered items such as honey and *madoras* (caterpillars) from the
bush areas on and around farms.[42] In addition, laborers gained
some degree of nutritional value from drinking beer. Van Onselen demonstrated that mine owners in both Southern
Rhodesia and South Africa used mine workers' desire for alcohol to enhance the process of proletarianization. He argued
that the presence of cheap alcohol, particularly beer, enticed
workers to freely spend their wages and ultimately forced
them to extend their periods of employment. The policy also
produced contradictory results, however, as it "tended to un-
dermine industrial discipline and productivity."[43] Although

tobacco farmers faced the same types of alcohol-related problems as mine owners, including fighting in the compounds and absenteeism, they also used beer as a means of attracting workers and stabilizing their work forces. In 1932 the government proposed a beer ordinance that would have restricted the legal brewing of beer on farms. The Banket Farmers' Association opposed the act on the grounds that they had "to compete with districts like Shamva, Mazoe [and] Bindura . . . for alien natives, and [the proposed act] might hamper our labour supply." This mirrored the earlier comments of the 1928 Native Labour Committee that "not only [is beer] necessary from a health point of view and that better work is obtained from the labourer, but it is a distinct attraction to him."[44]

For married workers or those laborers living with women, food preparation was not a major concern, as they expected their wives to do the cooking. That meant that even during the busiest times of the season married laborers anticipated a cooked meal when they returned to the compound. Single laborers faced a greater problem. This was because mealie meal takes some time to prepare properly and often, particularly during the more intense labor periods of the season, single men did not have adequate time to prepare a cooked meal. In an attempt to address this problem, single men living in the same hut occasionally joined together to take turns cooking for each other. Even that arrangement, however, may not have entirely alleviated the problem.[45]

Furthermore, on many tobacco farms rations were used to coerce workers' wives and children into "volunteering" as part time laborers at times when extra labor was deemed necessary. Some tobacco growers issued extra rations for laborers' families only during those months in which they were needed, and then only to those wives and children who actually worked. In other cases growers gave an extra amount of mealie meal every week to those workers with families. Farmers then believed that they had "some sort of pressure" on their labor-ers' wives and children to work when called on during peak labor periods of the year.[46]

Medical Care

An additional intrinsic component of the board-and-lodging myth as developed by farmers was that medical care was made available to laborers who were ill or injured. Although true to a certain extent, the majority of ill or injured farm laborers re-ceived only rudimentary first aid treatment on the farms of Southern Rhodesia. This practice was defended by most farm-ers and government officials alike by claiming that medical care was in reality rarely needed as farm labor in itself pro-duced healthy workers.[47]

Nevertheless, a variety of sources refute this and make it clear that farm laborers suffered from a wide range of illnesses directly related to their employment. Illnesses like pellagra (the result of a constant diet of maize), dysentery (resulting from eating unclean or uncooked vegetables and exposure to unclean water), and even ordinary diarrhea could be traced di-rectly to farm laborers' inadequate rations and generally poor living conditions. One of the most serious diet-related diseases suffered by farm laborers during this period was scurvy, which resulted from a deficiency of fresh vegetables and fruits in their diets. One observer estimated that their diet of mealie meal and beans could result in an outbreak of scurvy in three months. An irony of this disease in Southern Rhodesia was that it could have been prevented for much of the period under review. Citrus trees grew in the region long before the Euro-pean occupation of 1890, and oranges and other citrus fruits were grown on the BSAC-owned estates in Mazoe prior to the turn of the century. In 1929, the secretary of the Rhodesian Co-op Fruit Growers Association suggested that if the principal employers of labor, including farmers, promoted the year round use of oranges and orangeade for their employees, there would be a marked increase in the work efficiency of those employees. The savings in labor costs derived from that increased efficiency would, it was implied, more than offset the cost of the oranges and orangeade. This suggestion was not adopted by the great majority of farmers.[48]

It should also be noted that by the time migrants from the northern territories had signed on as workers on tobacco farms many were already suffering from malnutrition and physical exhaustion from the rigors of the journey. In addition, both these migrants and many indigenous people who worked on farms suffered from ailments such as hookworm, intestinal parasites, bilharzia, and tuberculosis before becoming farm workers.[49] Workers on tobacco farms also suffered from illnesses that were a direct result of their work. Respiratory problems such as pneumonia were common and were particularly prevalent during the reaping and grading periods of the season. This was largely the result of working in sheds with extremely high levels of tobacco dust and inadequate ventilation, but was exacerbated by the fourteen- to eighteen-hour work days, inadequate rations, poorly cooked meals, and generally unhealthy conditions associated with compound housing.[50]

In addition to common illnesses, farm laborers were also subject to a variety of diseases. For example, those employed in stumping and clearing virgin lands, as well as those who worked on previously unoccupied farms, were in great danger of being infected with malaria. Also, partly as a result of the crowded conditions found in most farm compounds, contagious diseases like influenza, measles, and smallpox often spread through laborers' compounds on individual farms and then to neighboring farms. For example, in 1929 at least three farms in the Banket area had to be quarantined when an outbreak of smallpox killed several workers. Ten years later a much more serious outbreak of the disease occurred on farms in a region of Lomagundi which encompassed the Sinoia, Banket, Trelawney, and Darwendale areas. The local native commissioner reported that the disease spread to such a large area because it had been allowed to "smoulder" on several farms for at least two months.[51] Farm laborers were also exposed to and suffered from a number of sexually transmitted diseases. In many cases these were a result of having had sex with prostitutes who traveled between farms. These women were in many cases the only women available for sexual release to a labor force of primarily unattached males. The problem was magnified by a lack of treatment centers and by the government policy of confining reported cases to a VD clinic for a period from six weeks to several months, depending on the severity of the case. Many workers reportedly associated these clinics with being put in jail and therefore did not report that they were suffering from the disease.[52]

In addition to the illnesses and diseases they contracted as a result of their jobs and living conditions, tobacco workers were also the victims of accidents. They could be injured or even killed falling from wagons or trucks during the reaping season, and occasionally a laborer was hurt or killed when a curing barn's walls, weakened from the constant heating and cooling, collapsed.[53]

Listing the diseases, illnesses, and accidents that farm workers were subject to begs the question of what kind of medical care farm laborers actually received. All farmers, or members of their families, were capable of treating minor illnesses and injuries, and throughout the period most did just that. Farmers then often requested that the government either furnish first aid supplies or reimburse them for the cost of treating laborers.[54] There were also a high number of instances when farmers demonstrated extreme callousness toward the physical sufferings of their workers. For example, farmers often ignored, and sometimes dismissed altogether, ill employees rather than attempt to get medical care for them. In other cases farmers "did not consider it of sufficient mental effort at the end of a long and hot day's work" to remember to provide medication to sick employees, medication they already had on hand. In yet other cases, farmers applied home remedies rather than seek proper medical attention, such as the case of a Mazoe farmer who treated a severely burnt laborer by applying motor oil to his burns rather than send for a doctor.[55]

In their own defense, farmers sometimes argued that sick or injured workers did not want to be taken to medical officers or the nearest clinic but preferred to be treated by their own *n'angas* (healers), friends, or relatives.[56] In some cases this was true, but in other instances they apparently had no other choice. When reporting on a number of cases in which sick laborers were being repatriated home to Nyasaland, a labor officer from that colony commented that the men who were the most sick had "to rely on their comrades . . . for cooking of food, drinking water, etc."[57] Another problem in districts like Lomagundi and Mazoe was the scarcity of doctors and clinics. Even when a farming area had an assigned district surgeon, the doctors would sometimes so restrict the hours they were willing to see African workers that there might as well not have been a local doctor. For example, in 1922 the surgeon assigned to the Bindura area had "a rooted objection to seeing [African laborers] out of surgery hours," which were from 9 A.M. to 10 A.M. weekdays only.[58]

Seasonal Work Discipline

Abuses of the ticket system, assigning make-up work, and physical assault were interrelated tactics used by farmers in their efforts to impose daily work discipline on African workers. Simultaneously, they also attempted to impose a more permanent form of work discipline, one that would keep laborers at the same job for longer periods of time. From the 1890s to 1945, tobacco farmers generally considered their efforts at imposing this second form of work discipline successful if they were able to keep the majority of their labor force employed for the length of the tobacco growing season. To accomplish this farmers used an assortment of practices, including advancing credit, and withholding or postponing the payment of wages and fines, in their attempts to control the length of laborers' employment.

All the methods used to increase the number of tickets worked by laborers were to some degree sanctioned by the day-to-day functioning of the legal system in Southern Rhodesia. For example, if a laborer gave a farmer notice that he wanted to quit, but was in debt to the farmer, that farmer had the legal right to file a civil suit against the worker to regain the debt. Local magistrates invariably found the debts legal and presented the laborer with the options of going to jail, somehow repaying the debt then and there, or returning to work until the debt was cleared. On other occasions farmers used the colonial legal system to their advantage by either threatening to bring or actually filing charges against laborers for practically any infraction of the Masters and Servants Act of 1901. In the latter case, farmers charged laborers with being absent without leave, refusing to obey orders or resume work, neglecting to perform an assigned task properly, or desertion. Some farmers became infamous for bringing charges against laborers as both a means of trying to control laborers on a daily basis and for trying to prolong laborers' contracts. For example, a Mr. Price of Glamorgam Farm in the Shamva region of eastern Mazoe district was considered "a most impossible man" by Africans as well as the local assistant native commissioner. He gained this reputation after initiating fifteen law suits against nineteen different laborers, between May 1936 and March 1938.[59]

In most cases, farmers filed charges in an attempt to intimidate their laborers with the authority of the local magistrate, impressing on them that they should not question the farmers' orders. Another reason was to place the laborer in financial debt to the farmer. As suggested above, laborers were almost always found guilty of the offenses charged against them and were sentenced to pay a fine or face time in jail. The fines imposed even for minor offenses were generally high for all Africans, not just farm workers, largely because of the racialist judicial philosophy that underpinned the Southern Rhodesian legal system. This philosophy was enunciated by Chief Native Commissioner C. L. Carbutt in 1935: "A native does not put the same value on money as a white man. . . . As far as Europeans are concerned . . . the mere fact of being hauled before a Court of Justice . . . is an indignity. . . . As far as the native is concerned . . . he is not embarrassed. . . . Fines are not a deterrent in the case of natives unless they are extremely severe and out of all proportion of their monetary income."[60]

The result for farm laborers was that they were almost always fined a much greater amount than it was possible for them to pay. It was at this point that many farmers magnanimously stepped forward and offered to pay the fines, providing laborers agreed to return to work, behave properly in the future, and have the amount of the fine deducted from future work tickets. Workers had little choice but to agree and were thereby forced to extend their period of employment, often for several months. In 1938, G. N. Burden, a Nyasaland labor officer, found that fines imposed on deserters from farms averaged between 10/– and 20/–, or fourteen days in jail. He added that many "employers pay the fine, take back the native and deduct the amount of the fine from his pay." (During the 1930s farm wages in the Lomagundi and Mazoe districts ranged between 8/– and 15/– per work ticket.) Burden's point was clear. When farmers paid workers' fines, they expected to add 35–45 working days to the length of the workers total period of employment.[61]

One additional point remains to be made regarding the functioning of the legal system. Farm workers had the right to complain about their treatment at the hands of farmers, and many did. Nevertheless, when a laborer wanted to complain to the police or local native commissioner, "in many cases they [were] prevented from so doing by threats and fear of what may happen to them if they report their employers."[62] Even when workers won cases, they were usually instructed by the magistrate to return to work for the very person who had imposed an illegal fine, withheld their wages, or assaulted them. They had little choice but to return. If they did not, they could have been charged with ignoring the lawful ruling of the court and fined or jailed for that offense. When they did return they were often "intimidated from again going to the Police to complain."[63] Their experiences with government authorities therefore often "combined to produce a generally unquestioning acceptance" of these acts by laborers.[64]

In addition to paying laborers' fines levied by the local magistrate's court, many farmers were also able to make at least some of their laborers financially beholden to them through the payment of the annual £1 tax. This usually worked in one of three ways. First, farmers advanced the tax payment to laborers by paying it for them and then deducting repayment from the next several completed tickets; or second, they retained part of a laborer's wages from each ticket, eventually collecting the tax. The third way was for farmers to forward tax payments to the local native commissioner after being given the £1 by laborers who had saved the amount themselves.[65] The first two of these practices benefited the farmer, while all three benefited the government. The native commissioner in Mazoe succinctly noted the problem that faced government officials if farmers did not cooperate in the collection of taxes: "You will, I am sure, quite appreciate the great trouble there would arise if no native paid tax unless it were personally demanded and fetched from him" by a government official.[66]

Supplemental to the collection of needed revenues, farmers' cooperation in collecting taxes also assisted the police in their duties, in that it helped to trace deserters and alleged criminals.[67] As with the ticket system, this practice was also subject to abuse. For example, in 1931 D. J. DeBeer of Sinoia had, according to a number of his African employees, deducted wages from several tickets with which he had promised to pay their taxes. He did not keep his promise, but used the money for other farm expenses. The result was that several employees who had worked on his farm for several years owed as much as £5 in past taxes. In most cases like DeBeer's, officials tried to reach some accommodation with the embezzling employer, but the employees still owed the late taxes, even though they had in effect paid it to their employer who had stolen the money. As for DeBeer, the investigating officer "respectfully suggest[ed] that he not be encouraged to deal with employee's tax money in future," but no criminal charges were proposed.[68]

Although it is important to remember that the colonial legal system tacitly supported farmers' efforts to lengthen the period of laborers' employment, the majority of methods used had little to do with the official world of the colonial court system. For example, one of the most common practices, one which became particularly notorious throughout Mazoe in the 1930s, was "the custom" adopted by many farmers "of failing to pay wages to their native employees as and when they become due."[69] Government officials generally agreed that this was detrimental to securing labor and was also illegal. Most officials, in effect, would probably have supported the Lomagundi native commissioner's belief that the practice of withholding wages was "a short sighted policy," which in the long run would create "an atmosphere at least of distrust . . . and tension . . . leading to ca-cammie [sic] actions by the labourer and annoyance to the employer."[70] On the other hand, farmers generally argued that "when owed a month or more wages, the native is less likely to desert and/or is more likely to perform his duties better being in fear that he may lose all the money due him."[71]

The general practice was to withhold wages from one to three completed tickets before paying, and then continue to keep workers' wages in arrears until the end of the season. In extreme cases, however, laborers were "only paid in full after the harvest ha[d] been reaped, although they are given advances on their tickets."[72] Reports of the practice became so prevalent in the mid-1930s that the acting chief native commissioner sent a circular to all Native Affairs department officials requesting information of its extent in their districts. The native commissioner in Concession noted that withholding wages had been "the fashion" for several years, while the assistant native commissioner in Bindura stated that it was a "fairly general practice in this sub-district."[73] It is important to make the distinction between unpaid wages and the practice of withholding wages. The practice of withholding wages was not a question of a farmer's inability to pay wages, but was rather a retaining of cash they had available in order to ensure that farm laborers "will not leave at a critical period in agricultural work."[74]

In writing about the working lives of mine workers in Southern Rhodesia, Van Onselen noted that "through extending credit to increasingly deprived black workers, [owners] found the means to lengthen the labor cycle and enhance the process of proletarianization."[75] The statement could just as easily have referred to tobacco growers in the period before 1945. Even those growers who might have opposed providing credit to workers in principle recognized that they could not attract and retain a labor force without advancing at least some small amount of credit.[76] The practice of advancing credit on farms took a number of forms, including establishing small stores, making purchases for laborers in town, and "advancing" cash loans, although the latter were usually given only to those laborers who had worked on a farm for at least one growing season. The first of these, farm stores, were generally found on the larger farms and in regions isolated from settlements or relatively far away from areas where stores might otherwise be found, such as on a reserve. On occasion, however, farm stores were found on smaller farms or on newly occupied farms and proved to be very advantageous to those farms' owners, particularly if there were no other stores nearby.[77]

In order to start a store a farmer obviously required a small amount of initial capital to buy a minimal amount of trade goods. These would have included items such as mealie meal, pots and pans, a few items of clothing, and a quantity of what one farmer called "that ghastly blue cloth that the women always wanted," *limbo*.[78] In addition, the farmer had to obtain a general dealer's license, which could usually be acquired pro forma from the nearest native commissioner's office. Once open for business a store sold to its own farm's workers and to laborers from neighboring farms. The operating expenses were low, as the store was usually run by a member of the farmer's family and open for only a few hours during the week, with the mark up on goods being 25–30 percent. Credit was usually freely extended to the farmer's own employees, but was usually restricted for employees from neighboring farms. Those laborers either had to pay cash or needed a note from their employer stating the amount of their wages and giving permission to provide credit. This policy served the dual purpose of keeping a farmer's own employees in debt and of providing an additional source of cash to help operate the farm. Michael Howell, who managed a large tobacco farm in the 1930s before taking up his own farm in 1940, commented that his store turned out to be extremely beneficial. He remembered that in the "first year, the store paid the farm wages."[79] Those farmers who did not establish stores on their own farms often made individual purchases for employees when they visited local settlements or went to Salisbury. These purchases, often recorded on pieces of paper called "square its," included blankets, shorts, shirts, shoes, an occasional bicycle, and soap and were credited against future tickets.[80]

In addition to credit, farmers sometimes gave cash advances or loans against future tickets to their workers who had been employed for some time. Although there were exceptions, this type of credit was almost always for the payment of the annual tax, for purchasing a bicycle, or for the payment of *lobolo* (bridewealth).[81] The practice of farmers providing advances for *lobolo* provides an interesting example of the use of credit to secure laborers. For example, one farmer gave advances for *lobolo* by paying half of the agreed amount to the prospective bride's father before the marriage and the remaining half after the birth of the first child. This particular practice had several advantages for the farmer. Not only was the laborer likely to extend his employment to pay off the ad-

vance, but it was generally considered by farmers and government officials that married workers, especially those with children, remained in wage employment longer than single men.
By paying the *lobolo* in this manner, the farmer cited here not
only secured the employment of several of his laborers for extended pay periods, but also secured the presence of a group of
people that were readily available as casual laborers, his employees' families.[82]

The actual amount of credit that farmers were willing to
advance varied greatly. The maximum amount on a single
ticket generally ranged from three-quarters to the full amount
of wages earned during that period. Although not common, it
was also not unheard of for farmers to give credit up to £10
and sometimes even more. Of course, as a laborer paid off his
debt with the earnings from one ticket, farmers were more
than willing to immediately grant new credit on the next
ticket.[83] It is impossible to know exactly how long it took laborers to pay off their debts, but in many cases it would have
left many in the same situation as the tobacco farm worker
from Bindura who, in 1928, had not drawn full wages from
completed tickets in at least six months, and in some months
he had not received any pay at all.[84] Perhaps the most truthful
answer regarding the amount of credit given, clearly reflect-
ing the situation from the farmers' point of view, was "never
more than necessary."[85]

There were, of course, ways of trying to secure a seasonal
labor force that did not involve direct economic coercion. For
example, many farmers merely held onto workers' registration certificates, both during the season and once it had ended.
In effect, they refused to let laborers terminate their employment. Of course, this practice was illegal unless farmers obtained a "working pass" for each worker whose certificate was
held. These could be relatively easily obtained from the local
native commissioner, who was supposed to ascertain that the

laborers involved understood that they retained the legal right to give a month's notice and quit. In practice, because most farms were located some distance from a native commissioners' office, many farmers simply ignored this regulation, held the registration certificates and issued their own "passes." In 1937 a Sinoia area tobacco farmer, after being notified by the local native commissioner that holding workers' registration certificates and issuing his own passes was illegal, stated the obvious, "that my holding the RC gives me no real hold on the native, but he appears to think it does."[86]

Illegal passes served a dual purpose for many tobacco farmers. First, they convinced many laborers that they remained legally employed during natural slack periods like the break between the end of grading and preparing fields for transplanting. Secondly, farmers often issued passes in those years when production levels fell off, from either natural causes or expected drops in international market demands. In those years farmers sometimes wanted to hold laborers until the end of the season in case conditions improved but did not want to pay regular wages. In those circumstances, farmers issued their own passes and told workers to return in several weeks, either to go back to work or be permanently dismissed. In 1928, following the collapse of the tobacco market, a tobacco farmer issued passes to his employees. The local native commissioner reported that "a great number of these natives were working before 20th March, but were on leave for various periods on account of work being slack. . . . [The] first ticket begins 26 February and ends 10 July."[87] After economic conditions began to improve in the early 1930s, some growers started to alter this practice by offering to pay laborers nominal wages, usually 5/- per calendar month, for the period they were away from the farm.[88]

In addition to the nominal wage, farmers used two other practices to try to attract and secure laborers for a season or

more. The first, private locations, were not unheard of on tobacco farms in the Lomagundi and Mazoe, but they were not
that common either. Some farmers allowed these African
homesteads, occupied by local Shona families, on their farms
because they believed that they could be "a big factor in keeping down cost," by allowing a group of workers to "stand off
for three or four months during the slack season" without
pay.[89]

The second of these practices only began to appear in the
mid-to-late 1930s. This new practice was for farmers to build
farm schools for their laborers' children. This practice developed because, as Arrighi argues, by that period "a major reorientation in the pattern of surplus absorption in the peasant
sector" had begun. One of the results of this reorientation was
a growing awareness by African laborers, foreign migrants
and indigenous Shona alike, that Western-style education provided their children with advantages in a wage economy.[90] As
Western-style education became more important to the general African population, tobacco farmers were among the first
to realize that they could attract labor by providing that type
of education on their farms. They learned that the cost was
low, merely the salary of a teacher and perhaps constructing a
shed to act as a school house. In return for these minimal expenses, they increasingly believed that they could secure a
more stable labor force, not to mention the presence of the
additional casual laborers that the children represented. The
first farm school in the Trelawney area was reportedly started
on a tobacco farm sometime in the late 1930s. Duda Thurburn
recounted that her husband started the school because "he
wanted something for his labourers; he thought it would be
rather nice to have a school . . . and, the other thing too, it
attracted the labour."[91] In 1942, R. D. James, who had farmed
in the Eldorado region of Lomagundi since the 1920s and had
grown tobacco since 1932, told a Natural Resources Board

inquiry committee that he was just then "thinking of starting a school for my juveniles." When asked why he was starting a school at that time, he answered, "to keep them on the farm."[92]

An examination of wage rates, rationing practices and medical care shows that farm laborers primarily worked for wages, although they also expected to be fed and, on most farms, to be given rudimentary medical attention if they became ill or were injured. In periods of severe labor shortages, farmers did not offer better rations but rather raised wages, no matter how begrudgingly or for how short a period. In addition, as time passed more and more tobacco farmers, in particular, tried using graduated pay scales, with increases offered to those who signed on for an entire season or remained for an additional season, and bonuses (called *bonsellas*) to attract laborers. There is no evidence of them offering greater amounts of mealie meal.[93] As for the practices developed by farmers in their attempts to secure a seasonal labor force, it is difficult to accurately assess the success of these practices. There is no doubt that over the years an unknown number of laborers deserted from farms rather than repay debts acquired as a result of fines or credit advances. Nevertheless, the great majority of growers believed that laborers would not desert before working or paying off their credit debts. On the other hand, there is also no doubt that these practices were extremely helpful in stabilizing labor on farms throughout the years between 1890 and 1945.[94]

6

The Life of the Compound

To succinctly describe the conditions of farm workers' compounds between 1890 and 1945 is relatively simple: they were generally extremely poor. In 1928, W. R. Benzies and Major Wane, the two native commissioners who made up that year's Native Labour Committee of Enquiry, aptly described compound conditions they found on a majority of tobacco farms. In their final report they condemned the "grass shelters and leaky hovels provided on many of the farms," and noted that the compounds were "detrimental to the health" of the laborer, and "militate[d] against his efficiency" and were "an active deterrent to labour." They concluded their findings by noting that a large majority of farm compounds left "much to be desired."[1]

Even though the purpose of farm compounds was ostensibly the same as for mining-camp compounds throughout southern Africa, their general organization was different. Charles Van Onselen has demonstrated that the intention behind the development of mine compounds had been to create a system of control and discipline over the labor force. He also noted that the forms eventually developed at Kimberly, on the Witwatersrand, and in Southern Rhodesia became increasingly more rigid as they adapted to their particular work environs. As a result of their location within the southern Africa regional economic system, and their vulnerable economic condition resulting from the low grade ores mined and the speculative nature of the mining industry in the early years, Van Onselen argues that the mines in Southern Rhodesia originally moved toward a "relatively 'closed compound' system." Other factors, however, including the lack of a local manufacturing industry and the relative isolation of most mines in rural areas caused mines to adopt "a more relaxed or 'open compound' system." Ultimately a system developed that combined elements of both "closed" and "open" compounds, a system Van Onselen called the "'three-tier' compound system." In this system the first tier was the most closed of the three, usually with a high fence and guards at the gates, and was used to confine short-term and recruited laborers. The second tier, made up of huts surrounding the inner compound, was where single laborers with some skills and work experience lived. The third tier was set away from the first two and was the home of married laborers and their families. Each tier reflected a perceived level of proletarianization of the laborers, with the inner compound having the least proletarianized and the married quarters housing the most proletarianized. This perception, shared by state officials and mine owners alike, was rooted in the idea that as laborers became more skilled and earned higher wages they were less likely to desert. The three-tier compound system developed primarily on the larger, better capitalized gold mines. Owners of less well-capitalized mines that paid their laborers at lower wage rates, such as the coal mines at Wankie and the mica mines in northern Lomagundi district, often utilized systems more similar to closed compounds in their attempts to exert control over laborers and prevent desertions.[2]

To follow the logic of the three-tier compound as described above, farm compounds would have been organized as closed compounds, or at the very least along lines similar to the inner compound of the three-tier system. Farm laborers were generally considered to be the least proletarianized of any group of African workers in the colony. Yet, the organization of farm compounds differed from both the closed compounds of the small mines and the three-tier compounds of the larger gold mines. Most farmers in Southern Rhodesia before 1945 were severely undercapitalized, with little cash on hand to spend on things other than land payments, capital equipment, and wages. Most farmers of the period could not afford to expend their limited capital resources on the building, maintenance, and requisite security personnel required for a closed compound.[3]

The nature of the work place itself must also be considered. Mine compounds were generally in close proximity, if not immediately adjacent to the mine itself, but such placement was not possible on farms. For example, between 1932 and 1945 the Mpandaguta Farm near Sinoia annually planted nearly 94 acres of tobacco. In addition, an unspecified number of acres would have been planted in maize, as rations for the labor force, and some type of silage crop to be used as feed for the farm's oxen. It can be assumed that between 250 and 300 acres were planted on the farm in any given year during that period. The tobacco crop alone would have required weeks of labor just for cultivating, with laborers working over a wide area of the farm. At any time during the working part of the day any number of African laborers could simply have walked away from the farm unnoticed. The organization of the compound could not have prevented them from exercising this option if they had chosen to do so.[4]

Furthermore, the extreme openness of the farm compounds benefited both farmers and laborers and was in effect agreed to, or at least acceptable to, both farmers and African laborers. The openness of the compounds became a recruiting device for farmers who argued they could not afford to match the higher wages paid at the mines. The ability of laborers to come and go more easily, and the knowledge that during non-working hours they were not under the ever watchful eyes of managers or private police would have given laborers on a farm a greater feeling of independence than mine laborers would ever have experienced. This view was hinted at in November 1940, when the compound inspector responsible for the northern regions of the country, reported that "it would never do to advocate the regimentation of farm compounds. Natives are happiest when living under conditions akin to kraal life and the married labourer likes to enjoy some privacy and unrestricted space for cultivation."[5] E. D. Palmer and Michael Howell, who both began farming in the mid 1920s, repeated this idea in comments made forty years later. Howell reflected that African laborers had "a community on the farm . . . a small village, and they were quite happy living in their own village." To this, Palmer added that "there was [no] doubt about that, they were contented, very contented living in their loosely supervised compounds."[6] What is striking about these statements is that they suggest an element in settler ideology quite different from, if not diametrically opposed to the view of labor held by mining officials and mine owners as presented by Van Onselen.[7] The existence of these two seemingly contradictory ideological views can be traced to the different material requirements and resources of mining and farming in Southern Rhodesia.

The specific location of compounds on individual tobacco farms was determined by a number of variables. The one constant was that they were located near a natural source of water for drinking, cooking, and other needs of laborers without costing the farmer the expense of digging a well or drilling a borehole. The downside to this was that compounds were occasionally located near *vlei* lands, which could sometimes prove to be dangerously unhygienic. In addition, they were usually situated no more than a few hundred meters from the farmer's homestead; far enough away so that the farmer's family could maintain feelings of privacy and security, yet close enough that problems could be dealt with quickly by the farmer.[8]

The size and number of compounds on a given farm depended on the number of laborers employed and the diversity of the work force. There were often two or more compounds on tobacco farms. This mirrored the practice of employing more laborers than farmers specializing in other cash crops, and the presence of laborers from at least two, and sometimes three or four, different ethnic groups within the labor force. Farmers generally allowed each group to establish their own cluster of huts, in effect forming separate compounds. Farmers often implied that this occurred naturally, that laborers from different groups who spoke different languages, prepared foods differently, and held different religious beliefs and practices merely "wanted their own compounds" so as to be with their own people during non-working hours. There is no doubt that an element of truth existed in this view; however, it should not be forgotten that the compounds were not just places of temporary residence for laborers but were also a means of controlling the labor force. Some farmers, therefore, separated ethnic groups into geographically distinct compounds in their attempts to keep conflicts from disrupting the functioning of their farms. When fights between groups did occur, they could interrupt work on a farm for several days. Jana Makumbira, a Malawian who had worked on Munemo Farm for over fifty years, recalled that the owner separated ethnic groups "because what would happen was that when we got drunk we would fight because we would scold each other using our different languages."[9] In addition to ethnic difference, compounds could be divided by occupation and marital status. Domestic servants working in the farmer's house would sometimes have their own cluster of huts separate from the field laborers' compounds, and on some farms married laborers and their families lived in compounds separate from single workers. There were also usually a few scattered huts located near the fields where "herd boys" or crop "guard boys" lived.[10]

Regardless of where it was located on a given farm, the laborers' actual housing was built out of materials from the farm. Although from the earliest years of the industry some growers built compound huts out of brick, the conditions native commissioners Benzies and Wane reported were much more common for the entire period. For example, in 1910, after visiting the Lochard tobacco plantation a government medical officer reported that "the huts are dirty, dilapidated,

Dr. Charles Jarron Sketchley's tobacco fields, laborers' compound, and barns, 1908.

and in their present state, unfit for occupation."[11] In a 1915 criminal case in Sinoia, farm laborers testified that even though they had been inside their hut, they had been able to witness a fight because they could look through gaps in the "walls" of the hut, walls that were made of coarse sacks hung loosely on a wooden frame and covered with a thatched roof. Thirteen years later we have Benzies' and Wane's report, and in 1938, G. N. Burden, a Nyasaland labor officer, reported that laborers on farms continued to live in "flimsy grass shelters which are little protection against the cold and damp."[12] In 1945, L. T. Tracey noted that the "housing of farm natives is very much in the experimental stage at present."[13] Finally, reports from two BSAP inquests into deaths on farms indicate the dangers housing conditions sometimes presented to laborers and their families. In July 1929, a sick laborer died from burns received when the grass hut he was sleeping in caught fire. Eleven months later another hut caught fire, resulting in the death of one child and another being severely burned. In both cases laborers had built larger than normal fires in their huts, one because of his illness and the other because his children were complaining of being cold, and the grass walls ignited, with tragic consequences.[14]

Farmers often asserted that they provided sufficient time and access to materials for laborers to build pole and dagga huts, not grass huts. This argument was supported by John Abraham, a Nyasaland official who investigated labor conditions in Southern Rhodesia in 1937. After consulting farmers in the tobacco producing area around Concession, Abraham reported that newly arrived laborers were "given a few days before commencing work to build their own housing accommodation on the farm. . . . The farmer provides the materials free."[15] Because the building of huts occurred "before commencing work," however, laborers were usually not paid for their labor to construct housing, and in some cases did not receive rations during these first few days on a farm. Also, in those situations when laborers were hired during times of peak labor demands such as planting, reaping, or grading, they were rarely given the time necessary to build adequate huts. Farmers said this was because during those periods workers' labor was required immediately. These circumstances meant that laborers often lived in poorly built huts when first employed. Later, those who were "particularly industrious" might "erect slightly more substantial huts of poles and mud, working at them on Sundays," while in some instances laborers were able to move into pre-existing pole and dagga huts left by other laborers.[16]

Some farmers did build brick housing for their laborers. Even then, farmers often argued it had been a waste of time and money because their African laborers would not live in them. The implication was that laborers preferred the grass huts. This argument was supported by T. H. Newmarch in testimony to the 1921 Native Labour Enquiry Committee. He stated that he had built brick huts for some of his laborers, but that "with the exception of two, they have all cleared out and built grass huts." He went on to claim that the grass huts reduced the danger of disease amongst his "boys," noting that "when we had the first visitation of influenza [1918] all my boys were living in brick compounds, and I lost nine boys. . . . Since putting my boys into grass huts I have had far less sickness amongst them." Newmarch was not alone in his opinions, for other farmers and the government publication *Native Affairs Department Annual* echoed the belief that grass huts were healthier than those made of brick because they were "easily and conveniently burnt when necessary, with the complete destruction of all bacteria and vermin."[17]

Other problems also existed. Sanitary arrangements were "a most serious defect on almost all farms" and were "usually in an objectionable state."[18] Because the time and money needed to build even primitive sanitary accommodations were considered excessive by most farmers during this period, they relied on what was euphemistically referred to as "bush sanitation," defecating in the fields around the compounds during the growing season, and using nearby *kopjes* or areas of uncleared bush during the winters. By the mid 1940s, some of the larger, more successful tobacco growers in Lomagundi had begun to install latrines, but an excerpt from a 1944 inspector's report of a tobacco farm compound indicates that sanitary conditions were hardly improving. There "are two sets of lavatories. . . . However, there are only nine toilets, which were all dirty. The ground around the latrines stank of decaying excreta."[19]

Another integral component of compounds on virtually all tobacco farms was an area provided by farmers where laborers, or members of their families, were allowed to plant their own crops. The product of these garden plots was then used to supplement the regularly issued rations. The practice was briefly explained in 1925 by a Mazoe farmer who noted that it was his "habit to give my boys some land for them to grow a few mealies for themselves to stabilize my labour."[20] Customarily, laborers worked these plots after completing their assigned work. An exception was made for the wives of laborers to spend "a few days each week" planting, weeding, cultivating, and otherwise tending individual plots. On other farms, farmers did not provide individual plots but instead plowed a few acres, planted maize and vegetables, and then allowed their laborers "to help themselves." Of course in these cases the laborers, or family members, were responsible for weeding, cultivating and harvesting the areas themselves when they were not working on the tobacco crop. In both methods, the main crop planted was maize, but depending on the size of the plots, soils and availability of water, people also planted other crops like *rapoko*, rice, and groundnuts.[21]

Most farmers of the period would have argued that these

plots were available to all laborers on their tobacco farms, but many single men did not have sufficient spare time to adequately attend to their own plots. This problem had an even greater impact on those laborers hired late in the season to work during reaping and grading. The actual circumstances faced by these laborers could be serious, as the additional food from garden plots was an important additional source of sustenance for most farm laborers, often determining whether laborers worked hungry and whether they were healthy. The only ways these workers would have been able to circumvent the problem was by working on the plots after their fieldwork had been completed, even if that was late at night, getting up very early before the official work-day began, or for a number of single men or newly hired laborers to join together and take turns working a plot.[22]

In addition to claiming that they provided the plots to all laborers, tobacco farmers also depicted their provision of plots as free to laborers. Laborers had a different perspective. Mugari Mandaza, a former farm laborer, when asked whether he was required to pay rent for the plot he had been provided, answered for many laborers when he responded that, "I was an employee so I paid through working."[23]

The importance of these garden plots cannot be understated. For most farmers, they were consciously viewed as an inducement for labor in circumstances where competition for labor was always keen. In addition, by providing garden plots, some farmers clearly hoped to reduce their ration costs and thereby help reduce overall operating costs. For the African laborers, the garden plots were a source of additional food necessary to supplement inadequate rations and, hopefully, provide better health.

A government that feared migrant laborers bypassing Southern Rhodesia for better employment conditions in South Africa would have tried to monitor conditions on farms with an aim to improving laborers' living conditions. After all, in 1900, following complaints about conditions found in mine compounds, the government began to regularly inspect those compounds. Compounds on farms, however, did not receive an equal level of scrutiny until the early 1940s, and even then not on a regular basis. Despite the absence of systematic inspection, the question of the necessity of inspecting farm compounds was fiercely debated by farmers and government officials throughout the period before 1945. Some farmers believed that the regular inspection of farm compounds would greatly benefit farmers because it would ultimately result in more African laborers seeking employment on farms. This idea was supported, at least in theory, by some government officials. After investigating the causes for shortages in the supply of labor in the country, the 1921 Committee of Enquiry concluded that "in the essential matters of housing and food . . . a system of farm inspection is, in our opinion, essential. [I]t is to ensure the contentment with their work and conditions that . . . natives should be subject to Government inspection."[24] In 1926, Alexander Thomson, a member of the Legislative Assembly, went even further in explaining why inspections of farm compounds would be beneficial to farmers: "The boys are naturally farmers, and they prefer farm work to mining work, but the conditions on some of the farms in the country are such that supervision is needed, as the conditions existing are very detrimental to native labour. . . . Official inspection might make the position such that we might have no complaints whatsoever."[25]

Charles Coghlan, Southern Rhodesia's first prime minister, also believed that the inspection of farm compounds would ensure "standard wages and proper housing accommodation and food," thereby rendering "conditions of labour on farms more attractive." Nearly a decade later, an assistant native commissioner in Sinoia reiterated Coghlan's view when he commented that "the inspection of farm compounds with a view to establishing and maintaining reasonable living conditions for native employees would do much to lay the labour shortage bogey."[26]

These positions supporting the inspection of farm compounds were not, however, representative of the prevailing views on the subject during the first half of the century. L. P. Leech, a farmer, asserted that government inspections "would add further burdens to a community already grossly over-governed."[27] Leech apparently spoke for a large number of farmers because in 1928 the Native Labour Committee reported that "probably the majority [of farmers], are distinctly opposed to inspection in any form whatsoever."[28] In addition, many government officials also agreed with Leech, as is demonstrated in a 1927 memo by Colonial Secretary William Leggate in which he reported that the majority of cabinet ministers believed "that the extension of the Compound Inspectors' duties to cover farms will be a mistake."[29]

In the end, regularizing the inspection of farm compounds was never seriously considered by the government before World War II. After examining the history of the inspections of mine compounds, Van Onselen observed that the "unwritten law of inspection was that regulations must only be enforced after the profitability and capitalization of the mine had been carefully considered."[30] Based on its lack of action, it is apparent that the government considered the profitability of farms in Southern Rhodesia and concluded that most farmers could not have survived the additional expenses that would have accrued had they been forced to meet the standards for rations and housing imposed on the mining industry. J. K. Rennie has argued that this lack of action on the part of the government was a form of financial assistance to farmers. Rennie's conclusion is particularly convincing since BSAP officers could have easily inspected farms during their annual official visits to farms to obtain lists of farm employees for tax purposes. If legislation had existed to regulate minimal conditions for just housing and rations, a short tour of the compound would have been sufficient to make the worst conditions obvious. The BSAP officer could then have issued a warning to improve conditions, which the local native commissioner could have checked on at a later date. Although the view of the BSAP was that there were too many farms for even this type of rudimentary inspection, it is interesting to note that the same officials did not believe that there were too many farms to visit to ensure that laborers' taxes were paid.[31]

Farm compounds differed from private locations, which existed on only a few farms. Private locations were basically those areas on alienated farms where indigenous Shona households were allowed to continue to reside in exchange for land rent or their labor at very low wages, or a combination of the two. G. Arrighi has characterized the conditions which existed between farmers and the residents of private locations as "semi-feudal relations" and argued that they acted as the most effective short-term solution for farmers who had plenty of land but lacked sufficient supplies of labor to work that land profitably. This argument implies that rent and labor agreements between farmers and indigenous Africans would be necessary only until that time when those political and economic pressures being directed at the local peasantry culminated in a large percentage of peasants being forced out of their reserves and into wage employment. At that time farmers would have sufficient laborers offering themselves for hire. With this free labor available to them, farmers could then fully develop their farms. No longer requiring private locations, the land they once occupied would be required for increased crop production. Palmer concurred in this interpretation and added that by 1908 the "general tendency" for indigenous Africans "in Mashonaland was to leave the farms as soon as they become occupied, and move into the reserves."[32]

The implication was that private locations were rare, and becoming rarer, in much of Mashonaland province by 1908. In addition, tobacco farmers often claimed that private locations did not exist on their farms in Mashonaland by the late 1920s. Nevertheless, various sources from the 1920s to 1945 indicate that private locations did exist on tobacco farms during those years. For example, in 1925, H. P. Forshaw, a Lomagundi tobacco grower, listed the conditions under which he would allow a private location on his farm:

1. That they work for me for three months each per annum on general work in lieu of rent, failing their working for me satisfactorily to pay me what they would have earned during that time—and thus pro rata.
2. They must not extend their lands beyond their present boundaries.
3. They must bring no more cattle on their location than I have already given permission.
4. Generally not make a nuisance of themselves.[33]

The next year a farmer wrote to W. A. Devine, the Mazoe native commissioner, to inform him that the people living in a private location on his farm were available to work for him during tobacco reaping. Testimony from a Sinoia magistrate's court case in 1934 provides not only evidence of a private location on a tobacco farm, but also a rare example of an African tenant stating the terms he had agreed to: "I agree[d] to work for the accused in consideration of his allowing me to reside on the farm. He [explained] I was to work three months in each year; two months I would be paid, and one month for no wages. I have never been to see the NC or ANC. . . . There are six of us in my kraal on the farm. They have agreed to the same terms as I have."[34] Lastly, in June 1942 Captain R.

D. James, a tobacco grower in the Eldorado region of Loma-gundi, testified that he had a private location on his farm because "it is a big factor in keeping down cost of production because they are quite willing to stand off . . . during the slack season."[35]

Social Relations

A visitor to almost any tobacco farm compound in Southern Rhodesia before 1945 would have found, in addition to the conditions already mentioned, a social hierarchy among the laborers living in the compound. An individual worker's positioning within that hierarchy was generally determined by the type of work performed. "Boss boys" were at the top of that social/labor pyramid and took their orders directly from farmers, although they were often consulted about what areas of the farm or sections of the tobacco crop needed priority attention.[36] Although farmers had slightly different expectations of what made a good "boss boy," the process of selecting one was fairly similar, albeit difficult to articulate. Laborers who demonstrated a "sense of responsibility" and "took a special interest" in the work, or gave "the impression of being an authority," or showed "an ability to control other labourers," were potential candidates when a new "boss boy" was needed. They were paid a wage 30 to 50 percent higher than the average field laborers' wage, and often received small privileges, such as an occasional day off with pay, and sometimes specially built housing.

Once picked, "boss boys" were often given a great deal of authority by farmers. On many tobacco farms they not only made daily work assignments and inspected the completed work, but in some instances were allowed to mark tickets. On other occasions they were sometimes left in charge of a farm when the tobacco grower and his family went away for a few days. Their authority went beyond the power to assign tasks or mark tickets. On many farms they were in charge of distributing rations. When this included distributing meat, which was infrequent on most farms during the period, there was the possibility for "boss boys" to play favorites with relatives and friends. In addition they could sometimes even develop a minor system of patronage. For example, during those periods of the season when women were employed as part time casual laborers to do suckering, topping, or grading, "boss boys" were in many cases allowed to choose the assistants who supervised the women. Again, these assistants usually came from among the "boss boys'" relatives or friends. Even though the pay for these short-term supervisors was increased only slightly, the positions were coveted because those appointed then worked less strenuous days than those who continued as field laborers.

With higher wages and extra privileges at stake, it is not surprising that "boss boys" sometimes resorted to bullying and even assaulting other workers in attempts to drive them to complete their assigned tasks. In their attempts to remain in a farmer's good graces, they often also acted as the farmer's eyes and ears in the compounds, reporting workers who refused to work, planned to steal livestock, or even talked about deserting for better paying jobs.[37]

"Drivers" were on the second tier of the workers' hierarchy and demanded almost as much prestige as "boss boys." They claimed such high status because of their skill at driving spans of oxen, a very difficult and trying task. Their mastering of this skill made them nearly indispensable on a farm during the period before 1945 because many farmers were recent immigrants to Southern Rhodesia and knew nothing about training or handling oxen. Without experienced drivers, these farmers could not have prepared their fields for planting, harvested crops, or even picked up supplies at the nearest railway depot. As for the other workers, a driver gained prestige partly because they were paid about 30 percent more than field laborers. In addition, their importance to the farmer was often accompanied with some of the privileges given to "boss boys," such as better housing or an occasional day off work. Like "boss boys," drivers often used their elevated status as an excuse for bullying other laborers, particularly the "plow boys" whose job it was to guide the span of oxen in a straight line.[38]

Below "boss boys" and drivers in status were two distinct groups of workers. The first was made up of the cooks and domestic servants who served the farmer and his family in the homestead. In addition to being paid at a higher rate than field workers, this group was usually given better housing and in many cases were provided with at least one set of relatively new clothes. The second group was made up of laborers who supervised specific tasks during the growing season. On many tobacco farms the most prominent member of this group was the chief tobacco grader. A person who was placed in charge of grading had demonstrated that he possessed a "sense and feel of tobacco." Although theoretically under the supervision of the tobacco farmer, a chief grader was the person who was really in charge of the grading sheds and made certain that each bale contained the same grade of tobacco.[39]

"Boss boys," drivers, cooks, domestics, and task supervisors commonly made up no more than about 10 percent of a tobacco farm's labor force. The majority of the rest of the people found in the compound were field laborers. These men had to be able to do "virtually everything on the farm."[40] Dake Choto, when recounting his experiences as a laborer on tobacco farms for over sixty years, remembered that "if you worked on the farm it was very important that you learned to do every type of job because you could be called to do anything." He explained that "the jobs were varied and many. We cleared tobacco fields, some days in *chirimo* (the post-harvest season), we were told to clear fields and on some days we worked with cattle to drag away the felled trees. We prepared the planting and all the rest that could be done before the planting and after planting like weeding and harvesting tobacco."[41] Even though this group of laborers all worked at basically the same tasks, they also made distinctions in the social hierarchy among themselves. Most commonly, this meant that those workers who had been recruited by either government or private agents experienced the same stigma that van Onselen has shown *chibaro* laborers endured on the mines.[42]

At the bottom of a tobacco farm's social/labor hierarchy were those few workers who had the least desirable jobs on the farms, and the part time casual laborers. The first group included "dairy boys," "cattle herds," and crop guards. The first two jobs were scorned by most other farm laborers because they meant no days off and earned very low wages. Crop guards also worked seven days-a-week and were paid at a low wage, but beyond that other workers did not trust and often disdained them because of the nature of their jobs. They reported strangers and even fellow laborers who might take some fresh vegetables from the farmer's personal garden or a few ears of maize from the farm's maize fields. The combination of the low wages and low status of these jobs meant that they were almost always filled by juveniles who were probably working for wages for the first time.[43]

The other group of workers below general field workers were casual laborers. On tobacco farms in Lomagundi and Mazoe this group was usually made up of a combination of migrants who did not want to sign on for the full season but needed food or some money before continuing further south, local Shona people, and the wives and children of the farm's full time employees. These workers were paid approximately two-thirds of what a seasonal worker earned, and while the wives and children of full time laborers lived in the farm compounds, the migrants in particular lived in extremely poor circumstances for the few months they were employed.[44]

Although the social/labor hierarchies as described existed on nearly every tobacco farm, on some of those farms a shadow authority acted as a counterbalance to the authority of "boss boys" and even farmers. This situation developed when a group of northern laborers, particularly Nyasalanders, chose their own leader to represent them as a single entity to a farmer. Farmers usually were not sure, but believed that the person chosen was perhaps someone with authority in the area where the workers came from, or someone who had previously worked in Southern Rhodesia. This leader usually had no official standing within the labor hierarchy but clearly spoke for the members of his group: negotiating their wages; voicing complaints or grievances about rations or compound conditions, and occasionally haggling over the amount of *mgwaza* assigned or questioning the behavior of a "boss boy." On some occasions it seems that these men even questioned a farmer's otherwise unchallenged authority and would threaten to give notice and quit, and take the entire gang with them, if rations, for example, were not increased. Most farmers, of course, would have found this type of behavior intolerable, but many would perhaps have acquiesced to some degree because if the leader's opinions were listened to, he was apparently willing to convince the gang to sign on for additional time. On other occasions, he might send letters home in attempts to help the farmer recruit additional laborers. Michael Howell noted that these leaders could be "very useful if you kept on the right side of them . . . so you [had] to be very careful with the one who was in charge."[45]

A truly accurate picture of what farm compound life was like for the workers and their families is perhaps impossible to depict. The task is difficult because the great majority of farm workers were illiterate and left no known personal records or diaries, while most archival materials dealing with the period reflect the concerns of farmers and government officials. On the other hand, those archival sources that do provide scattered glimpses into farm compound life often provide only pictures of conflicts between workers, not everyday types of activities and relationships. Of course, conflicts did arise among laborers, just as in any human community, but they were not the prevailing form of interaction between workers and members of their families.

The personal histories of retired or semi-retired tobacco farmers and farm workers can provide a clearer picture of what compound life may have been like. These tend to indicate that while the lives of laborers were difficult and frequently exhausting, the instances of conflict detailed in other sources were rare in the lives of most tobacco farm workers. Therefore it is possible to provide a general picture of what life was like in the workers' compound of a tobacco farm. That picture, described briefly, shows that the majority of people living in the compounds were young, adult males. Three or four of these men probably lived together in a hut and often shared cooking, wood gathering, and housekeeping chores. Laborers living with women, whether in certified marriages or not, and their families, generally had their own huts, sometimes separated from the huts of the single men on larger farms. When problems occurred the inhabitants of the compound attempted to solve them. If they could not, only then did they take it to the farmer for adjudication. When a majority in the compound felt strongly about the actions of an individual, workers and their families could practically force the farmer to dismiss the person or call in local authorities, by threatening to give notice and quit unless the person was told to leave the farm.[46]

Life in tobacco compounds was not, however, without serious problems. Workers and their families were victims of burglaries, accidental and intentionally set fires, and violent brawls between individuals and groups of laborers. Some of the thefts were no doubt committed by habitual criminals, but many more were by fellow workers who felt they needed money quickly, or apparently believed that they could steal clothing and other trade goods with little danger of being caught before leaving for their homes in the north or in a nearby reserve.[47] The trial records of those who were apprehended add some interesting details to our picture of compound life. Although some of those details we already know (i.e., that laborers and their families purchased blankets, shirts, blouses, trousers, shorts, dresses, and cloth) it is still worth noting that many laborers were able to acquire a fairly large variety of goods. For example, in one case a thief got away with items totaling over £9 in value, while in another a worker lost a pair of shorts, a jumper, three shirts, and three pairs of trousers. Additional trial records show that some workers were able to save relatively large amounts of money. In a 1924 case, a worker had a pocketbook containing his savings of £4 10/— stolen from his hut, while in 1938 another man had £7 10/— in cash stolen.[48]

Although farm compounds were free of conflict on most days, outbreaks of conflicts, some very violent, did occasionally take place. These almost always occurred on weekends when workers drank a good deal of beer. Many of the fights between individual laborers developed over quarrels concerning gambling debts and other money owed by one worker to another, and women. For example, in 1944 a drunken migrant farm worker attacked and raped a married woman living in his compound.[49] Less than a year later, in February 1945, the *Rhodesia Herald* reported a number of rapes of young girls and women following beer parties on farms northeast of Salisbury.[50]

Although unjustifiable, these conflicts can occur in almost any community of predominantly young, single adult males where consuming alcohol was one of the few recreations. Violent conflicts in farm compounds, however, went beyond getting drunk, fighting over debts, or violence directed toward women. They often related to work and laborers' perceived injustices.[51] For example, in 1921 a "herd boy" was killed in a fight with another youth when they quarreled over which one was responsible for losing two cows. The victim accused the other youth, who denied responsibility and a fight started, ending in murder. Witnesses testified that the fight became violent because neither youth wanted to be blamed and punished by the farmer who owned the cows.[52] In other cases, workers fought over who was in charge of certain tasks during the work day, or who had the authority to chastise other workers for not doing assigned tasks. There could also be violent confrontations when workers accused one another of shirking work, particularly in a gang labor situation, or stealing work materials or rations from farmers. Testimony from a number of cases suggests that fights often started because laborers resented being kept longer in the fields, or feared that the farmer's anger over missing goods or rations would be directed at the whole labor force. In those cases, once they returned to the compound, they directed their anger at the person they believed had caused the extension of work hours or placed them in jeopardy.[53]

As mentioned earlier, there were often several ethnically segregated compounds on tobacco farms. Occasionally rivalries and personal conflicts between individuals from different compounds developed into "faction fights" between these compounds. The fights generally followed derogatory comments and often ended in violence. While it appears that faction fights occurred fairly often on farms in general, involving large numbers of farm laborers in total, they were rare on any particular farm and involved relatively few laborers at any given time.[54]

Tobacco Farms and Their Indigenous Neighbors

Relations between those people who lived on tobacco farms, both tobacco growers and farm workers, and their Shona neighbors were never easily defined. For example, at the same time that farmers complained that Shona men refused to work on their farms because they lacked any sense of a work ethic, many growers in Lomagundi and Mazoe hired Shona men to train oxen, and both Shona men and women as casual laborers. In addition, farmers in all the tobacco growing districts consistently purchased quantities of maize and other grains from Shona peasant farmers to supplement workers' rations.[55]

On the other hand, conflicts occurred often and took a variety of forms. For example, although it was legal for the Shona to use established footpaths across European owned farms, farmers often attempted to bar them from using those paths. Farmers argued that the Shona were trespassing and only used the paths in order to steal from farm stores or crop fields. In many cases, following continuous threats from farmers that they would shoot trespassers, native commissioners would often warn Shona living near farms to avoid using the paths for their own safety. In addition to the rather petty nature of some of these complaints, there were also more serious conflicts such as the contentiousness that could develop between Shona peasants and farmers over the grazing of animals. In one case from 1916, a farmer near Concession killed eleven goats owned by a neighboring Shona peasant after he had repeatedly warned the peasant farmer to keep the goats on reserve lands. Shona peasants were not the only losers in quarrels over grazing. In 1921, two Shona peasant farmers were accused of burning down a tobacco curing barn, containing 10,500 pounds of tobacco, after a farmer had confiscated forty head of their cattle for grazing on his farm. Another peasant farmer, who worked part time on a European-owned farm adjacent to his land near Concession, killed a farmer's cow with an *assegai* (a short-handled, broad-bladed stabbing spear) after the animal had strayed into his crops for the third time.[56]

As for farm employees, relations with local Shona peoples were just as mixed. In many cases, foreign farm workers married Shona women. They did this for a number of reasons, including an attraction and desire to marry a particular woman, and, perhaps occasionally, "so that they would appear as part of the Shona society," and thereby hope to gain access to lands in a Shona reserve. In rare instances, after deciding to remain permanently in Southern Rhodesia, foreign workers even adopted Shona names in an attempt to fit into local Shona society. More commonly, farm workers visited nearby Shona reserves to purchase beer and food to supplement their farm rations. Of course, this could cause problems back on the farms, such as the time in the early 1930s when a number of farmers near the Chiweshe Reserve in Mazoe complained that their workers were consistently missing work because they were repeatedly becoming intoxicated during visits to Shona *kraals* in the reserve.[57]

In addition to being in trouble with their employers visiting Shona *kraals* could lead to more serious problems for farm workers. This situation usually had something to do with Shona women, and was often rooted in a general dislike many Shona men, particularly elders, held for foreign laborers. Sources from the period, as well as interviews conducted over fifty years later, indicate that Shona chiefs, headmen and male elders consistently complained to Mazoe and Lomagundi native commissioners that foreign farm workers were both debauching young women in the reserves and enticing them to run away from their homes.[58] For example, in July 1920 the native commissioner in Mazoe reported that Shona "locals complain of wives and daughters going with foreign natives."

Nine years later the native commissioner in Sinoia echoed that report when he informed his superiors that the chief of the Zwimba reserve, in southern Lomagundi, complained that a "considerable increase in trespass by non-indigenous Natives who work on farms adjoining the Reserve." He added that Zwimba reported that "intemperance and immorality attend the visits of these Natives and that they are having a bad effect on his people."[59]

Although it is important to keep in mind the physical organization and conditions of workers' compounds on tobacco farms, it is perhaps more pertinent to remember that the compounds were communities of working people. The people living in these communities experienced the same vagaries of life as people in any community would. They were subject to criminal acts like burglary, assault, and to disagreements with neighbors, some of which became violent. Nevertheless, it is also important to keep in mind that these were communities created for a specific purpose, to control the labor of those who lived in them. For example, the social hierarchy that all communities have was, in farm compounds, shaped by the work done by the members of the community. Most importantly, conditions of the compounds such as housing standards and sanitation facilities were, for the most part, not a reflection of the desires of the people living in the compounds, but rather resulted from the undercapitalized state of their employers.

7

Quick and Nimble Fingers

If a fellow arrived with two wives he was a godsend; there were three pairs of hands.[1]

Most of the farms used the wives because otherwise you would have to employ more actual workers.[2]

Women

Tobacco farmers, like some other groups of Europeans, held ambiguous ideas about African women during the period from 1890 to 1945. Elizabeth Schmidt has demonstrated that Europeans in Southern Rhodesia during this period generally believed that African women were "primarily responsible for the perceived depravity of African society." Colonial reports described them as "indolent," "lazy," "slothful," "immoral," "frivolous," "savage," and "uncivilized." One official went so far as to assert that "to any observer of the native, it is immediately apparent that their women are extraordinarily inferior to the men." One of the many reasons behind this extremely disparaging view of African women was their widespread refusal to work in the wage economy.[3] Even when women did work for wages these perceptions meant that women were usually not seen as "actual workers" and therefore did not receive wages equal to men.

On the other hand, by the early 1930s almost all tobacco farmers employed African women as casual laborers during the season for cultivating, tying and untying tobacco, and grading. Many of those farmers would have agreed with E. D. Palmer that "women played a very important part as very useful labor . . . [and] in the grading sheds they were invaluable."[4] This more appreciative view of African women seems to have been a corollary to an idea also held by many Europeans that African women were the principal agricultural workers in traditional African society. Therefore, they were, according to this mode of thought, well suited to certain tasks on a farm. Carol Summers pointed out that this second view of women did not originate "in a balanced analytic view, but in a . . . reinterpretation of the information . . . to justify the transfer of male labor from the African economy to the European economy."[5] Still, it did exist and because of it many farmers consistently encouraged women to work on their farms.

Despite the existence of the second of these contradictory perceptions of women's capabilities as workers, the historiography of labor in Southern Rhodesia has repeatedly ignored the role of women as workers. This is largely because studies of this kind have tended to focus on mining. By looking at women primarily in that context, the earlier studies restricted our understanding of the participation of African women in the developing wage economy of Southern Rhodesia before World War II.[6] Fortunately, a number of studies concerning other areas of colonial Africa provide alternative ways of looking at women's contributions to the development of wage economies in Africa. These studies demonstrate that African women have filled integral and necessary roles as both paid and unpaid labor in colonial economies throughout Africa. An examination of women's labor on tobacco farms in Southern Rhodesia adds to these by demonstrating that in addition to the unpaid labor performed by African women on farms, they also possessed, albeit in a limited fashion, the option of selling their labor directly to tobacco farmers.[7]

The number of African women who worked for wages on European-owned farms before 1945 is impossible to determine. The works of G. Arrighi, Robin Palmer, and Ian Phimister point out, however, that before the 1930s "the total number of black women in all categories of wage employment . . . was tiny."[8] It is also evident that following the implementation of the 1930 Southern Rhodesia Land Apportionment Act, the number of Shona women moving to farms, mine compounds, and urban centers increased. This was a consequence of a greater number of Shona men leaving the rural areas and entering wage employment. In order to make up for the absence of those young male workers in the rural areas, Shona women were forced to intensify their work loads. As their lives became more burdened in the rural areas an increasing number of women escaped to farms, mine compounds and towns throughout Southern Rhodesia. With the beginning of regular *Ulere* service in the mid 1930s these Shona women were joined by a growing number of foreign women.[9]

There are few official sources of statistics that noted the presence of women as workers, paid or unpaid. Those statistics that do exist from the late 1920s to the 1940s are problematic. This is because official African labor statistics generally included only information on full time workers and, as mentioned, when women worked they were routinely employed as part time laborers. The 1926 census, for example, reported that 588 women were employed on all commercial farms in the colony. That number is about 0.8 percent of the total of 72,706 Africans employed on farms that year. Later statistics indicate even fewer women in wage employment in the agriculture sector of the colonial economy. The 1938 *Statistical Yearbook of Southern Rhodesia* reported that a total of 204 women were employed in all of commercial agriculture in 1931. By 1936 the total had risen to only 209. According to the yearbook, 149 of those women were employed in Mashonaland province, the region of the country where the most tobacco was grown. The 1947 yearbook noted that 1,259 African women had been employed in 1941. That raised the percentage of women in the agricultural work force to 1.2 percent of the total reported (102,518).[10]

Comparative statistics from other regions of Africa suggest that these numbers are not only misleading, but are simply wrong. According to Deborah Fahy Bryceson women made up nearly 5 percent of the wage labor force in Tanganyika by the 1940s. The great majority of these women were employed in the commercial agriculture sector of that economy. Interviews with retired tobacco growers and former laborers, both men and women, suggest that the percentage given by Bryceson is applicable to Southern Rhodesian tobacco farms from the mid 1920s to 1945. That is, the number of women employed as casual laborers on farms would have been about 5 percent of the total work force. Applying that percentage to the total numbers of laborers cited above suggest that the number of women employed on commercial farms would have ranged from approximately 3,600 in 1926 to over 5,000 in 1941.[11]

Who were these women? Some foreign women, mostly from Nyasaland but also Northern Rhodesia and Mozambique, had always accompanied their husbands to Southern Rhodesia. Their numbers, however, were extremely low. In 1931, John C. Abraham, a Nyasaland official, estimated that less than one in every thousand Nyasaland migrants was a woman. That number increased somewhat in the late 1930s as a result of the opening of the *Ulere* transport system. Some of these women came to Southern Rhodesia after marrying men who had returned to their home villages after working in the

south. Many of these men had evidently returned north specifically to marry women from their original home areas. In
many instances they then returned to work again in Southern
Rhodesia, taking their new wives with them. For their part,
most of the women who married these men seem to have done
so in deference to their parents or to escape worsening economic conditions in the northern territories.[12]

This practice was often encouraged by officials in both regions. As mentioned in Chapter Two northern officials believed that women migrating south lessened the processes of
social disintegration that they saw as a result of male migration. In Southern Rhodesia government officials and employers believed that male laborers remained in employment for
longer periods once they had settled with their families. The
experiences of Emidres Monanji, a Malawian woman who had
lived in the south for over fifty years, confirm this belief. She
explained that "once we got settled with our families and children it was difficult to go [back] with the whole family." Fillimon Visani, a man who worked on the same farm with
Emidres' husband, added that "we had to make a lot of savings
to afford to travel [back home]. Yes, we wanted to go home,
but we got so use to this country that we just stayed."[13]

In some cases tobacco farmers and local native commissioners, who chronicled farmers' concerns about the availability of labor, did not merely sit and hope that male migrants
would bring their wives with them, but they often did all they
could to ensure that the wives of foreign migrants came south
to join their husbands. In 1938, A. W. Laurie, a tobacco
grower in the Concession area of Mazoe district, asked the
local native commissioner for help in attaining transport from
Fort Jameson (in Northern Rhodesia) for the wives of several
of his employees: "It is approaching the "signing off" time of
the year and these boys have been worrying me to find out if
you have been able to get into touch with their wives or

whether they will have to go for them themselves, which I would be very loth [sic] for them to do, in view of the shortage of labour. . . . I would sincerely appreciate any assistance you could give me." In response to this request, the native commissioner inquired about rail fares, took deposits from the laborers, and wired the passage fares for the men's wives to the Fort Jameson district commissioner. The women arrived several weeks later.[14]

Although there were foreign women on the farms of Southern Rhodesia the majority of women who lived in the compounds on tobacco farms throughout the period were indigenous Shona. Some of these Shona women were in the compounds because they were married to Shona men who worked on the farms. Others had left their traditional homesteads as single women and either moved in with family members or friends already living on a farm and eventually legally married, or lived as a temporary wife with a migrant farm worker. Schmidt pointed out that there were a number of reasons why Shona women abandoned their traditional lifestyles and sought alternatives on farms, mines and in urban centers. Shona women, regardless of their actual age, were legal minors under customary law and as such had no access to land and were completely dependent on their traditional male protectors (fathers or husbands). Shona women often attempted to escape the restrictions of this system by "attaching" themselves to migrant laborers. Chibaiso Mwandenga, who had lived with her husband and worked on a tobacco farm since the late 1930s, confirmed that some women "went to the farms in the hope of finding prospective husbands or to have live-in boyfriends [because] they wanted to survive the harsh times."[15] Some women were running away from arranged marriages while others were childless or had been accused of witchcraft. In some instances they were junior wives "whose status was low and work loads especially onerous." As noted above, after the implementation of the Land Apportionment Act rural Shona society began disintegrating and increasing numbers of Shona men took wage jobs. Schmidt argues that women's labor was then intensified by male elders "in a last-ditch attempt to stave off the necessity of male migration." Junior wives would have been particularly susceptible to this added level of work. An unknown number of these women then "responded to their lives of increasing hardship by running away to the emerging towns, mining centers, mission stations, and European farms."[16]

The majority of women, whether local or foreign, living in tobacco farm compounds were usually officially married. That is, their marriages had been countenanced by a government official, usually a native commissioner, under the terms of the Native Marriages Act of 1901. Nevertheless, there were also some single women. Once ensconced in a farm compound some of them married. Others entered into relationships with men that were similar to *mapoto* marriages found in the colony's major towns. Diana Jeater describes this type of relationship as a marriage that "did not involve any payment of bridewealth; nor did they require go-betweens to negotiate between lineages who could be hundreds of miles distant. . . . It allowed [women] to retain [their] independence, while gaining male protection."[17] Because they had voluntarily entered the relationship they were freer to abandon it if their personal interests no longer coincided with those of the men with whom they were living. Case transcripts from magistrate court hearings indicate that these relationships were generally monogamous, often lasting for periods ranging from a growing season to several years. *Mapoto*-style marriages meant that if the man decided to leave a farm for another job or to return home these women had the option of remaining in the farm compound. If their relationship with a man did end, the women nearly always established the same type of relationship with a new partner.[18]

The great difference between those African women who lived on farms and those who lived in mine compounds was that the former were able to sell their labor for wages. In 1925 the native commissioner for Lomagundi district reported that "until the advent of tobacco . . . there was no branch of industry whereby women could earn money. [These farmers] require quick fingered workers so that nowadays there is an opening for women."[19] While the vast majority worked part time, from at least the 1920s a few women worked full time on farms. Occasionally these jobs included one of the low status jobs, such as crop guard. More commonly, though, when women took full time jobs on farms they were employed as domestic servants or cooks. Although employing African women as domestics was considered inappropriate by many Europeans in Southern Rhodesian towns, it was apparently not as major a concern for those living on farms. In 1940, a government committee of inquiry reported that "the difficulties [i.e., immoral behavior] with which the employment of native girls in town is surrounded, do not occur in any serious form, if at all, in the country. . . . It is in rural areas that the practice of employing native females as domestic servants is best established."[20]

The percentage of women employed as domestics was, however, extremely small. The majority of women who worked on farms were casual laborers, primarily employed during the peak periods of the tobacco growing season. Although this type of work was always part time, on many tobacco farms it could be spread out over nearly the entire growing season. Even when tobacco farmers hired additional male laborers during peak periods, many of the extra workers were women. Farmers generally restricted this part time work to the wives and daughters of their full time male employees, although on farms located next to African reserves, farmers sometimes also employed women from the reserves. Because they were hired during the peak labor demand periods of the season, women most commonly worked at topping, suckering, tying and untying of hands of tobacco, and, in particular, grading. Many tobacco farmers also hired women to help during transplanting and to cultivate and weed the tobacco crop. In addition, women were often used to help harvest ration crops so that the farms' male laborers were free to work on the tobacco crop. Chibaiso Mwandenga remembered that "we [women] were part time workers and we could be called in at anytime for jobs such as planting, weeding, etc." Her co-wife, Senesai Chidemo, added that women generally worked "when the workload was acute" and that they "undertook the lighter tasks such as weeding . . . suckering of tobacco, harvesting, tying and untying tobacco and its selection [grading], and packing." She also noted, with some pride, "we were good and very fast."[21]

The amount of work women were required to perform as casual laborers was generally figured at between one-half to two-thirds of the work assigned to a male worker doing the same task, and they ordinarily completed their assigned tasks in about four hours. During grading, for example, women worked as graders in the mornings while men reaped tobacco in the fields. In the afternoons, the women generally returned to the compounds to prepare meals or work in garden plots. Senesai Chidemo stated that "as housewives we started relatively late, around eight in the morning and knocked off . . . to prepare lunch for our husbands" sometime in the early afternoon."

Casual male laborers always worked for cash wages on the thirty-day ticket system. Women's labor, on the other hand, was organized differently. Farmers did not commonly use the ticket system with women workers and they were sometimes paid in kind. When paid in this fashion they most likely received rations of salt or mealie meal. In a few cases they were not even paid in kind, but rather farmers considered women's labor as a repayment on advances of extra rations issued to their husbands. By the early 1920s, however, the general practice was to pay cash wages to women workers. Although some farmers paid women at the end of each working day, it was more common for them to be paid after completing a set number of workdays. The longest it seems that women went without being paid was a calendar month. This was evidently an attempt by farmers to maximize the number of days that women would work on the tobacco crop. Whichever method was used women's wages were generally "very paltry." At their highest levels women's wages mirrored the rate of work they were assigned, i.e., about two-thirds of what a full time male field laborer earned. Between 1890 and 1945 this meant that women were paid between 4/– and 12/6 for a calendar month.[22]

The extent to which women were able to influence how their wages were used within a family is difficult to determine. Retired tobacco farm workers, both men and women, generally agreed that in most cases women's wages became part of a family's total income. In those compound households where the men were selfish, men used the family's income without consulting with their wives. In other households, where the men were not considered selfish, the husband and wife would generally discuss how to use the money. It appears that in these households women's wages were used to buy household goods from either the farm store, if the farm had one, or from a store on a neighboring farm or reserve. To men household goods would have included items like matches, soap, and cooking oil. To women those items were on the list of household goods, but their list would have also included trade goods like salt, sugar, and sometimes extra mealie meal, goods that were necessary to supplement the rations provided by farmers. The point is not that compound households were examples of the absence of patriarchal attitudes and practices, but rather that women had some say in how their wages were to be utilized within the household.[23]

On most farms women could also make money by cooking meals, washing clothes, and performing other domestic chores for single male laborers. Included within these alternative ways of earning money there were three major sources of cash available to women on tobacco farms—beer brewing, prostitution, and selling surplus produce from family garden plots. The first, beer brewing, was traditionally done by women throughout Southern Rhodesia so it is not surprising that they brought that knowledge to the farms.[24] Most tobacco farmers had an ambiguous attitude toward beer brewing. On one hand they encouraged the practice, though they attempted to control it by restricting when and how much beer could be brewed. On the other hand, most farmers also believed that beer brewing led to fights in the compounds and absenteeism on Mondays. Which women should be allowed to brew beer was also a problem for many farmers. Their usual practice was to give permission to any woman who asked and who was married to or lived with one of the farm's full time male laborers. When too much beer was brewed, as determined by the farmer, or conflicts between women developed over who would brew for what weekend, farmers would create a register. In this register they kept the names of the women in their compounds who brewed beer and the dates they had been allowed to do so. The farmer would then rotate permission from week to week. Women favored using a traditional grain like *rapoko* to brew their beer because they believed it made a better-tasting beer. The beer was called "seven days beer" on many farms because it took that many days to ferment. According to Senesai Chidemo brewing beer could be extremely lucrative at times. "It was highly paying, even better than men's wages. In fact, we were major contributors to [our families'] incomes because of our involvement in the beer business." She added that women commonly had much greater control over the money they earned from brewing than they did over their wages. Although women would normally consult with their husbands first, they used this money for items that had value to them. Senesai Chidemo explained how this worked: "It was customary for every housewife to have her own belongings, like kitchen utensils and pots. So we used *our money* to buy these and other goods like clothing. But we would first consult with our husbands as a way of respect. If you did your things independently, without consulting your husband you were regarded as a bad housewife."[25]

Over a period of time some women were able to accumulate quite a bit of personal property. A list of such items could include chickens, scissors, mirrors, clothing items like dresses and chemises, sheets, a table cloth, a jacket, pieces of limbo, buttons, and beads. In addition to kitchen utensils and the items just listed it seems that women also used some of this money for clothing and, once schools began to appear on farms in the late 1930s, readers and exercise tablets for their children. The money that remained was then added to the family's overall income.[26]

Prostitution was the second way for some women to earn cash on farms. Many farm compounds in the Lomagundi and Mazoe districts were frequented by women prostitutes who lived in Salisbury but often visited farms. Some of these women made their way from Salisbury to the tobacco farms in the two districts by riding bicycles.[27] In addition, on some of the larger tobacco farms in the two districts there were also a few women who lived permanently in the farm compounds and earned their living as prostitutes. Although these women were generally self-employed, in some instances they worked with a man living in the compound. This man acted as both procurer and protector for the women.[28] For a number of reasons farmers usually made a conscious effort to ignore the presence of these women. Lawrence Vambe's comments on why Europeans officials acquiesced to prostitution in Salisbury also applies to tobacco farmers: they thought that "it safeguarded the chastity of white womanhood from the lust of their native" laborers.[29] Second, in her study of prostitution in Nairobi, Luise White has pointed out that in addition to sex, prostitutes also often "perform tasks that frequently include conversation, cooked food, and bathwater that restore, flatter, and revive male energies." These women met sexual needs and provided some degree of domestic life to male laborers. For farmers this meant more contented workers and the likelihood of fewer conflicts over access to women in their compounds. Fewer conflicts among workers, most farmers felt, was a good thing because it meant that all their laborers were available to work.[30]

Married African women did not generally like the presence of these women in the compounds. Although they did not always fault the prostitutes, they believed that the prostitutes threatened their marriages and, therefore, their security. Although the problems varied, most wives feared the possibility of contracting venereal disease from husbands who had sex with a prostitute and they strongly disapproval of the infidelity. In addition, there were the more serious cases when husbands would spend most, if not all, of their wages on prostitutes and beer, or even desert their wives and families for a prostitute. The lost wages made it difficult for the women to feed themselves and their children. If abandoned the married women could face the possibility of expulsion from the compound or be forced into finding another man to live with in the compound. These possibilities were frightening to married women and they believed that they could be avoided entirely if there were no prostitutes in the compounds.[31]

As discussed above, tobacco farms offered women opportunities to work for wages and earn cash by other means. Still, much of the work performed by women on tobacco farms was not directly related to the production of tobacco and did not earn them any cash. Nevertheless, the value of that work to both male farm laborers and farmers should not be underestimated. Work of this kind included raising children, preparation of meals, doing laundry, and collecting supplemental food from areas around the farm that were not being used by the farmer. The most important of these jobs was working in the garden plots provided to laborers on tobacco farms. Farmers only required women, when employed, to work half days so that they had time to work in the garden plots in the afternoons. Women grew maize, vegetables, and sometimes rice on these plots and were well aware of how this produce contributed to their families' well-being. Chibaiso Mwandenga remembered that "We grew vegetables, rice and grains in such plots. This was an important supplement to our meager rations and wages. We women labored so tirelessly in these plots and men simply enjoyed our efforts." Single men in the compounds also benefited from this particular form of women's unpaid labor because they could buy the surplus from the women.[32] There is little question that women's unpaid labor in working in the garden plots not only added additional quantity and quality to normal diets, but also improved the general health and perhaps saved the lives of some farm workers and their families. In addition, the women's labor on the garden plots was important for many farmers. Specifically, it allowed farmers the chance to reduce the costs associated with rationing their laborers by transferring a percentage of those costs to laborers' wives, registered or otherwise, through the unremunerated labor of those women.

One further point concerning women living in farm compounds during the period before 1945 bears reiterating. Whether as the result of sexual desires, jealousy or drunkenness, African women of all ages were the victims of violence at the hands of men. Additional examples include a case from 1921 in which a woman living in a farm compound near Bindura was raped by a laborer visiting from another farm. In 1935 a migrant farm worker called Isaac hit a woman in the head with an axe after she refused to sleep with him, and in 1937 a woman was nearly choked to death after attending a beer drink with her husband. She had apparently rejected the advances of another man, who then attacked both her and her husband.[33]

Children

As they did with women, tobacco growers also employed children as casual laborers throughout the period 1890–1945. Prior to the 1930s a large number of these children were young boys who came from neighboring Shona reserves. Although Shona reserves continued to be a source of juvenile labor after that time, beginning in the early 1930s a greater percentage of these young workers were the children of farm laborers.

Growers and government officials alike argued that child labor was essential to the successful operation of a tobacco farm because children were extremely cheap casual labor, earning from three pence a day to four or five shillings for a thirty day work period. They further explained the use of juvenile workers along three lines of thought. First, they stated that work on farms was actually less strenuous than that expected of the children in their traditional homesteads. The

1928 Native Labour Committee report clearly mirrored this idea: "It must be remembered that the native child in his kraal is put to work at a very early age and that the work which is usually expected of him on farms is lighter than that which he is set to perform at home."[34]

Secondly, they argued that children often worked at the instigation and approval of their parents. For parents who worked on the farms this meant an addition to the overall family income. As for Shona children, a 1934 report by the acting native commissioner in Urungwe explained the European perspective on why Shona parents approved of child labor: "[In] my experience the father does not object to his child seeking employment, in fact he rather encourages it as the child is relied on to a great degree to earn his tax. . . . [T]he main objection is that juveniles go off to work without his knowledge or consent."[35]

The third reason commonly espoused was that work on tobacco farms was better suited to children: "The opinion of the majority of tobacco growers, particularly those who do their own grading, is that Native Youths are even better suited and more satisfactory than the adults whose fingers are not so nimble or sensitive to the touch." As part of this third point, farmers and state officials also argued that children were better workers because it was easier for them to learn, and retain, "the habit of work." As one tobacco farmer put it: He did not "turn the young men off, those half grown, three-quarters grown, they were very valuable labour because they didn't forget what you trained them to do, where the older men forgot every year."[36]

Although the government tried to impose a legal minimum age of ten for juvenile employment in the mid 1920s, a number of reported cases dating from that same time indicate that children as young as six and seven years of age were regularly employed on farms. In some instances children of four to five years of age worked as cow herds on European-owned farms.[37] A contemporary observer reported that children, both boys and girls, were "extensively" employed on tobacco farms, where they worked on the "lighter tasks," such as tying and untying hands of tobacco, because they were "both neater and quicker than other [adult] natives." Juveniles also worked as "waiters," carrying tied tobacco from the tying sheds to the curing barns, and young boys were commonly employed as "leaders" of spans of oxen. They also occasionally worked in the tobacco fields. One farmer employed young boys and girls in an attempt to rid his fields of "mole crickets" which attacked young tobacco plants. The children used sharpened sticks to dig the crickets out of the earth and were paid three pence for a certain quota of dead crickets.[38]

As with the adult female employees, juvenile workers were also subject to violence at the hands of adult male workers. Both young girls and boys were sexually abused. In addition, numerous court cases indicate that boys who worked as leaders of oxen were particularly subject to being beaten by drivers as the latter took out their frustrations on the youngsters.

The economic weakness and low social status that African women and children experienced in their traditional homesteads continued in Southern Rhodesia under the dual patriarchies of their own indigenous societies and their European employers. Nevertheless, living in a farm compound offered an alternative to some African women, and with it some degree of control over their own lives. They could earn wages for working on the farms and had access to additional cash through beer brewing, prostitution, or selling produce from garden plots. As for the children, on one hand they provided farmers with an extremely cheap source of casual labor for tasks such as waiters and oxen leaders. On the other hand, by the end of the period, living on a farm with their parents provided some access to an education. Finally, the most important point to keep in mind is that women's and children's paid and unpaid work was essential for the successful operation of tobacco farms and for the reproduction of the labor employed on those farms.

8

Toward a Moral Economy

In examining a 1946 strike by black miners on the Witwatersrand, T. Dunbar Moodie provided a paradigm that enables
historians to develop a more subtle understanding of the socioeconomic relations that developed between employers and
laborers throughout southern Africa. Moodie argues that within
the moral economy of the Witwatersrand mines there were
"mutually 'acceptable' elements within a system of political
domination and economic appropriation." Moodie stresses
that the existence of such elements should not imply that
workers and their employers shared common values or interests. On the contrary, by persistently contesting one of their
employers' primary interests, the demand for labor, workers
could cause employers to alter those demands.[1]

Implicit in the concept of moral economy is the idea that
workers are capable of developing an awareness of their conditions of labor and a consciousness that enables them to determine the acceptability of those conditions. In historical
circumstances where people from pre-industrial societies
moved into ones dominated by capitalist relations, the emer-

gence of that consciousness was rooted in the material conditions of the workers' lives. It was also shaped by the practical skills, knowledge, and modes of thought those people brought with them to the workplace. Herbert Gutman supported this view in his inquiry into the early stages of proletarianization in the United States. "Men and women who sell their labor to an employer bring more to a new or changing work situation than their physical presence. What they bring . . . depends, in good part, on their culture of origin, and how they behave is shaped by the interaction between that culture and the particular society into which they enter."[2]

Raymond Williams, a British social philosopher who examined working-class culture, also contended that in order to understand the actions of workers new to wage labor, the changing conditions of labor and the society in which those workers find themselves must be carefully examined.[3] In the case of tobacco farm laborers in Southern Rhodesia this means examining both the material and socioeconomic conditions laborers found when they took jobs on those farms. Those conditions clearly shaped the demands that tobacco farmers made of their laborers. In addition, the beliefs and perceptions held by farmers also shaped the demands that were made of African laborers and their families.

Previous histories of Southern Rhodesia often attempted to define a consciousness common to all European settlers. These works rarely demonstrated an understanding of the socioeconomic differentiation that actually existed within settler society. As a result there has been little discussion of how different groups of settlers regarded African laborers. Although several studies examined government officials' and mine owners' perceptions of African labor, few works have attempted to ascertain how farmers viewed their African laborers.[4] Many farmers shared the ideas of Charles Coghlan, a member of parliament, who, in 1925, defined Africans as a "people who are backward in civilization [and] have to be taken care of against themselves just as in the case of children."[5] In 1934, Rawdon Hoare reiterated Coghlan's belief and spoke for many farmers when he wrote that "natives are not unlike children, and, if good results are to be gained [on farms], they must be treated as such."[6]

One term commonly used by farmers to describe farm workers was "raw." In 1915, the director of agriculture reported that farmers thought that "raw aliens . . . go back to their distant homes when they have begun to acquire a little usefulness, skill and civilization," implying that farm laborers had none of those qualities before working on a farm. Thirty years later African workers on tobacco farms were still thought to be "raw savages" who lived in "mud and straw huts . . . just as [if] they were in the native kraals in a dirty, cheerful, raucous community." Farmers used this particular word to convey the idea that Africans lacked even the rudimentary qualities they deemed necessary to be good workers on European-owned farms. "Raw" meant that an adult African man knew nothing about working as part of a group and that he was unable to do the simplest task without constant supervision, if then. Without mentioning the actual term Carol Summers has captured the general essence of the word, as used by farmers, when she points out that Southern Rhodesian employers believed that an African man was "the worst laborer on the face of the earth."[7]

Many farmers and government officials regularly augmented their use of "raw" with descriptive epithets like "retarded," "slothful," "primitive," "rude," and "barbarous." On occasion farm workers were dehumanized altogether, as when they were referred to simply as "defective material" or "animals." Farmers used these terms to reinforce in themselves, and to convey to government officials and African workers alike, their belief that Africans lacked the requisite skills and knowledge necessary to be skilled laborers. Farmers could then argue that the wages they paid and the rations, housing and medical care they provided were more than sufficient to maintain unskilled laborers. These conceptualizations were also used when farmers lobbied government officials to provide more labor, their rationale being that quantity would make up for the purported lack of quality.[8]

Another element inherent in most farmers' consciousness also allowed them to dismiss the material conditions found on many of their farms as unimportant. They argued that they were providing their African workers with something more valuable than wages, rations, housing or medical care. They were providing the opportunity to learn civilized behavior through "the dignity of labor." Of course, the use of the "dignity of labor" argument by employers extends back through labor history long before there were tobacco farmers in Southern Rhodesia. It is therefore not surprising that this ideological justification for demanding that certain groups of people be made to work should have entered into farmers' consciousness. An example of this doctrine was included in the findings of the 1910 committee of enquiry that reported that "it is only by becoming workers that the [Africans] can be elevated from barbarism." A 1924 letter to the editor of the *Rhodesia Herald* claimed celestial support for the idea, stating that work is "the remedy God and nature supplied to counteract the boredom [found in *kraals*] . . . and work is [an African male's] only salvation." Two years later a contributor to the same newspaper admitted that Southern Rhodesia's future development and the labor of Africans were tied together, but worried that "until the native learns the dignity of labour, there can be no real progress."[9]

Besides the "dignity of labor" argument, farmers and government officials who supported them also believed that farm work was itself beneficial for Africans. A 1923 letter to the

Rhodesia Herald summarized this idea when it reported that working on a farm was "a blessing" for an African, for labor on a European farm meant that "slavery, tribal war, massacre and even severe famines are not any longer to be dreaded by him."[10] Nearly a decade later a member of the legislative assembly reconfirmed this notion when he claimed that Africans preferred work on farms, as opposed to mines or their rural homesteads, because they could "learn from the white man."[11] Finally, in 1938, G. N. Burden reported to the Nyasaland governor that farm work was better than other types of employment for Nyasaland's migrants because "there are not the same temptations in the shape of the prostitutes, the gambler, the beer seller and the vender of trashy goods on credit such as exist in the towns and mining settlements, and the chances of the native returning to his village with a moderate percentage of his earnings after a year's work are considerably better."[12]

Despite such attitudes, the "dignity of labor" argument was not accepted without question. An opposing perspective was expressed in a *Rhodesia Herald* editorial in 1917: "Farmers are still talking at meetings and writing to the Press advocating forced native Labour . . . . The favorite stalking horse behind which the protagonist . . . conceal themselves and their true character is that of 'the dignity of Labour' . . . [it is] intended to hide the fact that they wish the State to exploit one set of citizens for the profit of another set."[13]

By the mid 1920s an antithesis to the idea of the "raw" farm worker and the "dignity of labor" doctrine began to enter into farmers' consciousness. This was the concept of a "gentlemen's agreement," and it implied that a mutually acceptable arrangement could be reached by farmers and their African employees. By 1935, the assistant native commissioner at Bindura could report that the idea was a "fairly general practice in this subdistrict." In his annual report he explained that farmers in that area "arrive at an understanding with natives seeking employment that they shall remain employed until the agricultural work for which they are engaged is completed." In 1984, Michael Howell remembered that when he was farming in the 1930s and 1940s this understanding worked rather simply, one "didn't sack them in the middle of the season and they didn't give notice."[14]

Notwithstanding, other sources indicate that many farmers believed that such an agreement was not as equitable as implied in Howell's statement. Those farmers believed that the agreement bound workers more forcefully to their jobs. In many cases these farmers only mentioned the existence of a gentlemen's agreement when attempting to deny farm workers their legal rights to give notice and quit before the end of the growing season. In 1936 Captain C. A. R. Shum, a tobacco grower near Sinoia, noted that the understanding established by a gentlemen's agreement meant that "once the crop is planted it is the duty of Natives employed to remain until it is reaped and graded." Four years later, E. Scott, a tobacco grower near Concession, wrote to his local native commissioner that "it is an understood rule that boys sign on for the whole season."[15]

Clearly, differences of opinion as to the obligations and responsibilities the gentlemen's agreement bestowed on workers and farmers existed. Just as clearly, its increasingly common use by many farmers contradicted the idea of "raw" or "ignorant" African workers. It did this by conveying the idea that African workers had the ability to understand what work they were agreeing to perform, the length of time they were willing to do that work, and what they could expect in return. Furthermore, the general acceptance of gentlemen's agreements by tobacco farmers and laborers demonstrates that by the mid 1920s a moral economy was emerging, if not already present, on many tobacco farms in Southern Rhodesia. This meant that in exchange for laborers agreeing to work for the duration of the tobacco season farmers agreed to pay wages at an acceptable level, provide a minimum amount of rations, and treat their workers civilly.[16]

Still, even after reaching such an arrangement farmers often continued to refer to their laborers as "raw," "ignorant," or "lazy." Obviously, workers on tobacco farms were not "lazy." On the contrary, for much of the year they worked long hours at tasks that were exceedingly tiring. They were also not "raw" or "ignorant." In many cases laborers actually brought practical skills and knowledge that related directly to tobacco growing to the farms where they sought employment. In addition they brought traditional cultural practices that they adapted to the labor process and to the social relations found on tobacco farms. By adapting their knowledge and social practices to conditions as wage laborers they were able to affect the types of both daily and seasonal disciplines tobacco farmers attempted to impose. For example, studies by Africanists and scholars of other regions of the world have shown that pre-industrial societies had well established concepts of time and work and what constituted legitimate demands upon both of those. These studies have also made evident that the people of those societies have relied on their concepts to facilitate their movements into wage economies. Keletso Atkins has argued that the "pre-industrial temporal concepts" of Zulu workers were "at the nexus of the 'kaffir labour problem'" on sugar plantations in Natal, South Africa, in the early nineteenth century. Their temporal sense partially determined what months of the year they would work and for how long they were willing to remain on those plantations. A Zulu "month," however, was defined by the lunar cycle and lasted for 28 days while their European employers defined a "month" as a period covering 28–31 days. This difference in the conceptualization of month resulted in on-going allegations of desertion from employers and countercharges of non-payment of wages by Zulu workers. Ultimately Natal sugar planters were forced to assign piece work in an attempt to increase the amount of daily production to compensate for their Zulu workers' short month. They also began "to teach such useful notions as the 'week', the 'weekend' and the proper time sequence of 'workdays' (euphemistically termed 'weekdays'), for which there were no words in Zulu." In the end, Natal planters "learned either to give way to traditional usages such as the lunar month, or do without local labour altogether."[17]

James C. Scott, in a study of Malayan peasant farmers, has shown that southeast Asia peasants developed "a perspective from which the typical peasant views the inevitable claims made upon his resources by fellow villagers, landowners, or officials. . . . Such claims are evaluated less in terms of their absolute level than in terms of how they complicate or ease his problem of staying above the subsistence crisis level."[18] When forced into circumstances where they had to sell their labor these peasants relied on this perspective to form judgments about the demands they faced in wage employment. John Higginson's history of labor policy in the Belgian Congo chronicled how African mineworkers used "some of the cultural mores of their villages to redefine the constraints imposed upon them by town life and wage labor."[19] Finally, Leslie Bessant and Elvis Muringai have written about how Shona peoples in Chiweshe, an area north of present-day Harare, had "ideas about what sorts of 'work' were reasonable." They discussed the role of communal work parties, known as *hoka* or *nhimbe*, among the people of Chiweshe. These *hoka* provide another example of how a preindustrial group of people determined what was a reasonable call on their labor. Anyone who required assistance to produce a subsistence crop could call a *hoka*. Elderly people or families who had suffered from illness and were late to begin field preparation, for example, could ask their neighbors to help them prepare or plant fields.

Nevertheless, hosting "a *hoka* created a web of obligation among the host family and the families who attended. When the guests called work parties at their homes, the host family was now obligated to attend, and to provide an equal number of workers. . . . If they failed to reciprocate, they ran the risk of having no one come to their party the next time they needed help. In other words, there was a clear idea in Shona society that providing labor under specific circumstances carried with it an expectation that those who participated would receive something in return."[20]

Workers on tobacco farms also judged the assigning of tasks and living conditions they encountered through the prism of the pre-existing social concepts and work experiences they brought with them to those farms. For example, during the period between 1890 and 1945 the largest group of workers on tobacco farms were migrants from Nyasaland. Many of these workers already possessed some knowledge of tobacco growing and skills related to working with tobacco, including knowledge of soils, leaf textures, and how to judge the tobacco's maturity. They also had the skills required for tying, handling, and grading cured leaves. They could have acquired all of these in one of two ways before ever emigrating from Nyasaland. First, Nyasaland Africans had been growing tobacco commercially as tenants on European-owned estates from the mid 1890s or as peasant farmers since 1909. Second, many Europeans had grown tobacco in Nyasaland from before the turn of the century. (The first Virginia flue-cured tobacco was grown there during the 1902/03 season.) A change in Nyasaland governmental policy in the early 1930s resulted in many of those European tobacco farmers abandoning their farms in that territory and relocating to Southern Rhodesia. In many cases, African laborers who had worked for these men either accompanied them south or later became labor migrants and went south to look for work on tobacco farms. A 1949 British Colonial Office report, though, indicates that the practice of migrating south with the hopes of finding jobs on Southern Rhodesian tobacco farms had begun long before the 1930s. The "habit" of Nyasaland migrants traveling to Southern Rhodesia, with the specific intention of finding work on tobacco farms, began as early as 1911 and had "continued and grown, a fact which has been of great help to production in that country."[21]

David Sinclair, who grew up on a tobacco farm near Banket during the late 1930s, recalled that when he was a child Nyasaland migrants "already had tobacco experience . . . so they were easy to adapt, and easy to teach because . . . they knew what the process involved."[22] Another tobacco grower, Trevor Gordon, also remembered that most laborers on tobacco farms prior to 1945 were from Nyasaland, "simply because they were experienced in tobacco growing because [Nyasaland] was a tobacco growing country."[23]

By the early 1930s Nyasaland workers who returned home were often replaced by relatives or friends from the north. Many of these laborers had previously worked on tobacco farms in Southern Rhodesia and were returning for a second, third, or even fourth period of farm work. This was particularly true in those cases where a farmer developed a reputation as a fair and reasonable employer. In those circumstances, it is safe to assume that the returning migrants would have told their replacements about the work that would be expected of them and to have suggested ways of dealing with those demands.[24]

Nyasaland migrants were not the only laborers who could have brought knowledge and experience which related directly to the growing of tobacco. Ackson Kanduza's work on the tobacco industry in Northern Rhodesia suggests that people from that territory could also have gained experience working with flue-cured tobacco before journeying south as labor migrants. Kanduza points out that Virginia flue-cured tobacco "emerged in 1912–1913 as a leading agricultural export crop for the white settlers centered around Fort Jameson . . . and an important additional source of income for the settlers along the line-of-rail" between Livingstone and Lusaka. As in Southern Rhodesia, the growth of the tobacco industry in that colony required large numbers of laborers, however Northern Rhodesian growers could not equal the wage rates offered in Southern Rhodesia and had a difficult time retaining laborers who moved south in search of higher wages. In addition, one of the principal labor migration routes south originated in the tobacco growing region around Fort Jameson and ran directly to the tobacco growing areas of Lomagundi and Mazoe.[25] These circumstances meant that many Northern Rhodesian migrants could have gained experience working with Virginia tobacco before migrating south.

As for indigenous Shona peoples, Barry Kosmin has shown that they too had some experience working with tobacco. People of the eastern regions of Southern Rhodesia had maintained a thriving trade in tobacco until it was largely displaced by European-grown tobacco in the 1930s. Although *inyoko* tobacco was a different variety than that grown on European-owned farms, some Shona also would have possessed a degree of the knowledge, and most of the skills, necessary to work with tobacco on European-owned farms.[26]

The works by Atkins and Bessant and Muringai demonstrate that Africans brought more than knowledge and skills relating to specific crops with them to wage employment. They also brought concepts of time and what constituted reasonable demands on their labor. Although specific examples are sparse it is clear that laborers on tobacco farms used similar concepts to develop a consciousness that allowed them to know exactly what work they agreed to perform, and for how long, when they signed on to work for tobacco farmers. In

August 1937, a dispute between the owners of Ebden Estates and ninety-eight of their Nyasaland employees arose around the question of the exact work those laborers had contracted to perform. On August 12, workers were assigned to sort through and grade the last remnants of the 1936/37 season's crop. When the steam boiler being used to condition the tobacco leaf scraps developed a serious problem the workers were told to stop work on the remaining leaf. After inspecting the boiler the estates' managers estimated that it would take at least ten days to order new parts and repair the boiler. They felt "compelled to find work other than handling leaf to keep the natives employed in the interval," at which time the final processing of the 1936/37 crop could be completed. The following morning the workers were organized into two groups. One group was assigned the task of clearing new fields, while the other was told to prepare new seed beds. All the workers were told they would have to do these tasks until the boiler had been repaired and they could return to the final processing of that season's tobacco. The great majority of the workers refused to do either of the tasks that morning and over the next several days they continued to refuse to work. On the morning of August 17, after consulting with their solicitors, Ebden's owners assembled the entire work force of one hundred and ten workers and asked each worker individually if he would work at whatever tasks were assigned until such time as the boiler was fixed. Ninety-eight of the men answered "no." Their contracts were terminated on the spot and they were told to leave the farm immediately.

For Ebden's owners the question was straightforward. The workers had refused direct orders to work and had therefore violated their contracts. For the workers the issue was just as straightforward. The fired workers all contended that they had agreed to work on the 1936/37 crop, and not on preparing lands or seed beds for the 1937/38 season's crop. To the laborers the tasks assigned following the problem with the boiler did not concern the 1936/37 tobacco crop so they refused to do them. The Ebden case is not the only instance of laborers refusing to perform tasks they believed they had not agreed to do when they initially agreed to work on a farm. The incident at Ebden Estates shows that farm workers had a distinct awareness of the work they had agreed to do and for how long they had agreed to perform it. When ordered to work at tasks that did not pertain to that specific agreement they would, on occasion, refuse to work.[27]

There were, of course, more subtle ways by which the moral economy between laborers and farmers was defined on a daily basis. When assigning daily tasks farmers and workers developed a mutual understanding regarding the amount of work each task should entail. Lance Smith, a Banket area farmer, explained that for cultivating he had learned to assign "so many yards of hoeing for a day, and if that was to be done properly it could only be a reasonable amount." He explained that a reasonable amount was worked out through a process of give-and-take between himself and his workers. He would assign the amount of hoeing he believed could be finished in a day. Workers would then work at what he referred to as a normal pace until the time of day they normally finished. If they had not completed the assigned work they would point out to Smith that he had obviously misread the situation and assigned more than it was possible to finish in a single workday. Smith said that if a large majority of workers could not finish "the tasks must have been too heavy because the weeds had grown more than [I] recognized."[28] Richard Colbourne supported Smith's view when he noted that the amount of work was negotiated on almost a daily basis. He called the assigning of daily tasks "a game that was played" between farmers and workers. He added that after taking the laborers to the fields and accessing the amount of work that he felt needed to be done he would say something like "right, this is six lines [rows] each." The workers would almost certainly respond with "Six lines, we're going to be here all day, and all night. We'll never finish, we'll sleep here." Like Smith, he admitted that "every now and then, of course, there's certain justification, because you have overdone it." Colbourne concluded that if farmers failed to listen to their workers' concerns and routinely assigned amounts of work considered unreasonable, then there was a strong probability that after several days workers would say "we're not going to do it, it's too much," and stop working.[29]

G. P. Purchase, whose tobacco career lasted over five decades, agreed with Smith and Colbourne, and added that in nearly every case he could recall farmers and laborers alike knew "there are certain jobs got to be done irrespective" of circumstances. Jobs like planting and reaping which could not be delayed. He contended that laborers "knew it had to be done" and did not complain or refuse to work as long as farmers recognized, in turn, that they "had to be reasonable about it." For Purchase that meant giving workers time off on "the next day you could get off."[30]

On those occasions when laborers and farmers failed to reach an acceptable solution to the workers' calls for reasonable work loads laborers were not beyond resorting to other means of adjusting the amount of work performed. For example, when weeding workers would turn over a clump of weeds, with the soil clinging to the roots, onto the adjacent patch of weeds. From even a short distance away it would appear as though the entire section had been properly weeded, while in fact only half the area had been cleared. Or, when assigned to cut and stack cords of wood laborers would place elbow-shaped branches in the middle of a cord so that "it was like a honeycomb; [they] got half a cord . . . of wood by building it strategically." Workers would also build a cord around a fallen section of tree trunk, filling the middle and making half a cord appear to be a full cord. Other means of addressing what workers judged to be unacceptable demands included picking unripe leaves during reaping and, when engaged in tying hands of tobacco, tying a smaller number of hands on a stick to make it look like it contained the full number.[31]

Occasionally the working of the moral economy broke down completely and many laborers evidently believed that they had only one option open, desertion. When writing about mineworkers Van Onselen has argued that desertions from mines should be understood primarily as migrant workers' attempts to "avoid as far as humanly possible the prospect of work in the zones of low wages [and] . . . to move as far south as possible."[32] Van Onselen's assessment of why mineworkers deserted was also undoubtedly true for many farm laborers. Still, a percentage of desertions from farms were also the result of the breaking down of the moral economy. As indicated previously, the moral economy on farms included understandings by migrants that they had agreed to sell their labor in return for rations, housing, an acceptable wage, and civil treatment. When a farmer reneged on any of these implicit agreements workers commonly believed that their contracts had been voided. They then often argued that they could leave the farm and look for work elsewhere. Although specific accounts of workers explaining why they deserted are rare, a few do exist. Testimony from a 1929 criminal case indicates that a farm worker deserted due to his employer's mistreatment, "he having threatened me several times with a sjambok."[33] In 1936, a tobacco farm worker named Gatsi recounted, through a court interpreter, the conditions which caused him to desert: "I completed six tickets and . . . earned one pound. I only received ten shillings and five shillings. . . . The reason I was not paid the wages in full was because I was told I had to compensate the master . . .

for the death of an ox. I herded cattle for some time, completing three tickets; whilst doing this one died of sickness. I didn't injure it at all but it was very thin, all the oxen were, and it died. I reported its death to the master and he went to see it. Then he said I would have to pay four pounds for it." Gatsi plainly thought that he had been wrongly accused of causing the oxen's death. The injustice was compounded when he was told he would have to pay the "master" for the dead ox and thereby lose the wages he believed he was owed.[34]

Obviously not all tobacco farm laborers deserted their jobs after encountering unacceptable conditions. This was particularly true in regards to their living arrangements in the compounds. In those cases farm laborers often resorted to traditional beliefs and practices in efforts to improve their living conditions as well as to regulate relationships with other workers in the compounds. For example, workers relied on their knowledge of constructing houses to build living quarters for themselves. The previous chapter described how women used the domestic skills they possessed to increase their families' total incomes through beer brewing, supplemented rations by cultivating garden plots and collecting wild produce from the bush, and helped to maintain the health of male workers by preparing proper meals. In addition, court records abound with examples of farm workers using traditional skills to improve the conditions they found on many tobacco farms. Hunting and trapping techniques, for example, were universally used by farm workers to supplement inadequate rations. Testimony given in court cases shows that laborers from tobacco farms would sometimes place *jero* roots in farm ponds to make the "fish jump up [so] you catch them." A witness in one of the cases testified that using *jero* roots to poison small ponds was a common means of catching fish in Nyasaland. The works of Michael Gelfand and Audrey Richards both indicate that indigenous Shona and migrants from Northern Rhodesia also used roots and other parts of wild plants to poison ponds as a way of catching fish.[35]

Laborers also adapted the beliefs they brought with them to wage employment to fit the new living conditions found on tobacco farms. A prime example of this process was farm workers' use of traditional medicines, talismans, and other "magical" powers to offset misfortunes associated with farm compounds. As noted previously laborers were at times victimized by thieves who stole both money and trade goods from workers' houses while they were working or otherwise absent. Although they usually reported these incidents to their employers and local police officials, workers also responded to burglaries with traditional remedies. In many cases workers used medicines similar to a traditional Shona remedy called *rukwa chibatirapakare*, which was used to guard crops by rendering thieves unable to walk or run. In farm compounds, however, its powers were meant to protect workers' homes, and the personal property in them, rather than crops. If protective medicines failed workers then often sought the services of an *n'anga*. Laborers believed that these healers could either provide more powerful medicines or exorcise the malevolent spirits that were causing their misfortune. The *n'anga* also claimed powers that could lead to discovering the identity of a thief, cause stolen property to be returned, or locate the hiding place of missing money or property.[36]

Just as intriguing were those occasions when laborers used time-honored methods of supernatural sanction in their relationships with other workers and tobacco farmers. In 1925 the *Rhodesia Herald* reported a case where work on a farm came to a standstill over a dispute between a laborer named Jemisi and his fellow workers. The newspaper noted that the workers and their families had become increasingly afraid to leave the compound for any reason, whether to work, attend garden plots, or gather wood and wild produce. All the residents of the farm's compound claimed that they had had trouble with Jemisi in the past and tensions got so bad that workers finally asked the farm's owner to make Jemisi leave the farm. At this point the number of misfortunes (such as accidents, fights, or quarrels between couples) evidently escalated to a new level. The workers blamed Jemisi with retaliating by summoning an *ngozi*, a malevolent and often vengeful spirit, to disrupt the compound. Jemisi was finally dismissed by the farmer and the workers called in an *n'anga* to drive the *ngozi* out of the compound.[37] Just as noteworthy is a 1936 case from the Darwendale area in which a woman who had been living in a farm compound was accused of using witchcraft against a man named Simon. The man believed that some kind of evil medicine was being used against him by someone in the compound. He testified that he was the farm's "boss boy" and was responsible for issuing work assignments and disciplining workers to make sure they completed their tasks. He suggested that he had perhaps alienated a number of the workers by being too critical when assessing how well they did their assignments. In his mind one or more of those disgruntled workers was retaliating by using witchcraft to keep him away from work. Simon concluded his testimony by pointing out that the accused had been seen picking up dirt from one of his footprints and that she intended to use it to make some type of talisman to harm him. Was it only a coincidence that Simon had been suffering from a sore leg for some time and had been unable to work for several days?[38]

Workers also used traditional practices in their relations with farmers. According to Michael Bourdillon, *n'angas* prepared several medicines that were supposed to help in finding employment or facilitate the establishment of good relations with employers. Workers also performed traditional ceremonies to benefit farmers. From the time Dake Choto began working on tobacco farms in the late 1920s, workers had

annually approached farmers with offers to perform ceremonies honoring the spirit guardians of the lands occupied by
the farms. According to Dake, these offers were commonly
made twice a year, once following the harvest and another
immediately before the rains were due. On most of those occasions the farmers gave their approval. Senior workers then
prepared special beer, or had their wives do the brewing, and
the first portions were poured on the fields to honor the spirit
guardians. The remaining beer was then consumed by the
workers in celebration of the coming rains. Bonifasio Kandiero confirmed that this was a common practice, stating that
"after each and every tobacco growing season and before the
rains came again, the start of the new season, we would brew
beer called *doro remukwerera* (a beer brewed to thank the an-
cestors and to ask for rain and blessings)."[39]

There are a number of ways to view the examples given
above. Most Europeans in Southern Rhodesia probably dismissed them as additional evidence that African farm workers
were "ignorant," "superstitious," and "uncivilized." On the other
hand, they can be viewed as attempts by workers to come to
terms with the circumstances they found as farm laborers.
Troublesome co-workers like Jemisi and demanding "boss
boys" like Simon created tensions and bad feeling among laborers and their families. Unless those problems erupted into
serious fights between workers, or work stoppages, farmers
generally did not want to deal with what they often believed
were petty jealousies. That meant workers had to resolve
those tensions themselves. To do that they turned to remedies
they believed would put an end to the problems, either by preventing thefts, recovering property, driving misfortune from
the compound, or keeping overly demanding supervisors out
of the fields. The same reasoning applies to laborers using traditional medicines and ceremonies in their relations with farmers. Finding an employer who would live up to his obligations

could be a problem. Why not resort to a talisman or medicine that, according to the workers, improved their chances of finding a good employer? As for the offers to perform ceremonies honoring the spirit guardians of the land, some farmers surely believed that these requests were merely poorly veiled attempts to have an additional beer party. On the other hand, for farm workers, good rains would have meant job security as well as a slight lessening of tasks during the transplanting phase of the season. As noted previously, one of the most hectic times on a tobacco farm came when the rains were late and farmers furiously drove their workers to plant as many acres as possible in a short time span. Good rains could benefit workers after reaping and grading, too, as some farmers gave bonuses to workers if they had a good season. Also, good and steady rains at the beginning of a season commonly meant that a greater supply of wild fruits and vegetables were available to supplement workers' basic rations.

When discussing the lives of African mine workers in Southern Rhodesia, Charles van Onselen demonstrated that "by systematically probing the response of African workers within the context of a specific industry, it seems possible to suggest that there was a well developed worker consciousness from the very earliest days in Southern Rhodesia."[40]

As the discussion above suggests there was also a developing form of worker consciousness among farm laborers in the period before 1945. It is reasonable to suggest that practices such as placing logs in cords of wood or using traditional medicines against African "boss boys" who assigned too much work were acts by workers who judged for themselves that an excessive amount of work was being demanded of them. Laborers consciously considered factors such as adequate rations, housing, and civil behavior by their employers when making their decisions. Farmers had to find the proper balance of those factors if they wanted to employ sufficient numbers of workers for the length of the growing season. Incidents like the one at Ebden Estates demonstrate that an awareness of what constituted legitimate demands was not restricted to individual workers, but was present throughout much of the agricultural labor force of Southern Rhodesia.

As early as 1920, a report submitted by the native commissioner for Lomagundi stated that more workers were acquiring ideas with which to judge their conditions of employment "which were unknown until now."[41] In 1938 a Nyasaland labor officer observed that Nyasaland migrants were "fully aware" of their value to Southern Rhodesia's farmers, and other employers, and were often unwilling to work for farmers who did not treat them as a valued resource. In short, farm laborers were not "raw" or "ignorant." They recognized that political and economic conditions had changed with the coming of Europeans to southern Africa. They understood that one result of those changes was that they had to increasingly work for wages. Tens of thousands chose farm work for numerous reasons. Some were afraid to work underground in mines, while others came to Southern Rhodesia with their wives and children and thought that a farm offered a better environment for their families than mine compounds or towns. Still others believed that without some degree of western education they lacked the skills needed to work in towns or on mines.[42] Nevertheless, for whatever reason they began working on farms once there workers developed a consciousness of themselves as wage laborers and judged farmers' actions from that perspective.

Conclusion

This study has attempted to meet E. P. Thompson's challenge by chronicling the circumstances under which African men, women, and children lived and worked on European-owned tobacco farms in Southern Rhodesia during the years 1890–1945. Only by examining the work, living conditions and socioeconomic relationships experienced by these people, will their lives be freed from "the enormous condescension of history."

In the early years of this period, the Southern Rhodesian colonial state instituted its agricultural policy and, in its attempts to insure the success of that policy, initiated financial and agronomic assistance programs for European settlers. By 1910, partially as a result of those programs Virginia flue-cured tobacco had ostensibly become the export crop earmarked as the agricultural commodity on which to bolster that policy. By the early 1930s those programs had helped European settlers establish hundreds of tobacco farms throughout the northeastern districts of Southern Rhodesia. In order to maintain those farms the state also launched programs like the *Ulere* transport system to try and secure "a sufficiency of labour" to work on tobacco farms. Adequate numbers of African laborers were absolutely necessary if farmers were to successfully grow a crop like tobacco. Although difficult to define, "a sufficiency of labour" meant enough workers to perform all the tasks of the tobacco growing season, such as transplant-ing, topping, suckering, and grading at the lowest possible cost to the farmer.

Tobacco farmers attempted to control their workers on a daily basis by assigning *mgwaza* (piece work) to individual workers, or by more directly supervising gangs of laborers. Most farmers used a ticket system similar to the one devel-oped on the mines of southern Africa to enforce whichever daily disciplinary system they used, and some resorted to vio-lence to try to get laborers to accomplish their assigned tasks. Simultaneously, farmers developed a variety of methods they believed would guarantee that their African laborers remained employed for the entire growing season. Although these in-cluded paying wages and providing basic housing, food ra-tions, and rudimentary medical care (albeit at substandard levels), they also included the withholding of wages and ad-vancing of credit. These practices were geared to keeping la-borers financially indebted to farmers, making it difficult for them to leave their jobs.

This study demonstrates that workers and their families were not merely powerless victims of tobacco farmers. To the contrary, African workers actively attempted to shape, or at least ameliorate, both the work and the living conditions they found on the European farms of Southern Rhodesia. Field workers slowed their pace of work, stacked cordwood loosely, and occasionally refused to work altogether. Women living in farm compounds endeavored to improve minimal rations by working in garden plots and gathering wild fruits and pro-duce. Women also improved male workers' health by prepar-ing meals and supplementing men's wages by working part time and selling beer they had brewed. One result of these ac-tions was the birth of a moral economy on most tobacco farms during the period before 1945. Within this moral economy workers utilized traditional skills and knowledge to help determine acceptable conditions of labor.

After World War II Southern Rhodesia's tobacco industry continued many of its prewar patterns. Between 1945 and 1948 it entered into a period of rapid growth and increased prosperity. The total acreage planted in Virginia flue-cured tobacco rose by almost 90 percent while the yields per acre and number of growers more than doubled. During the succeeding decade that level of growth continued, with the number of tobacco farmers rising from 1,778 in 1949 to nearly 3,000 in 1959. This rapid expansion of the tobacco industry was due in large measure to the continuation of state assistance. In addition, the government allowed European farmers to extend tobacco growing to areas like Centenary, in northern Mazoe district. The results of this expansionist trend were dramatic. For instance, the acres planted in flue-cured tobacco increased from approximately 125,000 acres in 1950 to over 215,000 acres by 1959. During those years production of flue-cured tobacco tripled and the export value quadrupled.[1]

Aided by continued government regulation, new agronomic research, and expanding overseas markets, this trend continued until the mid 1960s. In late 1965, the Rhodesian Front government of Prime Minister Ian Smith declared its Unilateral Declaration of Independence (UDI) from Great Britain. Britain immediately declared UDI illegal and called for international economic sanctions against Rhodesia. The tobacco industry, in particular, was greatly affected by the sanctions and once again experienced a period of retrenchment. Between 1966 and 1970 the number of registered tobacco farmers, acres planted, yields per acre, and market values all plummeted. By late 1972 Zimbabwean African liberation movements began to increase their activities inside the country, and one of their principal areas of operation was the tobacco growing regions of Mashonaland. The intensification of the liberation war in these areas, combined with the cumulative affects of sanctions, resulted in very low levels of tobacco production throughout the remainder of the 1970s.

After independence in April 1980 tobacco production once again entered a period of expansion. For the first time in the history of the industry the government of Prime Minister (and president since 1987) Robert Mugabe extended government-sponsored financial and agricultural assistance programs to African peasant farmers and encouraged them to grow Virginia tobacco. Although a few African farmers did begin to grow the crop on a small scale, the vast majority of flue-cured tobacco continued to be grown on European-owned commercial farms. By the mid 1980s record crops were once again being produced in the country. Those higher production levels and record exports, as well as the predominancy of European growers, continued through to the 1990s and both farmers and the government believed that tobacco was again "a most promising weed."[2]

What about the socioeconomic conditions on the farms? Even with the post-1965 downturn in production figured into the picture, it seems clear that the overall fortunes of tobacco farmers improved remarkably during the decades after World War II. Nevertheless, the same cannot be said about farm workers. Even though some fundamental changes in the nature of tobacco farm labor did occur, many of the conditions of labor discussed in this study continued, or worsened, over the years since 1945. For example, the composition of the labor forces on tobacco farms changed as tobacco farmers began to rely more on reproducing and maintaining their labor forces on the farms rather than on recruiting new laborers prior to each growing season. This shift to a more stabilized, resident labor force resulted in increases in both the number of African women living and working on tobacco farms and the number of families in the compounds during the 1950s and 1960s. Other changes affected the work done of tobacco farms, including the greater use of irrigation systems and farm machinery and the more extensive use of chemicals for seasonal tasks like topping, suckering, and weeding.[3]

Still, conditions that would have been familiar to tobacco laborers in the 1920s and 1930s continued to exist decades after 1945. Low wages, minimal rations, rudimentary medical care, poor compound sanitation and substandard housing were still common in the tobacco growing regions of the country in the early 1990s. In a study examining the lives of farm workers in the 1970s D. G. Clarke argued that "real wages in 1974 were possibly no better than wages in 1922." He added that "there is strong evidence . . . that real earnings have been stagnant for the last 50 years—except where they have declined."[4] Many farm workers expected that their low wages would change with independence. They were initially pleased when the newly installed government did raise the minimum wage for farm workers in 1981 and 1982. Nevertheless, even with those increases farm workers' wages remained well below subsistence levels. Indeed, in a recent examination of farm labor conditions in Zimbabwe, Rene Loewenson claimed that the real wages of farm laborers remained static from 1983 to the early 1990s.[5]

Farmers continued to provide rations for their laborers and, in most cases, their laborer's families, throughout the period before 1980. The level of rationing remained inadequate between 1945 and the 1970s, with the weekly ration to male workers consisting of "from 14 to 17 lbs. of mealie meal, 2 lbs. of beans or groundnuts . . . with regular issues of salt and vegetables in season."[6] These were, of course, substantially the same as the rations issued in the pre-1945 period. Following the increase of the wage rate in the early 1980s most farmers stopped rationing their laborers and workers were expected to use their higher wages to provide for themselves and their families. Thus, the new policy resulted in workers spending a greater proportion of their wages on food staples, although they buy smaller quantities than had been previously provided. In attempts to improve their increasingly meager diets, workers continued to rely heavily on the labor of their wives and children. Garden plots remained important as sources of additional food, and women and children continued to search the countryside, on almost a daily basis, for wild fruits and vegetables.[7]

Loewenson also demonstrates that the availability of "health care and development of new programmes evident in other areas of Zimbabwe has been weak or non-existent" in most commercial farming areas.[8] As for the housing used by farm workers, Clarke reiterated the findings of the 1928 Committee of Enquiry on Native Labor when he noted that "very little if any planning has gone into the layout of [farm] compounds from the viewpoint of creating a good living environment." He concluded his study by stating that "housing is almost universally poor—hut, mainly pole and dhaka [mud and straw], about 10 feet in diameter, improperly ventilated, windowless, rarely weatherproof, and generally with other occupants than [people]."[9] Fifteen years later Loewenson criticized farm compounds as being "a squalid conglomeration of poor quality mud and thatch housing on dry stoney soils or wet poorly drained areas, covered by a pall of woodsmoke, dust and insects."[10]

Unfortunately, though the industry has grown in scale and net worth, and individual tobacco farmers have become wealthy, workers' lives have not improved. The studies by Clarke and Loewenson demonstrate that many of the conditions of labor examined in this study have not changed substantially since 1945. Rather, those pre-1945 conditions became the foundations on which new levels of exploitation of farm workers have been built.

Notes

Preface

1. E. P. Thompson, *The Making of the English Working Class* (New York, 1968), 12.

2. See Richard Sandbrook and Robin Cohen, eds., *The Development of an African Working Class* (London, 1975); Peter Gutkind, Robin Cohen, and Jean Copans, eds., *African Labor History* (Beverly Hills, Calif., 1978).

3. Frederick Cooper, *On the African Waterfront* (New Haven, 1987), 5.

4. See John S. Galbraith, *Crown and Charter : The Early Years of the British South Africa Company* (Los Angeles, 1974); Richard Hodder Williams, *White Farmers in Rhodesia, 1890–1945* (London, 1983); Robin Palmer, *Land and Racial Domination in Rhodesia* (Los Angeles, 1977). Colonial nomenclature will be used for cities, towns, and countries in this study.

5. See Charles Van Onselen, *Chibaro: African Mine Labour in Southern Rhodesia, 1900–1933* (London, 1976); Ian Phimister, *An Economic and Social History of Zimbabwe 1890–1948: Capital Accumulation and Class Struggle* (London, 1988).

6. Statistics compiled from Southern Rhodesia, Reports of the Chief Native Commissioner, 1914, 1930, 1935; "Report of a Conference to Discuss the Formation of a Native Labour Organization, Salisbury, February 22, 1944, Public Record Office, London (hereafter referred to as PRO), Dominions Offices (hereafter referred to as DO) 35/1163/R217/6.

7. Ian Phimister, "A Note on Labour Relations in Southern Rhodesian Agriculture before 1939," *South African Labour Bulletin 3*,

no. 5 (May 1977): 94–104; D. G. Clarke, *Agricultural and Plantation Workers in Rhodesia* (Salisbury, 1977), ch. 1; G. L. Chavaunduka, "Farm Labour in Rhodesia," *Rhodesian Journal of Economics* 6 (1972): 18–25.

8. In October 1985, the district names "Lomagundi" and "Mazoe" were changed to "Makonde" and "Mazowe," respectively.

9. E. D. Palmer and Michael Howell, Harare, interview by the author, December 12, 1984; H. J. Quinton, Harare, interview by the author, October 2, 1984; Dake Choto, Mushangwe Estate, Marondera, interview by the author, August 22, 1996.

10. *Handbook for the Use of Prospective Settlers on the Land*, 6th ed. (Salisbury, 1935), 40.

11. G. Arrighi, "Labour Supplies in Historical Perspective: A Study of the Proletarianization of the African Peasantry in Rhodesia," *Journal of Development Studies* 6, no. 3 (1970): 225.

12. Phimister, *Economic and Social History of Zimbabwe*, 225–31.

13. Henrietta L. Moore, *Feminism and Anthropology* (Minneapolis, 1988), 43.

Chapter 1—*A Most Promising Weed*

1. Frank Clements and Edward Harben, *Leaf of Gold: The Story of Rhodesian Tobacco* (London, 1962), 70.

2. Robin Palmer, *Land and Racial Domination in Rhodesia* (Los Angeles, 1977), 80; John S. Galbraith, *Crown and Charter : The Early Years of the British South Africa Company* (Los Angeles, 1974), 286; L. H. Gann, *A History of Southern Rhodesia* (London, 1965), 166–67.

3. E. P. Mathers, *Zambezia: England's El Dorado in Africa* (London, 1891), 374.

4. Clements and Harben, *Leaf of Gold*, 48–49; *Rhodesia Herald*, November 19, 1892.

5. Lawrence Vambe, *An Ill-Fated People: Zimbabwe before and after Rhodes* (London, 1972).

6. British South Africa Company, *Directors' Report and Accounts* (London, 1897), 25.

7. H. W. Roberts, "The Development of the Southern Rhodesian Tobacco Industry," *South African Journal of Economics* 19, no. 2 (1951): 177–88.

8. Southern Rhodesia (hereafter referred to SR), Department of Agriculture, annual report, 1904, p. 32.

9. *Debates of the Legislative Council*, 3d Council, 1st sess., April 26, 1905.

10. SR, Department of Agriculture, annual report, 1904, p. 22.

11. F. A. Stinson, *Tobacco Farming in Rhodesia and Nyasaland, 1889–1956* (Salisbury, 1956), 1.

12. SR, Department of Agriculture, annual report, 1911, p. 2.

13. I. R. Phimister, "Zimbabwe: the Path of Capitalist Development," in David Birmingham and Phyllis M. Martin, eds., *History of Central Africa* (London, 1983), 269.

14. British South Africa Company, *Directors' Report and Accounts*, 1917, 6–7.

15. Ibid.

16. H. Weinmann, *Agricultural Research and Development in Southern Rhodesia, 1890–1923* (Salisbury, 1972), 49; D. D. Brown, "Seasonal Notes on Tobacco," *Rhodesia Agricultural Journal* 24 (1927): 1274–80.

17. W. Twiston Davies, *Fifty Years of Progress: An Account of the African Organization of the Imperial Tobacco Company, 1907–1957* (Bristol, 1958), 32.

18. Clements and Harben, *Leaf of Gold*, 100.

19. *South Africa Journal of Economics* 19, no. 2 (1951): 188

19. Brown, "Seasonal Notes," 1274.

20. Quinton interview.

21. *Votes and Proceedings of the Legislative Assembly and Acts*, 2d Parliament, 2d sess., 1930 and 6th sess., 1933; 3d Parliament, 1st sess., 1934; 4th Parliament, 1st sess., 1935 and 2d sess., 1936.

22. See Peter Scott, "The Tobacco Industry of Southern Rhodesia," *Economic Geography* 28, no. 3 (1952): 189–206.

23. W. E. Haviland, "Tobacco Farm Organization, Cost and Land-Use in Southern Rhodesia," *South African Journal of Economics* 21 (1953): 367–80; Rhodesia Tobacco Association Memorandum ("Imperial Preference on Tobacco"), August 1941, National Archives of Zimbabwe (hereafter referred to as NAZ) S482/114/39.

24. Clements and Harben, *Leaf of Gold*, 128, 130, 133; Annual Statement of Trade of Southern Rhodesia, 1946.

25. *Rhodesia Herald*, December 1, 1945.

26. Mr. Pemberton, Compound Inspector, to the Chief Native Commissioner, letter, 3 March 1938, NAZ S1542/L1 1938(2).

27. George Kay, *Rhodesia: A Human Geography* (London, 1970), 17.

28. "Future Development of the Lomagundi District," Mimeograph, January 7, 1908, NAZ L2/2/95/19.

29. SR, Native Commissioner, Lomagundi, annual report, 1898, NAZ N9/1/4.

30. Colin Black, *The Legend of Lomagundi* (Salisbury, 1976), 31; C. T. C. Taylor, "Lomagundi," *Rhodesiana* 10 (1964): 17–44; SR, Native Commissioner, Lomagundi, annual reports, 1909 and 1911, NAZ N9/1/12 & 14.

31. SR, District Surgeon, Lomagundi, annual report, 1912, NAZ H2/4/23; Taylor, "Lomagundi," p32.

32. SR, Native Commissioner, Lomagundi, annual report, 1921, NAZ N9/1/23.

33. SR, 1926 census forms, Lomagundi District, NAZ C7/2/9.

34. John Scott and Nina Wise, Rainbow Nursery Farm, Banket, interview by the author, May 11, 1985; Duda Thurburn, Stroud Farm, Trelawney, interview by the author, May 9, 1985; Governor E. Baring to Viscount Cranborne, Dominions Office, Dispatch no. 162, 5 August 1944, PRO DO35/1169/R392/8.

35. SR, 1911 census returns, Lomagundi, NAZ C5/3/2.

36. SR, Department of Agriculture, annual report, 1912, p. 3.

37. "Additional Reports on Available Farms in Lomagundi District to 30 May 1913," NAZ L2/2/95/32; "Review of Agricultural Conditions," report, April 30, 1927, NAZ S881/485/1.

38. Victor Machingaidze, "Bankrupt Settler Farmers, Unemployment and State Response in Colonial Zimbabwe in the 1930s," paper presented at the Conference on Zimbabwean History: Progress and Development, University of Zimbabwe, August 23–27, 1982.

39. SR, Native Commissioner, Lomagundi, annual report, 1931, NAZ S235/509; B. Carr, 3D/Sgt. CID, to the Assistant Superintendent, CID, Salisbury, letter, May 10, 1939, NAZ S1226; SR, Native Commissioner, Lomagundi, annual report, 1938, NAZ S235/516.

40. Mazoe Farmers' Association, Minute Book, August 1907, NAZ Historical Manuscripts, MA4/1/1.

41. Kay, *Rhodesia*, 17, 21; Scott, "Tobacco Industry in Southern Rhodesia," 193, 200–201.

42. Scott, "The Tobacco Industry of Southern Rhodesia," 194.

42. *Rhodesia Herald*, August 7, 1925.

43. Oliver Ransford and Peter Steyn, *Historic Rhodesia* (Salisbury, 1975), 50.

44. *Rhodesia Herald*, August 7, 1925.

45. SR, Native Commissioner, Mazoe, annual report, 1903, NAZ N9/1/8; Mazoe Farmers' Association, Minute Book, August 11, 1907. The Mazoe Farmers' Association was founded in 1904.

46. Gann, *Southern Rhodesia*, 169.

47. *Rhodesia Herald*, August 7, 1925.

48. SR, Agricultural Department, annual report, 1907, pp. 9–10.

49. SR, Native Commissioner, Mazoe, monthly report, April 1908, NAZ N9/1/11; SR, Native Commissioner, Mazoe, annual report, 1908, ibid.

50. SR, Native Commissioner, Mazoe, annual report, 1920, NAZ N9/1/22.

51. *Rhodesia Herald*, May 4, 1920.

52. Weinmann, *Agricultural Research*, 48.

53. *Rhodesia Herald*, February 19, 1926.

54. SR, Native Commissioner, Mazoe, annual report, 1930, NAZ S235/508.

55. SR, Native Commissioner, Mazoe, annual report, 1933, NAZ S235/511; Scott, "Tobacco Industry of Southern Rhodesia," 193; Quinton interview.

56. Van Onselen, *Chibaro*, 120.

57. Palmer, *Land and Racial Domination*; Phimister, *Economic and Social History of Zimbabwe*; E. D. Palmer and Michael Howell, Harare, interview by the author, 12 December 1984; Thurburn interview; *Report of the Committee of Enquiry in Connection with the Supply of Native Labour in Southern Rhodesia* (Salisbury, 1921), pp. 12–13, NAZ SRG Miscellaneous Reports 1921; Report of the Committee Appointed by His Excellency the Governor to Enquire into Emigrant Labour, 1935 (Zomba, 1936), p. 2, PRO, CO525/161–80988.

58. SR, Native Commissioner, Mazoe, annual report, 1899, NAZ N9/1/5.

59. SR, Native Commissioner, Mazoe, annual report, 1908, NAZ N9/1/11.

60. SR, Native Commissioner, Lomagundi, annual report, 1909, NAZ N9/1/12.

Chapter 2—Salisbury Lends a Hand

1. Statement of W. M. Leggate, *Rhodesia Herald*, July 23, 1926.

2. Land and Agriculture Bank of Southern Rhodesia, annual report, 1926, NAZ S/AG 06.

3. Native Commissioner, Sinoia, to J. Robb, letter, 13 March 1929, NAZ S307/1929; British South Africa Company, *Directors' Report and Accounts*, 1896, pp. 25–26; A. Williams to the Secretary, Department of the Prime Minister, letter, 15 February 1934; Review of Agricultural Conditions in Southern Rhodesia, June 1929 and March 1930, NAZ S881/485/2; *Debates of the Legislative Council*, 5th Council, 3rd sess., April 7 and 23, 1913.

4. Peter Scott, "Migrant Labor in Southern Rhodesia," *Geographic Review* 44, no. 1 (1954): 29–48.

5. Eric A. Nobbs, Director of Agriculture, "Agricultural Credit in Southern Rhodesia," report, 1911, NAZ T2/29/48.

6. See Palmer, *Land and Racial Domination in Rhodesia*, 81–84; "Schemes of Assistance to Farmers," memorandum, NAZ S1246/S30H v. 1; Victor Machingaidze, "The Development of Settler Capitalist Agriculture in Southern Rhodesia, with Particular Reference to the Role of the State, 1908–1939" (Ph.D. diss., University of London, 1980), 71–72.

7. W. Olive, "The Rhodesia Land Bank," *Rhodesia Agricultural Journal* 9 (1911): 838.

8. British South Africa Company, *Directors' Report and Accounts*, 1913–23.

9. Machingaidze, "Development of Settler Capitalist Agriculture," 59–61; *Rhodesia Herald*, March 2, 1923; ibid., April 25, 1924.

10. "Assistance to Tobacco Industry," March 29, 1931; O. C. DuPont, Secretary to the Minister of Agriculture and Lands, to the Premier, letter, 27 March 1928, NAZ LE3/1/1.

11. Clements and Harben, *Leaf of Gold*, 100–108.

12. SR, Native Commissioner, Mazoe, annual report, 1928, NAZ S235/506.

13. Assistant Native Commissioner, Amandas, to the Chief Native Commissioner, letter, July 12 1928, NAZ S622/1928.

14. Chief Native Commissioner to the Secretary to the Treasury, letter, November 13, 1928, NAZ S235/406.

15. SR, Native Commissioner, Lomagundi, annual report, 1928, NAZ S235/506.

16. *Debates of the Legislative Assembly*, vol. 7, 1928, p. 29.

17. Native Commissioner, Mazoe, to the Chief Native Commissioner, letter, September 6, 1928, NAZ S138/40/28–29.

18. Secretary to the Treasury to the Chief Native Commissioner, letter, November 14, 1928, NAZ S235/406.

19. Principal Revenue Examiner to the Native Commissioner, Sinoia, letter, May 8, 1930, S307/1929; Assistant Native Commissioner to the Native Commissioner, Sinoia, letter, March 25, 1938, NAZ S307/1938.

20. George M. Odlum, *The Culture of Tobacco* (London, 1905), 164.

21. SR, Secretary of Agriculture, annual report, 1905, p. 25.

22. Director of Agriculture to J. S. Loosely, letter, August 21, 1910, NAZ G1/2/5/2.

23. *Rhodesia Herald*, June 30, 1922.

24. Evidence given by L. A. M. Hastings, Enquiry into the Position of Agriculture in Southern Rhodesia, 1934, NAZ S1246/S30(c).

25. Clements and Harben, *Leaf of Gold*, 55; SR, Department of Agriculture, annual report, 1904, p. 22.

26. See H. Weinmann, *Agricultural Research and Development in Southern Rhodesia, 1924–1950* (Salisbury, 1975); SR, Report of the Manager of the Tobacco Experiment Station, 1926–27, NAZ S1196; *Rhodesia Agricultural Journal* 28 (1931): 658; SR, annual reports of the Tobacco Research Board, 1935, 1936, and 1937.

27. R. Reynolds, "The British South Africa Company's Central Settlement Farm, Marandellas, 1907–1910: The Papers of H. K. Scorror," *Rhodesiana* 10 (1964): 1–16; Richard Hodder-Williams, *White Farmers in Rhodesia, 1890–1965* (London, 1983), 44–48.

28. Shepard Masocha, "The Tobacco Research Board, 1935–1965: A History with Special Reference to the Flue-Cured Virginia Tobacco Industry of Southern Rhodesia" (unpublished seminar paper, Department of Economic History, University of Zimbabwe, 1996), 10–11.

29. SR, Department of Agriculture, annual reports, 1922, p. 8, and 1925, p. 9.

30. See H. Weinmann, *Agricultural Research and Development in Southern Rhodesia, 1890–1923* (Salisbury, 1972).

31. SR, Secretary of the Department of Agriculture, annual reports, 1925–30.

32. Murray C. Steele, "The African Agricultural Labour Supply Crisis, 1924–1928," paper presented at Department of Economics, University of Rhodesia, October 4, 1973, p. 4.

33. SR, Native Commissioner, Lomagundi, annual report, 1899, NAZ N9/1/5.

34. *Rhodesia Herald*, April 28, 1911.

35. *Rhodesia Herald*, September 4, 1925.

36. Minutes of the Rhodesia Tobacco Association Executive Council meeting, held December 7, 1943, NAZ Historical Manuscripts RH27/8/4/4.

37. Van Onselen, *Chibaro*, 25–26, 103–107.

38. H. J. Taylor, Chief Native Commissioner, to the Secretary to the Department of the Administrator, letter, March 11, 1919; *Rhodesia Herald*, April 20, 1920; C. L. Carbutt, Chief Native Commissioner, to the Minister of Native Affairs, letter, March 24, 1934.

39. SR, Supervisor of Facilities for Passage of Northern Natives, annual report, 1926, NAZ S235/431.

40. Capt. G. N. Burden, "Report on Nyasaland Native Labour in Southern Rhodesia" (Salisbury, 1938), NAZ GEN-P/BUR.

41. "Re: Dispatch, Secretary of State, to the Governor, Lusaka," memo, August 11, 1936, PRO CO795/79/45007.

42. Sir Hubert Young, Governor of Northern Rhodesia, to W. G. A. Ormsby-Gore, letter, July 24, 1936, PRO CO795/83/45109/1.

43. "Provisional Agreement Between the Governments of Southern Rhodesia, Northern Rhodesia and Nyasaland," NAZ S482/524/39.

44. Official Report on the Annual Congress of the Rhodesia Agricultural Union, 1936, NAZ S1542/A6(2).

45. SR, Native Commissioner, Lomagundi, annual reports, 1931, 1932, and 1938, NAZ S235/509, 510, 516; B. Carr, 3D/Sgt. CID, to the Assistant Superintendent, CID, Salisbury, letter, May 10, 1939, NAZ S1226.

46. Report of the Committee of Enquiry, 1928, NAZ S480/36–38.

47. A. L. Holland, Supervisor of Facilities for the Passage of Northern Natives, to the Secretary of the Department of the Colonial Secretary, letter, May 27, 1930, NAZ S138/40/3–34.

48. Minutes of the Rhodesia Tobacco Association Executive Committee meeting, October 19, 1932, NAZ Historical Manuscripts RH27/8/4/1.

49. E. W. Lionel Noakes, Secretary of the Rhodesia Tobacco Association, to the Colonial Secretary, letter, November 14, 1932, NAZ S246/696.

50. *Debates of the Legislative Assembly*, v. 18, 1938, p. 2284; A. L. Holland, Supervisor of Facilities for the Passage of Northern Natives, to the Secretary of the Department of the Colonial Secretary, letter, May 27, 1930, NAZ S138/40/3–34.

51. *Bulawayo Chronicle*, January 20, 1938.

52. *Debates of the Legislative Assembly*, v. 18, 1938, pp. 2280–86; Nyasaland Labour Officer, to the Native Commissioner, Concession, letter, August 23, 1939, NAZ S1059/1938; John C. Abraham, Senior Provincial Commissioner, Blantyre, Nyasaland, Report on Nyasaland Natives in the Union of South Africa and in Southern Rhodesia, 22 February 1937.

53. SR, Controller, Stores and Transport Department, annual report, 1939, p. 6.

54. Victor Machingaidze, "The Development of Settler Capitalist Agriculture," pp. 65–66.

55. SR, Controller, Stores and Transport Department, annual report, 1941, pp. 6–8; SR, Supervisor of Native Labour Immigration, annual report, 1945, p. 256; SR, Secretary for Labour, Social Welfare, and Housing, annual report, 1958, p. 20.

56. Scott, "Migrant Labour in Southern Rhodesia," 36; Secretary to the Treasury, to the Auditor General, letter, January 23, 1941, NAZ S1539/A95/1.

57. *Report of the Secretary for Labour, Social Welfare and Housing* (Salisbury, 1959), 20.

58. Official Report on the Annual Congress of the Rhodesia Agricultural Union, 1936, NAZ S1542/A(2); E. Baring, Governor of Southern Rhodesia, to Viscount Cranbourne, Dominions Office, May 8, 1944, confidential dispatch no. 83, PRO DO35/1163/R217/6.

59. Leroy Vail, "The State and the Creation of the Colonial Malawi Agriculture Economy," in Robert I. Rotberg, ed., *Imperialism, Colonialism and Hunger: East and Central Africa* (Lexington 1983), 57–59; "Report of Conference to Discuss the Formation of a Native Labour Organisation," Salisbury, February 22, 1944, PRO DO35/1163/R217/6.

60. *Rhodesia Herald*, August 6, 1938.

61. SR, Native Commissioner, Lomagundi, monthly report, November 1938, NAZ S1619.

62. Minutes of a meeting held at the Colonial Office, October 16, 1938, PRO CO525/173/44–53/10; *Nyasaland Times*, December 15, 1938.

63. *Debates of the Legislative Assembly*, v. 18, 1938, p. 2282.

64. SR, Minutes of the Meeting of the Executive Council of the Rhodesia Agricultural Union, November 8, 1938, NAZ RH27/8/4/2; SR, Report of the Compound Inspector, Salisbury, January 1940, NAZ S1610.

65. Chief Native Commissioner, to Native Commissioner, Concession, letter, October 24, 1938, NAZ S1059/1938.

66. F. Wane, Native Commissioner, Concession, to the Chief Native Commissioner, letter, October 24, 1938, NAZ S1059/1938.

67. H. A. Cripwell, Assistant Native Commissioner, Shamva, to the Native Commisssioner, Mazoe, letter, October 12, 1938, NAZ S1059/1938.

68. G. Arrighi, "Labour Supplies in Historical Perspective: A Study of the Proletarianization of the African Peasantry in Rhodesia," *Journal of Development Studies* 6, no. 3 (1970): 197–234.

Chapter 3—Farms and Farmers

1. V. Vincent and R. G. Thomas, with R. R. Staples, *An Agricultural Survey of Southern Rhodesia—Part I: The Agro-Ecological Survey* (Salisbury, 1959), 45.

2. W. E. Meade, "Review of Agricultural Conditions in Southern Rhodesia to 28th October [1926]," NAZ S482/114/39; W. E. Haviland, "Tobacco Farm Organization, Cost and Land-Use in Southern Rhodesia," *South African Journal of Economics* 21 (1953): 368.

3. Nina Wise, Banket, farm account books.

4. D. C. H. Parkhurst, Compound Inspector, to the Native Commissioner, Salisbury, confidential memorandum, November 15, 1940, NAZ S482/510/39.

5. Palmer and Howell interviews, December 12, 1984 and February 25, 1985.

6. See SR, *Handbook for the Use of Prospective Settlers on the Land* (Salisbury), 3d ed. (1924), 4th ed. (1927), 5th ed. (1930), and 6th ed. (1935).

7. Quinton interview.

8. Scott and Wise interview.

9. Ibid.

10. Meade, "Review of Agricultural Conditions"; Quinton interview.

11. Roberts, "Development of the Southern Rhodesian Tobacco Industry," 185.

12. Parkhurst memorandum; Quinton interview; Palmer and Howell interview, December 12, 1984; Dick Colbourne, Woodleigh Farm, Banket, interview by the author, May 13, 1985.

13. Palmer and Howell interview, February 25, 1985.
14. SR, Department of Agriculture, annual report, 1907, p. 11; SR, Report of the Native Labour Enquiry Committee, 1906, NAZ Miscellaneous Reports, 1901–1908; SR, Report of the Native Affairs Committee of Enquiry, 1910/11, NAZ Miscellaneous Reports, 1909–16; SR, Report of the Committee of Enquiry in Connection with the Supply of Native Labour in Southern Rhodesia, NAZ SRG4 Miscellaneous Reports, 1921; SR, Report of the Native Labour Committee, 1928, NAZ S480/36–38; SR, Report of the Committee of Enquiry into the Economic Position of the Agricultural Industry of Southern Rhodesia, 1934, NAZ SRG4 Miscellaneous Reports 1933–40.
15. SR, Report of the Compound Inspector, Salisbury, November 1940, NAZ S1610.
16. *Rhodesia Herald*, January 4, 1907; ibid., February 22, 1907; ibid., October 4, 1912; ibid., January 7, 1921; Mr. Wright, Land Inspector, report, September 19, 1936, NAZ S2111/26.
17. Manager, Land and Agricultural Bank of Southern Rhodesia, to Captain the Honorable F. E. Harris, Minister of Agriculture and Lands, memorandum, December 13, 1935, NAZ S482/93/40.
18. H. W. Taylor, Tobacco Expert, "Memorandum on Closer Settlement under Irrigation," April 1919, NAZ T2/29/91.
19. Clements and Harben, *Leaf of Gold*, 53.
20. P. H. Haviland, *Flue-Curing Tobacco Barns, Bulking and Grading Sheds* (Salisbury, 1926), 7; C. S. Jobling, "Notes on Tobacco Growing and Curing under Local Conditions," *Rhodesia Agricultural Journal* 9 (1910/11): 678–79.
21. P. H. Haviland, *Flue-Curing Tobacco Barns*, 4–5; Taylor Memorandum; *Handbook[s] for the use of Prospective Settlers on the Land*, 1924, p. 25; 1927, p. 40; 1930, p. 45; 1935, p. 40.
22. Ibid., 1935, p. 40.
23. *Rhodesia Herald*, January 26, 1917; ibid., October 8, 1926; Assistant Road Engineer, to the Native Commissioner, Sinoia, letter, December 8, 1924, NAZ S307.
24. *Rhodesia Herald*, July 18, 1924.
25. Jennings, Assistant Director Lands, to the Secretary, Office of the High Commissioner for Southern Rhodesia, letter, September 22, 1927, NAZ S1801/2537.
26. Land Settlement Officer, London, to the Secretary, Office of the High Commissioner for Southern Rhodesia, letter, October 21, 1927, NAZ S1801/2537.

27. "Tobacco Production Cost," *Rhodesia Agricultural Journal* 25 (1928).

28. Charles Cartwright and Guy Cartwright papers, Waltondale Farm, Marondera.

29. Quinton interview.

30. Van Onselen, *Chibaro*, 34.

Chapter 4—Making the Grade

1. *Handbook for the Use of Prospective Settlers on the Land* (Salisbury) 3d ed. [1924], 24.

2. Quinton interview.

3. Bruce Keevil, Dodhill Farm, Chegutu, interview by the author, March 30, 1985; Richard Colbourne, Woodleigh Farm, Banket, interview by the author, May 13, 1985; John Brown, Chegutu, interview by the author, March 30, 1985; Scott and Wise interview; V. M. Wadsworth, "Native Labour in Agriculture, pt. 1—Tobacco," *Rhodesia Agricultural Journal* 47, no. 3 (1950): 243; idem, "Native Labour in Agriculture, pt. 2—Maize," *Rhodesia Agricultural Journal* 47, no. 6 (1950): 489.

4. Clements and Harbin, *Leaf of Gold*, 87.

5. G. T. Purchase, Vainona, Harare, interview by the author, February 4, 1985.

6. Trevor Gordon, Audley End Farm, Darwendale, interview by the author, May 11, 1985; Colbourne interview.

7. Purchase interview.

8. *Rhodesia Herald*, November 12, 1926.

9. Ibid.

10. Palmer and Howell interview, December 12, 1984.

11. Odlum, *The Culture of Tobacco*; E. A. Nobbs, *Handbook of Tobacco Culture* (Salisbury, 1913); D. D. Brown, "Seasonal Notes on Tobacco Culture in Southern Rhodesia," *Rhodesia Agricultural Journal* 26 (1929): 1274–80.

12. SR, Department of Agriculture, annual report, 1922, p. 1.

13. Sinoia Magistrate's Court, case 201/22, 1922, NAZ D3/2/19.

14. Palmer and Howell interview, December 12, 1984.

15. *Rhodesia Herald*, January 9, 1925; "Review of Agricultural Conditions in Southern Rhodesia" [February 1927], NAZ S881/

485/1; George Scott, Land Inspector, report, July 31, 1928, NAZ S2111/26; Quinton interview, December 17, 1984; Colbourne interview.

16. Brown, "Seasonal Notes," 1274; C. S. Jobling, "Notes on Tobacco Growing and Curing under Local Conditions," *Rhodesia Agricultural Journal* 9 (1911/12): 677.

17. Brown, "Seasonal Notes," 1274; Colbourne interview.

18. D. D. Brown, "Seedbeds," *Rhodesia Agricultural Journal* 27 (1930): 1032–34; Nobbs, *Handbook of Tobacco Culture; From Seedbed to Smoker: Southern Rhodesian Tobacco, Its Growth and Manufacture* (London, 1928).

19. Dake Chote, Mushangwe Farm, interview by the author, Marondera, August 22, 1996; SR, Report of the Native Labour Committee, 1928, NAZ S480/36–38.

20. Nobbs, *Handbook of Tobacco Culture*, 19.

21. Ibid.; C. S. Jobling, "Tobacco Sale—Some Hints and Suggestions" *Rhodesia Agricultural Journal* 9 (1911/12): 507–19.

22. Jobling, "Notes on Tobacco Growing," 677.

23. Clements and Harben, *Leaf of Gold*, 88.

24. Z. C. Marangwanda, Katena, Chiweshe, interview by L. Leslie Bessant and Elvis Muringai, December 6, 1984.

25. Brown, "Seasonal Notes," 1276.

26. Colbourne interview.

27. Jobling, "Notes on Tobacco Culture," 677; Nobbs, *Handbook on Tobacco Culture*, 21.

28. Brown, "Seasonal Notes," 1276.

29. Ibid., 1276–77; Nobbs, *Handbook on Tobacco Culture*, 9.

30. Ibid., 23–24.

31. Keevil interview.

32. Mr. Muvura, Grove Farm, Arcturus, interview by the author, January 23, 1985; Purchase interivew; *Debates of the Legislative Assembly*, v. 6 (1927).

33. Clements and Harben, *Leaf of Gold*, 201; Jobling, "Notes on Tobacco Growing," 679.

34. Colbourne interview.

35. Muvura interview; Keevil interview; SR, Report of the Compound Inspector, Salisbury, April 15–30, 1940, NAZ S1610; Haviland, "Tobacco Farm Organization," 371.

36. Report on Public Health, 1928, pp. 13–14, NAZ SRG3.

37. Clements and Harben, *Leaf of Gold*, 64, 70; J. S. Loosley, to Dr. E. Nobbs, letter, August 9, 1910, NAZ G1/2/5/2; Odlum, *Culture of Tobacco*, 20; *Rhodesia Herald*, March 19, 1913.

38. Clements and Harben, *Leaf of Gold*, 83.

39. SR, Secretary for Agriculture, annual report, 1920, p. 8; *Rhodesia Herald*, June 30, 1922.

40. SR, Secretary for Agriculture, annual reports, 1923, p. 12; ibid., 1927, p. 6; *Rhodesia Herald*, October 8, 1926.

41. SR, Secretary for Agriculture, annual report, 1926, p. 1.

42. W. E. Meade, Periodic Report Regarding the Agricultural Conditions in Southern Rhodesia (Office of the High Commisssioner for Southern Rhodesia, October 1927), NAZ S881/485/1.

43. Palmer and Howell interview, February 25, 1985.

44. Mr. Murambwa and Ashley Staunton, Grove Farm, Arcturus, interviews by the author, January 23, 1985; Cartwright and Cartwright papers.

Chapter 5—Labor and Discipline

1. John C. Abraham, Senior Provincial Commissioner, Nyasaland [Blantyre 1937], "Nyasaland Natives in the Union of South Africa and Southern Rhodesia," National Archives of Malawi.

2. Rawdon Hoare, "Rhodesian Jottings," *Cornhill Magazine* 150, no. 898 (October 1934): 467–76.

3. Quinton interview, October 2, 1984.

4. Peter M. Lamb to the Native Commissioner, Sinoia, letter, May 18, 1936, NAZ S307/1935–6.

5. Colbourne interview; Thurburn interview, May 9, 1985; Purchase interview; C. Bullock, Native Commissioner, Lomagundi, correspondence, 1929, NAZ S307/1929.

6. L. W. Morgan, to the Committee of Enquiry into the Economic Position of the Agricultural Industry of Southern Rhodesia [1934], letter, January 11, 1934, NAZ S1246/30(E).

7. Palmer and Howell interviews, December 12, 1984, February 25, 1985.

8. *Rhodesia Herald*, February 4, 1921; Van Onselen, *Chibaro*, 98.

9. *Rhodesia Herald*, January 2, 1924; SR, Report of the Native Affairs Committee of Enquiry, 1910–11, NAZ A3/3/18.

10. SR, Chief Native Commissioner to Superintendent of Natives, Bulawayo, letter, November 26, 1931, NAZ S138/40/30–34.

11. Van Onselen, *Chibaro*, 143.

12. Colbourne interview; Wilson Mtikira, Grove Farm, Arcturus, interview by the author, January 23, 1985; Native Commissioner, Amandas, to S. W. Kemp, letter, September 19, 1928, NAZ S622/1928; S. E. Collings, Public Prosecutor to the Assistant Magistrate, Amandas, letter, July 2, 1929, NAZ S622/1929.

13. SR, Report of the Native Labour Committee, 1928, NAZ S480/36–38.

14. Cartwright and Cartwright papers.

15. *Rhodesia Herald*, January 9, 1925.

16. *Rhodesia Herald*, March 12, 1909.

17. Hoare, "Rhodesia Jottings," 470.

18. *Rhodesia Herald*, January 19, 1912; ibid., April 2, 1915; Sinoia Magistrate's Court, case 199/22, NAZ D3/2/19.

19. *Rhodesia Herald*, January 26, 1912; Jeannie M. Boggie, *A Husband and a Farm in Rhodesia* (Gwelo, 1959), 104–105.

20. Sinoia Magistrate's Court, case 176/15, NAZ D3/2/9.

21. Bindura Magistrate's Court, case 62/22, NAZ D3/10/3.

22. SR, Director of Agriculture, annual report, 1910, NAZ SRG 3.

23. SR, Native Commissioner, Mazoe, monthly report, April 1938, NAZ S1619.

24. Palmer and Howell interview, February 25, 1985.

25. *Rhodesia Herald*, May 5, 1911; SR, Assistant Native Commissioner, Shamva, annual report, 1925, NAZ S235/503; SR, Chief Native Commissioner, monthly report, March 1936, NAZ S235/529.

26. *Rhodesia Herald*, November 5, 1926.

27. Letter from "Lomagundi Farmer," *Rhodesia Herald*, January 6, 1911; Report of the meeting of the Banket Farmers' Association, *Rhodesia Herald*, October 8, 1926; *Rhodesia Herald*, November 12, 1926; ibid., November 28, 1926.

28. SR, Native Commissioner, monthly reports, NAZ S235/525; S235/509; S235/511; S235/515; N9/1/6–11; S138/40/24, 28–29; S307/1924 and 1926; S622/1928–32; Clements and Harben, *Leaf of Gold*, 83; Quintin interview; Purchase interview; Colbourne interview.

29. SR, Department of Native Affairs, annual report, 1935, NAZ S1542/L1 v. 3, table 1; SR, Native Commissioner, Lomagundi,

monthly reports, June, July, October, and November 1934, NAZ S235/527.

30. SR, Native Commissioner, Lomagundi, monthly reports, October and November 1934, NAZ S235/527.

31. Assistant Native Commissioner, Bindura, to the Chief Native Commissioner, letter, June 12, 1940, NAZ S1059.

32. Concession Magistrate's Court, case 135/19, NAZ D3/15/5; *Rhodesia Herald,* April 1, 1921; J. W. Brigden, *Trade Conditions in Southern Rhodesia, 1932* (London, 1932), 9.

33. Cartwright and Cartwright papers.

34. SR, Cost of Living Committee, report, 1921, NAZ SGR 4.

35. SR, Native Labour Committee, report, 1928, NAZ S480/36–38.

36. Report of the Committee appointed by his Excellency, the Governor, to Enquire into Emigrant Labour, 1935 (Zomba, 1936), PRO CO 525/161/80988 (hereafter referred to as Report to the Nyasaland Governor, 1935).

37. Ganda Chivandire, Shopo, Chiweshe, interview by L. Leslie Bessant and Elvis Muringai, December 19, 1984.

38. SR, Report of the Native Labour Committee, 1928, NAZ S480/36–38.

39. Van Onselen, *Chibaro,* 73; Ralph Drew Palmer, transcript of interview, NAZ Oral History Transcripts, Oral/PA 4.

40. SR, Report of the Compound Inspector, Salisbury, 5–23 April 1940, NAZ S1610.

41. G. N. Burden, *Nyasaland Native Labour in Southern Rhodesia* (Salisbury, 1938); Pemberton, Compound Inspector, to the Chief Native Commissioner, letter, March 3, 1938, NAZ S1542.L1 1938(2); SR, Report of the Compound Inspector, Salisbury, March 1940, NAZ S1610; Fillimon Visani, Fraser Rali, Bonifacio Kandiero, Sani Binali, Divarsion Mazombe, and Issac Mwandela, Gabaza Farm, Beatrice, interviews by the author, September 5, 1996.

42. Palmer and Howell interview, February 25, 1985; Gordon interview; Handina Makonyonga, Chihota village, interview by Elizabeth Schmidt, February 15, 1986; Hamundidi Mhindurwa, Chaitezyi village, interview by Elizabeth Schmidt, January 26, 1986; Murambwa interview. See also Sipolilo Magistrate's Court, cases 210/30 and 211/30, NAZ 1979; Bindura Magistrate's Court, case 618/32, NAZ D3/10/13; Darwendale Magistrate's Court, case 341/33, NAZ S660.

43. Van Onselen, *Chibaro*, 166–67.

44. Chairman, Banket Farmers' Association, to the Native Commissioner, Sinoia, letter, 3 January 1932, NAZ S307/1932; SR, Report of the Native Labour Committee, 1928, NAZ S480/36–38.

45. Audrey I. Richards, *Land, Labour and Diet in Northern Rhodesia* (1939; reprint London, 1961), 406–408; Concession Magistrate's Court, case 659/29, NAZ S583.

46. Keevil interview.

47. SR, Report of the Native Labour Committee, 1928, NAZ S480/36–38; W. E. Haviland, "The Use and Efficiency of African Labour in Tobacco Farming in Southern Rhodesia," *Canadian Journal of Economics and Political Science* 20, no. 1 (1954): 100–106; G. St. J. Orde-Browne, "The African Worker," *Africa* 3 (1930): 13–31.

48. "Minutes from the Conference on the Incidence of Scurvy on Certain Farms and Tobacco Plantations," Salisbury, January 10, 1939, NAZ S482/447/39; Report on Inspection of Farm Labourers, Native Commissioner, Gwibi, February 25, 1913, NAZ N3/22/1/1; Palmer, "Agricultural History of Rhodesia," 223; H. Weinmann, *Agricultural Research and Development in Southern Rhodesia, Under the Rule of the British South Africa Company 1890–1923*, Department of Agriculture [University of Rhodesia] Occasional Paper No. 4 (Salisbury, 1972), 11; Secretary, Rhodesia Co-op Fruit Growers' Association, to the Medical Director, letter, July 4, 1929, NAZ S1173/238.

49. Major Wane, Native Commissioner, Amandas, to the Chief Native Commissioner, letter, July 6, 1928, NAZ S622/1928; Compound Inspector, Salisbury, to the Chief Native Commissioner, letter, March 2, 1938, NAZ S1542/L1 1938(2); David Kiddrie, "The Road to Work: A Survey of the Influence of Transport on Migrant Labour in Central Africa," *Rhodes-Livingstone Journal* 15 (1954): 31–42; SR, Report to the Nyasaland Governor, 1935; *Rhodesia Herald*, September 15, 1944; ibid., February 16, 1945.

50. SR, Report on Public Health, 1928, pp. 13–14, NAZ SRG3.

51. SR, Reports on Public Health, NAZ SRG3; annual reports of the Mount Darwin Clinic, 1930–35, NAZ S1820/C; Assistant Magistrate, Sinoia, to the Medical Director, letter, December 14, 1929; SR, Native Commissioner, Lomagundi, annual report, 1939, NAZ S235/517.

52. E. T. Palmer, Native Commissioner, Sinoia, to the Chief Native Commissioner, letter, July 25, 1935, NAZ S1542/D5; SR,

Report of the Compound Inspector, Mashonaland, September 1942, NAZ S1610.

53. Inquest into the death of Forosa, farm laborer, S622/1931; British South Africa Police, Inquest 3/33, Inquest into deaths, 1928–33, NAZ S1969; British South Africa Police, Inquest 1/31, Inquest into deaths, 1928–33, NAZ S1969.

54. Medical Director, to Deputy Colonial Secretary, letter, August 26, 1929, NAZ S1173/238; C. T. C. Taylor, Nyarapinda Farm, Banket, to the Medical Director, Salisbury, letter, September 11, 1931; Medical Director, Salisbury, to C. T. C. Taylor, letter, September 15, 1931, NAZ S1173/239.

55. *Rhodesia Herald*, May 14, 1914; ibid., January 9, 1925; Major Wane, Native Commissioner, Amandas, to Ivor Southey, letter, October 8, 1928; G. Brisley, to the Native Commissioner, Mazoe, letter, March 19, 1928, NAZ S622/1928; F. G. Southey, to the Native Commissioner, Mazoe, letter, October 13, 1925, NAZ S622/1925.

56. Lance Smith, Pindi Park Farm, Banket, interview by the author, May 8, 1985; SR, Report on Public Health, 1931, NAZ SRG3; SR, Native Commissioner, Lomagundi, annual report, 1917, NAZ N9/1/19; Bindura Magistrate's Court, case 1468/35, NAZ S1026.

57. Abraham Report, p. 21.

58. District Surgeon, Bindura, to the Native Department, memorandum, January 11, 1922, NAZ NSB 1/1/1.

59. Assistant Native Commissioner, Shamva, to Native Commissioner, Mazoe, letter, May 12, 1938, NAZ S1059/1938.

60. Text of a speech delivered by Col. C. L. Carbutt, Chief Native Commissioner, to the Conference of Senior Native Commissioners, Salisbury, March 27–29, 1935, NAZ S235/488.

61. Burden Report.

62. SR, Native Commissioner, Mazoe, monthly report, February 1933, NAZ S235/526.

63. monthly report, Native Commissioner, Mazoe, July 1934, NAZ S235/527.

64. Van Onselen, *Chibaro*, 145.

65. SR, Native Commissioner, Mazoe, monthly report, September 1921, NAZ N9/4/41; SR, Native Commissioner, Mazoe, annual report, 1928, NAZ S235/506; Native Commissioner, Sinoia, to N. P. van Biljon, letter, December 5, 1930, NAZ S307/1930; SR, Report of the Compound Inspector, Salisbury, April 5–23, 1940, NAZ S1610;

Managing Director, Darwendale Estates, to the Native Commissioner, Sinoia, letter, February 4, 1933, NAZ S307/1933.

66. Native Commissioner, Mazoe, to A. Stead, letter, December 21, 1925, NAZ S622/1925.

67. Text of speech presented by Mr. Howman, Native Commissioner, Goromonzi, to the Conference of Superintendents of Natives and Native Commissioners, 1927, NAZ SRG 4.

68. NCO i/c, Sinoia, to the Native Commissioner, Sinoia, letter, November 25, 1931, NAZ S307/1931.

69. SR, Native Commissioner, Mazoe, monthly report, June 1932, NAZ S235/525.

70. SR, Native Commissioner, Lomagundi, annual report, 1936, NAZ S235/515. See also Native Commissioner, Salisbury, to the Acting Chief Native Commissioner (ACNC), letter, July 12, 1935; Native Commissioner, Rusapi, to the ACNC, letter, July 10 1935.

71. SR, Native Commissioner, Mazoe, annual report, 1930, NAZ S235/508.

72. Native Commissioner, Concession, to the Acting Chief Native Commissioner, letter, July 11, 1935, NAZ S1542/L1/1935; Sinoia Magistrate's Court, case 183/34, NAZ S2181; Pemberton, Compound Inspector, to the Chief Native Commissioner, letter, March 3, 1938, NAZ S1542/L1/1938(2).

73. Assistant Native Commissioner, Bindura, to the Acting Chief Native Commissioner, letter, July 13, 1935, NAZ S235/356.

74. C. Bullock, Acting Chief Native Commissioner, Circular Minute no. 25, July 4, 1935, NAZ S235/356.

75. Van Onselen, *Chibaro*, 162.

76. Palmer and Howell interview, 12 December 1984; W. A. Devine, Native Commissioner, Mazoe, to the Chief Native Commissioner, letter, January 30, 1925, NAZ S622/1925.

77. Burden Report.

78. Palmer and Howell interview, February 25, 1985.

79. Ibid.; Bindura Magistrate's Court, case 586/35, NAZ D3/10/20.

80. Thurburn interview; Cartwright and Cartwright papers.

81. Interview with Ashley Staunton, Grove Farm, Arcturus, January 23, 1985; SR, Report of the Native Labour Committee, 1928, NAZ S480/36–38; Native Commissioner, Sinoia, to N P. Biljon, letter, December 5, 1930, NAZ S307/1930; Statement by Mphande, to

NCO i/c Darwendale, British South Africa Police Report, April 14, 1933, NAZ S307/1933.

82. Quinton interview, October 2, 1984.

83. Palmer and Howell interview, December 12, 1984; Purchase interview; Muvura, Kachepa Khamiso, and Wilson Mtikira, Grove Farm, Arcturus, interview by the author, January 23, 1985; Cartwright and Cartwright papers.

84. Concession Magistrate's Court, case 305/28, NAZ D3/15/16.

85. Thurburn interview.

86. SR, Report of the Native Affairs Committee of Enquiry, 1910/11, NAZ A3/3/18; *Rhodesia Herald,* May 25, 1945; SR, Report of the Native Labour Committee, 1928, NAZ S480/36–38; F. W. Winskill, to E. T. Palmer, Native Commissioner, Sinoia, letter, December 2, 1937, NAZ S307/1937.

87. *Rhodesia Herald,* May 25, 1945; Native Commissioner, Salisbury, to the Chief Native Commissioner, letter, February 6, 1929, NAZ S235/406.

88. SR, Native Commissioner, Lomagundi, monthly report, July 1933, S235/526; Scott and Wise interview.

89. Capt. R. D. James (ret.), evidence given before the Natural Resources Board, June 23, 1942, NAZ 987/1.

90. Arrighi "Labour Supplies in Historical Perspective," 212, 219.

91. Thurburn interview.

92. Capt. R. D. James (ret.), evidence given before the Natural Resources Board, June 23, 1942, NAZ 987/1.

93. SR, Chief Native Commissioner, monthly report, November 1919, NAZ N9/4/37; D. W. Parkhurst, Compound Inspector, to the Chief Native Commissioner, report, November 15, 1940, NAZ S482/510/39.

94. Palmer and Howell interview, February 25 1985.

Chapter 6—The Life of the Compound

1. Report of the Native Labour Committee, 1928. Mimeograph. NAZ S480/36–38.

2. Van Onselen, *Chibaro,* 128–36; J. K. McNamara, "The Development of a Labour Infrastructure: Migration Routes to the Witwatersrand Gold Mines and Compound Accommodation, 1889 to

1912," *South African Labour Bulletin* 4, no. 3 (May 1978): 7–28; Sean Moroney, "The Development of the Compound as a Mechanism of Worker Control 1900–1912," *South African Labour Bulletin* 4, no. 3 (May 1978): 29–49; Rob Turrell, "Kimberly: Labour and compounds, 1871–1888," in Shula Marks and Richard Rathbone, eds., *Industrialisation and Social Change in South Africa* (Essex, U.K., 1982), 45–76; Ian Phimister, *Wangi Kolia: Coal, Capital and Labour in Colonial Zimbabwe 1894–1954* (Johannesburg, 1994), 71–73, 79–80.

3. Victor Machingaidze, "Bankrupt Settler Farmers, Unemployment and State Response."

4. Wise account books.

5. D. C. H. Parkhurst, Compound Inspector, to the Native Commissioner, Salisbury, confidential memorandum, November 15, 1940, NAZ S482/510/39.

6. Palmer and Howell interview, December 12, 1984.

7. Van Onselen, *Chibaro*, 132–36.

8. SR, Report of the Compound Inspector, January 1940, NAZ S1610. A *vlei* is an area where water collects below the immediate surface.

9. Scott and Wise, interview; Staunton interview; Jana Makumbira, Munemo Farm, Marondera, interview by author, August 22, 1996.

10. T. H. Newmarch to the Secretary, Native Labour Commission of Enquiry, letter, April 15, 1921, NAZ A3/3/19/1; Bindura Magistrate's Court, case 618/32, NAZ D3/10/13; Sinoia Magistrate's Court, cases 119/20 to 122/20, NAZ D3/2/17.

11. Native Commissioner, Gwebi, "Report on Inspection of Farm Labourers," February 15, 1913, NAZ N3/22/1/1; Assistant Medical Director, Bulawayo to Medical Director, Salisbury, letter, February 23, 1910. NAZ A3/18/30/2.

12. Sinoia Magistrate's Court, case 176/15, 1915, NAZ D3/2/9; Burden Report.

13. L. T. Tracey, *Approach to Farming in Southern Rhodesia* (Salisbury, 1945), 354.

14. British South Africa Police Inquests into Deaths, cases 1/29 and 4/30, 1928–1933, NAZ S1969.

15. Abraham report, p. 20.

16. Burden report; Keevil interview; SR, Report of the Compound Inspector, Salisbury District, for the period April 5th to 23rd

1940, NAZ S1610; Saidi, Grove Farm, Arcturus, interview by the author, January 23, 1985.

17. T. H. Newmarch to the Secretary, Native Labour Commission, letter, April 15, 1921, NAZ A3/3/19/1; response to Letter to the Editor, in *Native Affairs Department Annual* 6 (1928): 79; Palmer and Howell interview, December 12, 1984.

18. SR, Report of the Native Labour Committee, 1928, p. 8, NAZ S480/36–38.

19. Compound Inspector to Medical Director, letter, 10 October 1944, NAZ S2104/1.

20. F. Allen to Native Commissioner, Mazoe, letter, November 17, 1925.

21. Mhindurwa interview; Makonyonga interview; Senesai Chidemo and Chibaiso Mwadenga, Choto homestead, Hwedza, interviews by the author, August 31, 1996; SR, Report of the Compound Inspector, Salisbury, for January 1940, NAZ S1610.

22. F. Allen to Native Commissioner, Mazoe, letter, November 17, 1925.

23. Mugari Mandaza, Nyakudya, interview by L. Leslie Bessant and Elvis Muringai, December 13, 1984.

24. SR, Report of the Committee of Enquiry in connection with the Supply of Native Labour in Southern Rhodesia [1921], NAZ SRG4 Miscellaneous Reports, 1921.

25. *Debates of the Legislative Assembly*, v. 5 (Salisbury, 1926), p. 1676.

26. Charles P. J. Coghlan, Premier and Minister of Native Affairs, memorandum for meeting with Sinoia Farmers Association, March 17, 1927, NAZ S235/431; Assistant Native Commissioner, Sinoia, to the Chief Native Commissioner, Salisbury, letter, October 25, 1935, NAZ S1542/D5.

27. L. P. Leech, Tuli Farm, Gwanda, to the Colonial Secretary, letter, [ca. January 20, 1927,] NAZ S235/430.

28. SR, Report of the Native Labour Committee, 1928, NAZ S480/36–38.

29. W. Leggate, Colonial Secretary, to the Premier, letter, April 20, 1927, NAZ S235/431.

30. Van Onselen, *Chibaro*, 69.

31. J. K. Rennie, "White Farmers, Black Tenants and Landlord Legislation: Southern Rhodesia 1890–1930," *Journal of Southern African Studies* 5, no. 1 (1978): 86–98; Smith interview.

32. G. Arrighi, "Labour Supplies in Historical Perspective," 208–209; Palmer, *Land and Racial Domination in Rhodesia*, 286.

33. H. P. Forshaw to E. C. Howman, Native Commissioner, Lomagundi, letter, September 8, 1925, NAZ S307/1925.

34. Sinoia Magistrate's Court, case 29/34, NAZ S2181; C. J. Wilke to Native Commissioner, Mazoe, letter, April 30, 1926, NAZ S622/1926; Native Commissioner, Sinoia, to C. H. Stanger, Banket, letter, December 31, 1930, NAZ S307/1930.

35. SR, Report of the Compound Inspector, Salisbury, November 1940, NAZ S1610; James, evidence given before the Natural Resources Board.

36. The term "boss boys" is both dated and pejoritive in nature, but its use is consistent with other historical terms used throughout the text.

37. Palmer and Howell interview, February 25, 1985; Purchase interview; Quinton interview; Lyman Makina, Muvura and Murambwa, Grove Farm, Arcturus, interview by the author, February 23, 1985; case 243/26, Concession Magistrate's Court, NAZ D3/15/10; Bindura Magistrate's Court, case 110/22, NAZ D3/10/3; J. H. Farmer, to the Magistrate, Bindura, letter, May 24, 1923, NAZ NSB 1/1/1.

38. *Rhodesia Herald*, January 9, 1925; Sinoia Magistrate's Court, case 8/26, NAZ D3/2/24; Bindura Magistrate's Court, case 263/26, NAZ D3/10/5.

39. Cartwright and Cartwright papers; Palmer and Howell interview, February 25, 1985; Purchase interview.

40. Eddison Mkondwa, Munemo Farm, interview by the author, Marondera, August 22, 1996.

41. Choto interview.

42. Van Onselen, *Chibaro*, 99; Colbourne interview; Quinton interview; Scott and Wise interview.

43. Boggie, *A Husband and a Farm in Rhodesia*, 104–105; SR, Report of the Native Labour Committee, 1928, NAZ S480/36–38; Muvura interview; Sinoia Magistrate's Court, case 157/23, NAZ D3/2/20; Concession Magistrate's Court, case 181/24, NAZ D3/15/7.

44. Colbourne interview; Quinton interview; Burden Report; SR, Report of the Compound Inspector, Salisbury, April 5th to 23rd 1940, NAZ S1610.

45. Palmer and Howell interview 25 February 1985.

46. Keevil interview; Purchase interview; Smith interview.

47. Concession Magistrate's Court, case 6/16, NAZ D3/15/3; ibid., case 22/20, NAZ D3/15/5; Attorney-General to the Senior Judge, letter, July 15, 1920, NAZ D3/2/17; Bindura Magistrate's Court, case 44/19, NAZ D3/10/2; Concession Magistrate's Court, case 36/25, NAZ D3/15/8.

48. Sinoia Magistrate's Court, case 213/20, NAZ D3/2/17; Concession Magistrate's Court, case 422/44, NAZ S1569; ibid., case 396/24, NAZ D3/15/7; ibid., case 632/38, NAZ S624.

49. Concession Criminal Court, case 532/44, NAZ S1569.

50. *Rhodesia Herald*, February 2, 1945.

51. For an example of conflicts over gambling, see Sinoia Magistrate's Court, case 360/37, NAZ S1079. For examples of conflicts over debt, see Sinoia Magistrate's Court, case 226/20, NAZ D3/2/17; and ibid., case 357/29, Concession Magistrate's Court, NAZ S583. For examples of conflicts over women, see Sinoia Magistrate's Court, case 210/18, NAZ D3/2/15; ibid., case 211/18; Bindura Magistrate's Court, case 258/26, NAZ D3/10/5; Darwendale Magistrate's Court, case 269/38, NAZ S1574.

52. Concession Magistrate's Court, case 141/21, NAZ D3/15/6.

53. Bindura Magistrate's Court, case 88/23, NAZ D3/10/3; ibid., case 546/34, NAZ D3/10/17; Concession Magistrate's Court, case 20/23, NAZ D3/15/7; Darwendale Magistrate's Court, case 113/38, NAZ S1574.

54. Concession Magistrate's Court, case 98/15, NAZ D3/15/3; ibid., case 194/21, NAZ D3/15/6; Bindura Magistrate's Court, case 265/26, NAZ D3/10/5; Sinoia Magistrate's Court, case 215/35, NAZ S581; Jana Makumbira, Munemo farm, interview by the author, Marondera, August 22, 1996.

55. Carol Summers, *From Civilization to Segregation—Social Ideals and Social Control in Southern Rhodesia, 1890–1934* (Athens, Ohio, 1994), 63; Ganda Chivandire, Shopo, Chiweshe, interview by Leslie Bessant and Elvis Muringai, December 19, 1984; John Brown, Chegutu, interview by author, March 30, 1985; SR, Native Commissioner, Sipolilo, annual report, 1932, NAZ S235/510.

56. Concession Magistrate's Court, case 373/19, NAZ D3/15/5; ibid., case 122/25, NAZ D3/15/8; ibid., case 165/16, NAZ D3/153; J. R. Trevor, Secretary of the Shamva Farmers' Association to the Secretary of the Concession Farmers Association, letter, January 7, 1926, NAZ S622/1926; Secretary of the Department of Administra-

tion, memorandum, February 8, 1916, NAZ A3/2/8 v. 2; SR, Native Commissioner, Mazoe, monthly report, October 1919, NAZ N9/4/37.

57. Makina and Muvura interviews; transcript of a speech delivered by Major Wane, Mazoe native commissioner, to the 1930 Native Commissioners' Conference, NAZ S235/488.

58. Chakanyuka Chindawi, Chiweshe Communal Land, interview by Leslie Bessant and Elvis Muringai, December 12, 1984; Kaviya, Gweshe, and Chiweshe, interviews; Philemon Gatsi, Gato, Chiweshe, interview by Leslie Bessant and Elvis Muringai, December 7, 1984; Chari Chiwocha, Mukodzongi, Chiweshe, interview by Leslie Bessant and Elvis Muringai, December 17, 1984.

59. SR, Native Commissioner, Mazoe, monthly report, July 1920, NAZ N9/4/39; Native Commissioner, Sinoia to the Chief Native Commissioner, letter, January 29, 1929, NAZ S307/1929.

Chapter 7—Quick and Nimble Fingers

1. Quinton interview.
2. Gordon interview.
3. Elizabeth Schmidt, *Peasants, Traders, and Wives: Shona Women in the History of Zimbabwe, 1870–1939* (Portsmouth, N.H. 1992), 99–101.
4. Palmer and Howell interview, February 25, 1985.
5. Summers, *From Civilization to Segregation*, 63.
6. Van Onselen, *Chibaro*; Phimister, *Wangi Kolia*; Per Zachrisson, *An African Area in Change, Belingwe 1894–1946* (Gothenburg, 1978).
7. Deborah Fahy Bryceson, "The Proletariznization of Women in Tanzania," *Review of African Political Economy* 17 (1980): 4–27; George Chauncey Jr., "The Locus of Reproduction: Women's Labour in the Zambian Copperbelt, 1927–1953," *Journal of Southern African Studies* 7, no. 2 (1981): 135–64; Jane L. Parpart, *Labor and Capital on the African Copperbelt* (Philadelphia, 1983); Janet M. Bujra, "'Urging Women To Redouble Their Efforts . . .': Class, Gender, and Capitalist Transformation in Africa," in Claire Robertson and Iris Berger, eds., *Women and Class in Africa* (New York, 1986), 117–40.
8. Phimister, *An Economic and Social History of Zimbabwe 1890–1948*, 203. See also, G. Arrighi, *Political Economy of Rhodesia* (The Hague, 1967); Palmer, *Land and Racial Domination in Rhodesia*.

9. Schmidt, *Peasants, Traders, and Wives,* 119; Chief Native Commissioner to the Native Commissioner, Sinoia, letter, August, 18, 1938, NAZ S307/1938; Secretary to the Treasury, to the Auditor General, letter, January 23, 1941, NAZ S1539/A95/1.

10. SR, *Report of the Director of Census, 1926* (Salisbury, 1927), 47; *Statistical Yearbook of Southern Rhodesia* (Salisbury, 1938), 38–39; *Statistical Yearbook of Southern Rhodesia* (Salisbury, 1947), 48.

11. Bryceson, "Proletarianization of Women in Tanzania," 16–17; Colbourne interview; Quinton interviews, October 2, 1894, December 17, 1984; Thurburn interview; Namazo Nwandela, Emidres Monanji, and Erina Liwakwa, Gabaza Farm, Beatrice, interviews by the author, September 5, 1996.

12. Abraham report; Eddison Mkondwa, Munemo Farm, Marondera, interview by the author, August 22, 1996; Bonifasio Kandiero and Fillimon Visani, Gabaza Farm, Beatrice, interviews by the author, September 5, 1996; Monanji interview.

13. Ibid.; Visani interview.

14. A. W. Laurie to the Native Commissioner, Concession, letter, June 21, 1938, NAZ S1059/1938.

15. Chibaiso Mwandenga and Senesai Chidemo, Choto homestead, Hwedza, interviews by the author, August 31, 1996; Mwandela, Monanji, and Liwakwa interviews.

16. Schmidt, *Peasants, Traders, and Wives,* 7, 92–94, 98–99, 117–19.

17. Mwandenga interview; Joan May, *Zimbabwean Women in Colonial and Customary Law* (Gweru 1983); Diana Jeater, *Marriage, Perversion, and Power: The Construction of Moral Discourse in Southern Rhodesia 1894–1930* (Oxford 1993), 179.

18. Sinoia Magistrate's Court, case 210/18, NAZ D3/2/15; ibid., case 211/18; ibid., cases 164/20, NAZ D3/2/17.

19. SR, Native Commissioner, Lomagundi, annual report, 1925, NAZ S235/503.

20. Concession Magistrate's Court, case 417/44, NAZ S1569; Bindura Magistrate's Court, case 152/14, NAZ D3/10/1; Mhindurwa interview; "The Employment of Native Female Domestic Labour in European Households in Southern Rhodesia, 1940," report, Salisbury, 1941.

21. Mwandenga and Chidemo interviews; Saidi interview; Makonyonga interview; Quinton interview; Palmer and Howell interview, December 12, 1984; Colbourne interview.

22. Chidemo interview; Liwakwa interview; Choto interview; *Report of Public Health*, 1928, pp. 13–14, NAZ SRG 3.

23. Mwandenga and Chidemo interviews; Nwandela, Monanji, and Liwakwa interview; Kandiero interview; Makonyonga interview.

24. Schmidt, *Peasants, Traders, and Wives*, 25–26; Purchase interview; Mwandenga and Chidemo interviews; Kandiero interview.

25. Chidemo interview.

26. Concession Magistrate's Court, case 645/29, NAZ S583; Sinoia Magistrate's Court, case 536/34, NAZ 2181.

27. Southern Rhodesia. *Report on Public Health*, 1927, 20–21, NAZ SRG 3; E. T. Palmer, Native Commissioner, Sinoia, to the Chief Native Commissioner, letter, July 25, 1935, NAZ S1542/D5; Lawrence Vambe, *An Ill-Fated People* (London, 1972), 200–201.

28. Palmer and Howell interview, February 25 1985.

29. Vambe, *An Ill-Fated People*, 185.

30. Luise White, *The Comforts of Home: Prostitution in Colonial Nairobi* (Chicago, 1990), 11.

31. Chidemo interview; Mwandela, Monanji, and Liwakwa, interview.

32. Kandiero and Visani, interview; Monanji interview; Mwandenga and Chidemo interview.

33. Bindura Magistrate's Court, case 135/21, NAZ D3/10/2; Concession Magistrate's Court, case 196/25, NAZ D3/15/8; ibid., case 532/44, NAZ S1569; Sinoia Magistrate's Court, case 189/35, NAZ S581; ibid., case 1058/37 NAZ S1081.

34. J. W. Posselt, Transcript of a speech delivered to the 1935 Native Commissioners' Conference, NAZ S235/488; SR, Report of the Native Labour Committee, 1928, NAZ S480/36–38.

35. Acting Native Commissioner, Urungwe, to the Native Commissioner, Lomagundi, letter, March 9, 1934, NAZ S307/1934.

36. SR, Report of the Native Labour Committee, 1928, NAZ S480/36–38; Quinton interview; Mary Blackwood Lewis, "Letters about Mashonaland, 1897–1901," *Rhodesiana* 5 (1960): 14–53.

37. *Debates of the Legislative Assembly*, vol. 5, 1926, p262; Acting Chief Native Commissioner to the Secretary of the Law Department, letter, September 22, 1926, NAZ S138/255; Chief Native Commissioner to the Secretary to the Premier, letter, June 8, 1928, NAZ S138/255.

38. SR, Native Commissioner, Sipolilo, annual report, 1931, NAZ

S235/509; ibid., 1932, NAZ S235/510; Colbourne interview; Purchase interview; Palmer and Howell interview, December 12, 1984.

Chapter 8—Toward a Moral Economy

1. T. Dunbar Moodie, "The Moral Economy of the Black Miners' Strike of 1946," *Journal of Southern African Studies* 13, no. 1 (1986): 1–35.

2. Gutman, *Work, Culture and Society in Industrializing America*, 18.

3. E. P. Thompson, "The Moral Economy of the English Crowd in the Eighteenth Century," *Past and Present* 50 (1971): 76–136; Raymond Williams, *Culture and Society, 1780–1950* (New York, 1983).

4. For government officials, see William Rayner, *The Tribe and Its Successors* (London, 1962), 179–81; Montague Yudelman, *Africans on the Land* (Cambridge, Mass., 1964), 101–102; Martin Loney, *Rhodesia: White Racism and Imperial Response* (Baltimore, 1975), 40–43. For mine owners, see Per Zachrisson, *An African Area in Change*, 74–75; Van Onselen, *Chibaro*.

5. *Debates of the Legislative Assembly*, 1925, v. 3.

6. Hoare, "Rhodesian Jottings," 467–76.

7. SR, Director of Agriculture, annual report, 1915, p. 3, NAZ SRG3; Clements and Harben, *Leaf Of Gold*, 148–49; Summers, *From Civilization to Segregation*, 65.

8. Boggie, *A Husband and a Farm in Rhodesia*, 324; William Brown, *On The South African Frontier* (New York, 1899), 317; SR, Native Commissioner, Mazoe, annual report, 1911, NAZ N9/1/14; Thurburn interview; Scott and Wise interview; E. Morton, Secretary of the Lomagundi West Farmers' Association, to the Native Commissioner, Sinoia, letter, December 15, 1935, NAZ S307/1935–36; and, lecture by Dr. Hewetson, reported in the *Rhodesia Herald*, pt. 1, September 24 1926, pt. 2, October 1, 1926.

9. SR, Report of the Native Affairs Committee of Enquiry, 1910/11 (Salisbury, 1911), p. 52, NAZ Miscellaneous Reports, 1909–16; *Rhodesia Herald*, August 15, 1924; ibid., February 19, 1926.

10. *Rhodesia Herald*, February 2, 1923.

11. Statement made by Capt. Downes, *Debates of the Legislative Assembly*, 1932, v. 12, p. 725.

12. Burden report.

13. *Rhodesia Herald*, February 2, 1917.

14. SR, Assistant Native Commissioner, Bindura, annual report, 1935, NAZ S235/356; Palmer and Howell, December 12, 1984.

15. Captain C. A. R. Shum to the Native Commissioner, Sinoia, letter, February 29, 1936, NAZ S307/1935–6; E. Scott to the Native Commissioner, Concession, letter, 10 December 1940, NAZ S1059/1940.

16. Smith interview.

17. Keletso E. Atkins, *The Moon Is Dead! Give Us Our Money! The Cultural Origins of An African Work Ethic, Natal, South Africa, 1843–1900.* (Portsmouth, N.H.: 1993), 80–95. See also E. P. Thompson, "Time, Work-Discipline, and Industrial Capitalism," *Past and Present* 38 (1967): 56–97.

18. James C. Scott, *The Moral Economy of the Peasant, Rebellion and Subsistence in Southeast Asia* (New Haven, 1976), 29.

19. John Higginson, *A Working Class in the Making—Belgian Labor Policy, Private Enterprise and the African Mineworker, 1907–1951* (Madison, 1989), 61.

20. Leslie Bessant and Elvis Muringai, "Peasants, Businessmen, and Moral Economy in the Chiweshe reserve, Colonial Zimbabwe, 1930–1968," *Journal of Southern African Studies*, 19, 4 (1993): 551–592.

21. S. S. Murray, "Report on Tobacco, with Particular Reference to the Prospects of Increased Production in Central and East Africa," London, 1949; W. H. J. Rangeley, "A Brief History of the Tobacco Industry in Nyasaland," *Nyasaland Journal* 10, no. 1 (1957): 62–83, and no. 2 (1957): 32–51; Martin Chanock, "The Political Economy of Independent Agriculture in Colonial Malawi: The Great War to the Great Depression," *Journal of Social Science* 1, no. 1 (1972): 1–17; F. A. Stinson, *Tobacco Farming in Rhodesia and Nyasaland, 1889–1956* (Salisbury, 1957), 2; John McCracken, "Planters, Peasants and the Colonial State: the Impact of the Native Tobacco Board in the Central Province of Malawi," *Journal of Southern African Studies* 9, no. 2 (1983): 172–92.

22. SR, [Department of] Native Affairs, Report on Nyasaland Farm Labour, 1910, NAZ A3/18/30/15 v. 3; David Sinclair, Solario Farm, Banket, interview by the author, May 13, 1985.

23. Gordon interview.

24. Abraham report.

25. Ackson Kanduza, "The Tobacco Industry in Northern Rhodesia, 1912–1938," *International Journal of African Historical Studies* 16, no. 2 (1983): 201–30.

26. Barry A. Kosmin, "The Inyoko Tobacco Industry of the Shangwe People: A case Study of the Displacement of a Pre-Colonial Economy in Southern Rhodesia, 1898–1938," *African Social Research* 17 (1974): 554–77.

27. Information on this case was taken from: Honey and Blanckenberg, Solicitors, to the District Commissioner, Blantyre, letter, August 28, 1937, NAZ S1542/L1 1937; Chief Native Commissioner, to the Native Commissioner, Sinoia, letter, September 15, 1937, ibid.; and Office of the Attorney General, Opinion #231, 1937, ibid.

28. Smith interview.

29. Colbourne interview.

30. Purchase interview.

31. Palmer and Howell interview, February 25, 1985; Colbourne interview.

32. Van Onselen, *Chibaro*, 228.

33. Concession Magistrate's Court, case 538/29, NAZ S583.

34. Gatsi, statement to the Assistant Native Commissioner, Sipolilo, July 10, 1936, NAZ S307/1935–36.

35. Sipolilo Magistrate's Court, cases 210/30 and 211/30, NAZ S1979; Darwendale Magistrate's Court, case 341/33, NAZ S660/1933; Sinoia Magistrate's Court, case 302/20, NAZ D3/2/17. See also, Michael Gelfand, *Diet and Tradition in an African Culture* (Edinburgh 1971), 160–61; Audrey I. Richards, *Land, Labour and Diet in Northern Rhodesia* (London, 1969), 330–31.

36. J. R. Crawford, *Witchcraft and Sorcery in Rhodesia* (London, 1967); Michael Gelfand, *The African Witch* (Edinburgh, 1967); Lawrence Vambe, *From Rhodesia to Zimbabwe* (London, 1976); Gelfand, *Diet and Tradition*; Concession Magistrate's Court, case 36/25, NAZ D3/15/8; ibid., case 396/24, NAZ D3/15/7; Bindura Magistrate's Court, case 46/19, NAZ D3/10/2.

37. *Rhodesia Herald*, January 9, 1925.

38. Darwendale Magistrate's Court, case 159/36, NAZ S1574.

39. Michael Bourdillon, *The Shona Peoples* (Gweru, 1987), 151; discussion between the author, translator Oliver Masakura, and Dake Choto, Choto homestead, Hwedza, August 31, 1996; Kandiero interview.

40. Charles Van Onselen, "Worker Consciousness in Black Miners: Southern Rhodesia, 1900–1920," *Journal of African History* 14, no. 2 (1973): 254.

41. SR, Native Commissioner, Lomagundi, annual report, 1920, NAZ N9/1/22.

42. Khamiso, Saidi, and Murambwa interviews; Makonyonga interviews.

Conclusion

1. Phimister, *Economic and Social History of Zimbabwe*, 225; Trish Mbanga, *Tobacco: A Century of Gold* (Harare, 1991), 226.

2. Ibid., 226–27.

3. Ibid., chs. 7–10; Colbourne interview; Gordon interview; Eric Palmer and Michael Howell, Harare, interview by the author, February 25, 1985; Keevil interview; Ian Burton, interview by the author, Gabaza Farm, Beatrice, September 5, 1996.

4. D. G. Clarke, *Agricultural and Plantation Workers in Rhodesia* (Gwelo, 1977), 38.

5. Rene Loewenson, *Modern Plantation Agriculture: Corporate Wealth and Labour Squalor* (London, 1992), 76.

6. Clarke, *Agricultural and Plantation Workers*, 272.

7. Loewenson, *Modern Plantation Agriculture*, 72–74.

8. Ibid., 98–114.

9. Clarke, *Agricultural and Plantation Workers*, 125, 272.

10. Loewenson, *Modern Plantation Agriculture*, 68.

Bibliography

Published Sources

Official Documents

BRITISH SOUTH AFRICA COMPANY (PRE-1923)
Annual Directors' Report and Accounts, 1897, 1914–41.

Debates of the Legislative Council, 1899–1923.

Handbook of Tobacco Culture for Planters in Southern Rhodesia. Salisbury, 1913.

Information for Settlers (Cape Town, 1905).

A Land of Sunshine: Southern Rhodesia: Unique Openings for Farmers. London, 1911.

Minutes of Proceedings and Ordinances. Legislative Assembly, 1899–1923.

Reports, Department of Agriculture, 1900–1906.

Reports of the Director of the Census. Salisbury, 1911 and 1921.

Report of the Labour Board. Salisbury, 1901.

Report of the Native Affairs Committee of Enquiry, 1910–11.Salisbury, 1911.

Report of the Secretary for Agriculture, 1907–24.

GOVERNMENT OF SOUTHERN RHODESIA (POST-1924)
Annual Reports of the Chief Native Commissioner, 1907–45.

Annual Reports of the Controller, Stores and Transport Department, 1939–45.

Annual Reports of the Director of Native Development, 1929–34.

Annual Reports of the Land and Agricultural Bank of Southern Rhodesia, 1924–45.

Annual Reports of the Native Commissioner, Lomagundi District, 1895–15, 1917–33, 1935–36, 1938–39.

Annual Reports of the Native Commissioner, Mazoe District, 1895–1936, 1938–39.

Annual Reports on the Public Health, 1924–36.

Central African Statistical Office. Official Yearbooks, 1924, 1930, 1932, 1952.

Debates of the Legislative Assembly, 1924–45.

Department of Statistics. Statistical Yearbooks, 1938 and 1947.

Government Gazette. 1935.

Handbooks for the Use of Prospective Settlers on the Land, 1924, 1927, 1930, and 1935.

Report of the Committee of Enquiry into the Economic Position of the Agricultural Industry of Southern Rhodesia. Salisbury, 1934.

Report of the Committee of Enquiry To Investigate the Economic, Social, and Health Conditions of Africans Employed in Urban Areas. Salisbury, 1944.

Report of the Conference of Superintendents of Natives and Native Commissioners of the Colony of Southern Rhodesia. Salisbury, 1928.

Reports of the Director of the Census. Salisbury, 1926, 1936, 1941, and 1947.

Report of the Economic Development Committee, 1939. Salisbury, 1939.

Report of the Farmers' Debt Adjustment Board, 1941. mimeo. Salisbury, 1941.

Report of the Secretary for Labour, Social Welfare and Housing,1958.

Reports of the Secretary, Department of Agriculture and Lands, 1925–45.

Reports of the Secretary, Department of Justice, 1933–45.

Reports of the Tobacco Research Board, 1936–50.

Report on the Railway System of Southern Rhodesia, by F. D. Hammond. Salisbury, 1925.

Reports on Unemployment and the Relief of Destitution in Southern Rhodesia, by G. E. Wells. Salisbury, 1934 and 1935.

Votes and Proceedings of the Legislative Assembly and Acts, 1926–46

GOVERNMENT OF THE COLONY OF NYASALAND

Burden, G. N. Nyasaland Native Labour in Southern Rhodesia. Zomba, 1938.

GOVERNMENT OF THE FEDERATION OF THE RHODESIAS AND NYASALAND

The Tobacco Industry of Rhodesia and Nyasaland. Salisbury, 1961.

GREAT BRITAIN

Department of Overseas Trade. *Trade Conditions in Southern Rhodesia, 1932*, by J. W. Brigden. London, 1932.

Department of Overseas Trade. *Trade and Economic Conditions in Southern Rhodesia, Northern Rhodesia and Nyasaland, 1933*, by J. W. Brigden. London, 1934.

Department of Overseas Trade. *Economic Conditions in Southern Rhodesia, Northern Rhodesia and Nyasaland, 1935*, by J. W. Brigden. London, 1936.

Department of Overseas Trade. *Economic and Commercial Conditions in Southern Rhodesia, Northern Rhodesia and Nyasaland, 1939*, by A. W. H. Hall. London, 1939.

Colonial Office. *Report on Tobacco with Particular Reference to the Prospects of Increased Production in Central and East Africa*, by S. S. Murray. London, 1949.

Secretary of State for Dominion Affairs. *Southern Rhodesia—Papers Relative to the Southern Rhodesia Native Juveniles Employment Act, 1926, and the Southern Rhodesia Native Affairs Act, 1927*. London, 1928.

Books and Pamphlets

Anderson, R., with R. R. Staples. *An Agricultural Survey of Southern Rhodesia, Part II—The Agro-Economic Survey*. Salisbury: Government Printer, 1959.

Arrighi, G. *The Political Economy of Rhodesia.* The Hague: Manton, 1967.

Atkins, Keletso E. *The Moon Is Dead! Give Us Our Money! The Cultural Origins of an African Work Ethic, Natal, South Africa, 1843–1900.* Portsmouth, N.H.: Heinemann, 1993.

Black, Colin. *The Legend of Lomagundi.* Salisbury: North-West Development Association, 1976.

Boggie, Jeannie M. *A Husband and a Farm in Rhodesia.* Gwelo: Catholic Mission Press, 1959.

Bourdillon, Michael. *The Shona Peoples*, rev. ed. Gweru: Mambo Press, 1987.

Brown, William Harvey. *On the South African Frontier.* New York: Charles Scribner's Sons, 1899.

Chanock, Martin. *Unconsummated Union; Britain, Rhodesia and South Africa 1900–1945.* Manchester: Manchester University Press, 1977.

Clarke, Duncan G. *Contract Workers and Underdevelopment in Rhodesia.* Salisbury: Mambo Press, 1974.

———. *Agricultural and Plantation Workers in Rhodesia.* Salisbury: Mambo Press, 1977.

Clements, Frank and Edward Harben. *Leaf of Gold: The Story of Rhodesian Tobacco.* London: Methuen and Company, 1962.

Cooper, Frederick. *On the African Waterfront.* New Haven: Yale University Press, 1987.

Crawford, J. R. *Witchcraft and Sorcery in Rhodesia.* London: Oxford University Press, 1967.

Cripps, Arthur S. *An Africa for African.* London: Longmans, Green and Company, Ltd., 1927.

Davies, W. Twiston. *50 Years of Progress; An Account of the African Organisation of the Imperial Tobacco Company, 1907–1957.* Bristol: Mardon, Son and Hall, 1958.

De Kock, E. Plewman. *Various Outspans: Incidents in the Life of an Early Settler in Southern Rhodesia.* Bloemfontain: A. C. White Printing and Publishing Company, 1949.

Dunlop, H. *The Development of European Agriculture in Rhodesia 1945–1965.* Salisbury: University of Rhodesia, 1971.

Evans, Morgan O., ed. *The Statute Law of Southern Rhodesia*. Salisbury: Argus Printing and Publishing Company, 1899.

Fielding, Ann Mary. *The Noxious Weed*. London: Heinemann, 1951.

Fripp, Constance E. and V. W. Hiller, eds. *Gold and Gospel in Mashonaland, 1888*. London: Chatto and Windus, 1949.

From Seed-bed to Smoker: Southern Rhodesian Tobacco, Its Growth and Manufacture. London: Office of the High Commissioner of Southern Rhodesia, 1928.

Galbraith, John S. *Crown and Charter—The Early Years of the British South Africa Company*. Los Angeles: University of California Press, 1974.

Gann, L. H. *A History of Southern Rhodesia*. London: Chatto and Windus, 1965.

————. *The Birth of a Plural Society*. Manchester: University of Manchester Press, 1958.

Gelfand, Michael. *Tropical Victory: An Account of the Influence of Medicine on the History of Southern Rhodesia, 1890–1923*.Cape Town: Juta and Company, Ltd. 1953.

————. *The African Witch*. Edinburgh: Livingstone, 1967.

————. *A Service To The Sick: A History of the Health Services for Africans in Southern Rhodesia (1890–1953)*. Salisbury: Mambo Press, 1976.

Gutkind, Peter, Robin Cohen, and Jean Copans, eds. *African Labor History*. Beverly Hill: Sage, 1978.

Gutman, Herbert G. *Work, Culture, and Society in Industrializing America*. New York: Vintage Press, 1977.

Harries, Patrick. *Work, Culture, and Identity: Migrant Laborers in Mozambique and South Africa, c. 1860–1910*. Portsmouth, N.H.: Heinemann, 1994.

Harris, John H. *The Chartered Millions, Rhodesia and the Challenge to the British Commonwealth*. London: Swarthmore Press Ltd., 1920.

Haviland, P. H. *Flue-Curing Tobacco Barns, Bulking and Grading Sheds*. Salisbury: Argus Printing and Publishing Company,1926.

Hemans, H. N. *The Log of a Native Commissioner*. London: H. F. and G. Witherby, 1935.

Higginson, John. *A Working Class in the Making—Belgian Colonial*

Labor Policy, Private Enterprise and the African Mineworker, 1907–1951. Madison: University of Wisconsin Press, 1989.

Hoare, Rawdon. *Rhodesian Mosaic.* London: John Murray, 1934.

Hodder-Williams, Richard. *White Farmers in Rhodesia, 1890–1965.* London: Macmillan Press, Ltd., 1983.

Hone, Percy F. *Southern Rhodesia.* London: Bell and Sons, 1909.

Jeater, Diana. *Marriage, Perversion, and Power: The Construction of Moral Discourse in Southern Rhodesia 1894–1930.* Oxford: Clarendon Press, 1993.

Johnson, R. W. M. *The Labour Economy of the Reserve.* Salisbury: University College of Rhodesia and Nyasaland, 1964.

Kanduza, Ackson M. *The Political Economy of Underdevelopment in Northern Rhodesia, 1918–1960.* Lanham: University Press of America, 1986.

Kay, George. *Rhodesia: a human geography.* London: University of London Press, 1970.

Knight-Bruce, G. W. H. *Memories of Mashonaland.* London: Edward Arnold, 1895.

Lessing, Doris. *The Grass is Singing.* London: M. Joseph, 1950.

———. *African Laughter.* New York: Harper Collins, 1992.

Leys, Colin. *European Politics in Southern Rhodesia.* Oxford: Clarendon Press, 1959.

Loney, Martin. *Rhodesia; White Racism and Imperial Response.* Baltimore: Penguin Books, 1975.

Loewenson, Rene. *Modern Plantation Agriculture: Corporate Wealth and Labour Squalor.* London: Zed Books, 1992.

Mack, Peter H. *The Golden Weed.* Southampton: Newman Neame, Millbrook Press, Ltd., 1965.

Marx, Karl. *Capital.* New York: Vintage Books, 1977.

Mason, Philip. *The Birth of a Dilemma.* London: Oxford University Press, 1958.

Mathers, E. P. *Zambesia: England's El Dorado in Africa.* London: King, Sell and Railton, Ltd., 1891.

Mbanga, Trish. *Tobacco: A Century of Gold.* Harare: ZIL Publications, Ltd., 1991.

McClymont, D. S. *Bonanza, 75 Years of Flue-Cured Tobacco Advice.* Bulawayo: Books of Zimbabwe, 1981.

Moore, Henrietta L. *Feminism and Anthropology*. Minneapolis: University of Minnesota Press, 1988.

Mosley, Paul. *The Settler Economies*. Cambridge: Cambridge University Press, 1983.

Murray, D. J. *The Governmental System in Southern Rhodesia*. Oxford: Clarendon Press, 1970.

Mutambirwa, James A. C. *The Rise of Settle Power in Southern Rhodesia (Zimbabwe), 1898–1923*. New Jersey: Association of University Presses, 1980.

Nobbs, E. A. *Handbook of Tobacco Culture*. Salisbury: Argus Printing and Publishing Company, Ltd., 1913.

Northrup, David. *Beyond The Bend in the River: African Labor in Eastern Zaire, 1865–1940*. Athens, Ohio: Center for International Studies, 1988.

Odlum, George M. *The Culture of Tobacco*. London: British South Africa Company, 1905.

Orde-Browne, G. St. J. *The African Labourer*. London: Oxford University Press, 1933.

Outposts: Stories of the Police of Rhodesia. Cape Town: Books of Africa, 1970.

Palley, Claire. *The Constitutional History and Law of Southern Rhodesia 1888–1965, with Special Reference to Imperial Control*. Oxford: Clarendon Press, 1966.

Palmer, Robin H. *Land and Racial Domination in Rhodesia*. Los Angeles: University of California Press, 1977.

Parpart, Jane L. *Labor and Capital on the African Copperbelt*. Philadelphia: Temple University Press, 1983.

Penvenne, Jeanne Marie. *African Workers and Colonial Racism: Mozambican Strategies and Struggles in Lourenco Marques, 1877–1962*. Portsmouth, N.H.: Heinemann, 1995.

Perrings, Charles. *Black Mineworkers in Central Africa*. London: Heinemann, 1979.

Phimister, Ian. *An Economic and Social History of Zimbabwe, 1890–1948: Capital Accumulation and Class Struggle*. London: Longman, 1988.

———. *Wangi Kolia: Coal, Capital and Labour in Colonial Zimbabwe 1984–1954*. Johannesburg: Witswatersrand University Press, 1994.

Ranger, Terence O. *African Voice in Southern Rhodesia, 1898–1930.* London: Heinemann, 1970.

————. *The Invention of Tribalism in Zimbabwe.* Gweru: Mambo Press, 1985.

Ransford, Oliver. *"Bid the Sickness Cease": Disease in the History of Black Africa.* London: John Murray, 1983.

Rayner, William. *The Tribe and Its Successors: An Account of African Traditional Life and European Settlement in Southern Rhodesia.* London: Faber and Faber, 1962.

Richards, Audrey I. *Land, Labour and Diet in Northern Rhodesia.* Oxford: Oxford University Press, 1961.

Richards, Hylda M. *Next Year Will Be Better.* Cape Town: H. B. Timmins, 1952.

Rubert, Steven C. and R. Kent Rasmussen. *Historical Dictionary of Zimbabwe,* 3d ed. Lantham, Md.: Scarecrow Press, forthcoming.

Schmidt, Elizabeth. *Peasants, Traders, and Wives: Shona Women in the History of Zimbabwe, 1870–1939.* Portsmouth, N.H.: Heinemann, 1992.

Schoffeleers, J. Matthew. *River of Blood: The Genesis of a Martyr Cult in Southern Malawi, c. A.D. 1600.* Madison: University of Wisconsin Press, 1992.

Scott, James C. *The Moral Economy of the Peasant, Rebellion and Subsistence in Southeast Asia.* New Haven: Yale University Press, 1976.

Simson, Howard. *Zimbabwe, A Country Study.* Uppsala: Scandinavian Institute of African Studies, 1979.

Speight, Arthur. *The Statute Law of Southern Rhodesia from 1 January, 1911 to 31 March, 1922.* Salisbury: Government Printer, 1923.

Stichter, Sharon. *Migrant Labourers.* Cambridge: Cambridge University Press, 1985.

Stinson, F. A. *Tobacco Farming in Rhodesia and Nyasaland, 1889–1956.* Salisbury: Tobacco Research Board of Rhodesia, 1956.

Thompson, E. P. *The Making of the English Working Class.* New York: Penguin Books, 1968.

Tracey, L. T. *Approach to Farming in Southern Rhodesia.* Salisbury: Ministry of Agriculture, 1945.

Vambe, Lawrence. *From Rhodesia to Zimbabwe.* London: Heinemann, 1976.

Van Onselen, Charles. *Chibaro: African Mine Labour in Southern Rhodesia, 1900–1933.* London: Pluto Press, 1976.

———. *Studies in the Social and Economic History of the Witwatersrand 1886–1914,* 2 vols. Harlow: Longman, 1982.

Vincent, V., and R. G. Thomas, with R. R. Staples. *An Agricultural Survey of Southern Rhodesia,* Part 1. Salisbury: Government Printers, 1959.

Weinmann, H. *Agricultural Research and Development in Southern Rhodesia, 1890–1923.* Salisbury: University of Rhodesia,1972.

———. *Agricultural Research and Development in Southern Rhodesia, 1924–1950.* Salisbury: University of Rhodesia, 1975.

Williams, Raymond. *Culture and Society: 1780–1950.* New York: Columbia University Press, 1983.

Yudelman, Montague. *Africans on the Land.* Cambridge, Mass.: Harvard University Press, 1964.

Zachrisson, Per. *An African Area in Change; Belingwe, 1894–1946.* Gothenburg: University of Gothenburg, 1978.

Articles

"Agricultural Native Labour, Ltd.: The Outcome of the First Year of Operation." *Vuka* 1, no. 10 (June 1944): 61–63.

P. E. T. "Native Labour." *Native Affairs Department Annual* 4 (1926): 122–23.

Arrighi, G. "Labour Supplies in Historical Perspective: A Study of the Proletarianization of the African Peasantry in Rhodesia." *Journal of Development Studies* 4 (1970): 197–234.

Berg, Elliott J. "Backward-Sloping Labor Supply Functions in Dual Economies—The Africa Case." *Quarterly Journal of Economics* 75 (1961): 468–92.

Bessant, Leslie and Elvis Muringai. "Peasants, Businessmen, and Moral Economy in the Chiweshe Reserve, Colonial Zimbabwe, 1930–1968." *Journal of Southern African Studies* 19, no. 4 (1993): 551–92.

Bozzoli, Belinda. "Marxism, Feminism and South African Studies." *Journal of Southern African Studies* 9, no. 2 (April 1983): 139–71.

Brown, D. D. "The Development of the Tobacco Industry in Southern Rhodesia." *Rhodesia Agricultural Journal* 26(1929): 768–92.

————. "Seasonal Notes on Tobacco Culture in Southern Rhodesia." *Rhodesia Agricultural Journal* 26 (1929): 1274–80.

Bryceson, Deborah Fahy. "The Proletarianization of Women in Tanzania." *Review of African Political Economy* 17 (April 1980): 4–27.

Bujra, Janet M. "'Urging Women To Redouble Their Efforts . . .': Class, Gender, and Capitalist Transformation in Africa." In *Women and Class in Africa*, ed. Claire Robertson and Iris Berger. New York: Africana Publishing, 1986.

Burke, E. E. "Mazoe and the Mashona Rebellion, 1896–97." *Rhodesiana* 25 (1971): 1–34.

Chanock, Martin. "The Political Economy of Independent Agriculture in Colonial Malawi: The Great War to the Great Depression." *Journal of Social Science* 1, no. 1 (1972): 1–17.

Chauncey, George Jr. "The Locus of Reproduction: Women's Labour in the Zambian Copperbelt, 1927–1953." *Journal of Southern African Studies* 7, no. 2 (April 1981): 135–64.

Chavunduka, G. L. "Farm Labour in Rhodesia." *Rhodesia Journal of Economics* 6 (1972): 18–25.

Christiansen, Robert, and Jonathan Kydd. "The Return of Malawian Labour from South Africa and Zimbabwe." *Journal of Modern African Studies* 21, no. 2 (1983): 311–26.

Cohen, Robin. "From Peasants to Workers in Africa." In *The Political Economy of Contemporary Africa*, ed. Peter Gutkind and I. Wallerstein. Beverly Hills: Sage, 1976.

————. "Resistance and Hidden Forms of Consciousness Amongst African Workers." *Review of African Political Economy* 19 (September–December 1980): 8–22.

Davies, Robert, and David Lewis. "Industrial Relations Legislation: One of Capital's Defences." *Review of African Political Economy* 7 (1976): 56–68.

Duncan, J. R. "Native Food and Culinary Methods." *Native Affairs Department Annual* 11(1933): 101–106.

Du Toit, F. P. "The Accommodation of Permanent Farm Labourers." *Rhodesia Agricultural Journal*, Technical Bulletin 17 (1977): 1–61.

Edwards, J. A. "The Lomagundi District—An Historical Sketch." *Rhodesiana* 7 (1962): 1–21.

Emmanuel, A. "White-Settler Colonialism and the Myth of Investment Capitalism." *New Left Review* 73 (1972): 35–57.

Garbett, G. K. "Circulatory migration in Rhodesia: Towards a decision model." In *Town and Country in Central and Eastern Africa*, ed. David Parkin. Oxford: International African Institute, 1975.

Gelfand, Michael. "Migration of African Labourers in Rhodesia and Nyasaland [1890–1914]." *Central African Journal of Medicine* 7, 8 (1961): 293–300.

Gluckman, Max. "How the Bemba Make Their Living: An Appreciation of Richards' Land, Labour and Diet in Northern Rhodesia." *Rhodes-Livingstone Journal* (1945): 55–75.

Good, Kenneth. "Settler Colonialism: Economic Development and Class Formation." *Journal of Modern African Studies* 14, no. 4 (1976): 597–620.

Harris, Marvin. "Labour Emigration Among the Mozambique Thonga: Cultural and Political Factors." *Africa* 29, no. 1 (January 1959): 50–66.

Haviland, W. E. "The Tobacco Industry of Southern Rhodesia: An Economic Analysis. Part 1—Economic History and its Lessons." *Rhodesia Agricultural Journal* 49, no. 6 (November-December 1952): 365–81.

———. "Tobacco Farm Organization, Cost and Land-Use in Southern Rhodesia." *South African Journal of Economics* 21(1953): 367–80.

———. "The Use and Efficiency of African Labour in Tobacco Farming in Southern Rhodesia." *Canadian Journal of Economics and Political Science* 20, no. 1 (February 1954): 100–106.

Hoare, Rawdon. "Rhodesian Jottings." *Cornhill Magazine* 150 (October 1934): 467–76.

Hooker, James R. "Shortages Among the Surpluses: European Views of African Unemployment in British Central African Between the Wars." *Canadian Journal of African Studies* 3, no. 2 (1969): 421–29.

Howman, B. "The Native Labourer and His Food." *Native Affairs Department Annual* 19 (1942): 3–24.

Jeeves, Alan. "The Control of Migratory Labour on the South African Gold Mines in the Era of Kruger and Milner." *Journal of Southern African Studies* 2, no. 1 (1975): 3–29.

Jobling, C. S. "Notes on Tobacco Growing and Curing Under Local Conditions." *Rhodesia Agricultural Journal* 9 (1911/12): 675–80.

Johnson, David. "Settler Farmers and Coerced African Labour in Southern Rhodesia, 1936–46." *Journal of African History* 33 (1992): 111–28.

Kosmin, Barry A. "The Inyoka Tobacco Industry of the Shangwe People: A Case Study of the Displacement of a Pre-Colonial Economy in Southern Rhodesia, 1898–1938." *African Social Research* 17 (1974): 554–77.

Krishnamurthy, B. S. "Economic Policy: Land and Labour in Nyasaland, 1890–1914." In *Early History of Malawi*, ed. B. Pachai. Evanston, Ill.: Northwestern University Press, 1972.

Leitner, Kersten. "The Situation of Agricultural Workers in Kenya." *Review of African Political Economy* 6 (May-August 1976): 34–50.

Lewis, Mary Blackwood. "Letters about Mashonaland, 1897–1901." *Rhodesiana* 5 (1960): 14–53.

Mackenzie, J. M. "African Labour in the Chartered Company Period." *Rhodesian History* 1 (1970): 43–58.

Makambe, E. P. "The Nyasaland African Labour 'Ulendos' to Southern Rhodesia and the Problem of the African 'Highwaymen,' 1903–1923: A Study in the Limitations of Early Independent Labour Migration." *African Affairs* 79 (October 1980): 548–66.

Malaba, Luke. "Supply, Control and Organization of African Labour in Rhodesia." *Review of African Political Economy* 18 (May/August 1980): 7–28.

McCracken, John. "Planters, Peasants and the Colonial State: The Impact of the Native Tobacco Board in the Central Province of Malawi." *Journal of Southern African Studies* 9, no. 2 (1983): 172–92.

McNamara, J. K. "The Development of a Labour Infrastructure: Migration Routes to the Witswatersrand Gold Mines and Compound Accommodation—1889 to 1912." *South African Labour Bulletin* 4, no. 3 (May 1978): 7–28.

Mintz, Sidney W. "The Rural Proletariat and the Problem of the Rural Proletarian Consciousness." In *Peasants and Proletarians*, ed. Peter Gutkind, Robin Cohen, and P. Brazier. New York: Monthly Review Press, 1979.

Mitchell, J. Clyde. "The Causes of Labour Migration." *Inter-Africa Labour Bulletin* 6, no. 1 (1959): 12–47.

———. "Wage Labour and African Population Movements in Central Africa." In *Essays on African Population,* edited by K. M. Barbour and R. M. Prothero. New York: Praeger, 1961.

Moodie, T. Dunbar. "Migrancy and Male Sexuality on the South African Gold Mines." *Journal of Southern African Studies* 14, no. 2 (January 1988): 228–56.

———. "The Moral Economy of the Black Miners' Strike of 1946." *Journal of Southern African Studies* 13, no. 1 (October 1986): 1–35.

Moroney, Sean. "The Development of the Compound as a Mechanism of Worker Control 1900–1912." *South African Labour Bulletin* 4, no. 3 (May 1978): 29–49.

Morris, R. M. "Bindura in the 1920s." *Rhodesiana* (March 1977).

Munger, Edwin S. "Rhodesian Pioneer—Tobacco Farm Microstudy." *American Universities Field Staff Report* (Central and Southern African series) 2, no. 15 (1953): 2–20.

Murapa, Rukudzo. "Geography, Race, Class and Power in Rhodesia, 1890 to the Present." *Journal of Southern African Affairs* 3, no. 2 (1978): 159–72.

Niddrie, David. "The Road to Work: A Survey of the Influence of Transport on Migrant Labour in Central Africa." *Rhodes-Livingstone Journal* 15 (1954): 331–43.

Nobbs, E. A. "Farms and Farming in Rhodesia: Mazoe." *Rhodesia Agricultural Journal* 8 (1910).

Olive, W. "The Rhodesia Land Bank." *Rhodesia Agricultural Journal* 9 (1911/12): 837–41.

Orde-Browne, G. St. J. "The African Labourer." *Africa* 3 (1930): 13–31.

Palmer, Ralph Drew. "Native Labour: Its Source and Its Worth." *Rhodesian Farmer Yearbook* (December 1953): 189–90.

Palmer, Robin. "Land Alienation and Agricultural Conflict in Colonial Zambia." In *Imperialism, Colonialism, and Hunger: East and Central Africa,* edited by Robert I. Rotberg. Lexington: Lexington Books, 1983.

———. "Working Conditions and Worker Responses on Nyasaland

Tea Estates, 1930–53." *Journal of African History* 27, no. 1 (1986): 105–26.

Perrings, Charles. "'Good Lawyers but Poor Workers': Recruited Angolan Labour in the Copper Mines of Katanga, 1917–1921."*Journal of African History* 18, no. 2 (1977): 237–59.

———. "Consciousness, Conflict and Proletarianization: An Assessment of the 1935 Mineworkers' Strike on the Northern Rhodesian Copperbelt." *Journal of Southern African Studies* 4, no. 1 (October 1977): 31–51.

Philpott, R. "The Mulobezi-Mongu Labour Route." *Rhodes-Livingstone Journal* 6 (1945): 50–54.

Phimister, Ian R. "Peasant Production and Underdevelopment in Southern Rhodesia, 1890–1914." *African Affairs* 73, no. 291 (1974): 217–28.

———. "A Note on Labour Relations in Southern Rhodesian Agriculture before 1939." *South African Labour Bulletin* 3, no. 5 (May 1977): 94–104.

Rangely, W. H. J. "A Brief History of the Tobacco Industry in Nyasaland." *Nyasaland Journal*, pt.1, 10, no. 1 (1957): 62–83; pt.2, 10, no. 2 (1957): 32–51; "Additional notes," 11, no. 2 (1958): 24–27.

Rennie, J. K. "White Farmers, Black Tenents and Landlord Legislation: Southern Rhodesia 1890–1930." *Journal of Southern African Studies* 5, no. 1 (1978): 86–98.

"Report on Native Labour Conditions in the Province of Mozambique, Portuguese E. A. [1922]." *South African Labour Bulletin* 2, no. 2 (1975): 14–27.

Reynolds, R. "The British South Africa Company's Central Settlement Farm, Marandellas, 1907–1910—From the Papers of H. K. Scorror." *Rhodesiana* 10 (1964): 1–16.

Richardson, A. S. R. "Farm Labour in Rhodesia." *Rhodesia Agricultural Journal* 3 (1905/06): 537–41.

Rita-Ferreira, A. "Labour Emigration Among the Mocambique Thonga: Comments on a Study by Marvin Harris." *Africa* 30, no. 2 (April 1960): 141–52.

Roberts, H. W. "The Development of the Southern Rhodesian Tobacco Industry." *South African Journal of Economics* 19 (1951): 177–88.

Sanderson, F. E. "The Development of Labour Migration from Nyasaland." *Journal of African History* 11, 2 (1961): 259–71.

Scott, Peter. "The Tobacco Industry of Southern Rhodesia." *Economic Geography* 28, no. 3 (July 1952): 189–206.

———. "Migrant Labor in Southern Rhodesia." *Geographical Review* 44, no. 1 (1954): 29–48.

———. "The Role of Northern Rhodesia in African Labor Migration." *Geographical Review* 44, no. 3 (1954): 432–34.

"Seasonal Notes on Tobacco Culture—Seed Beds." *Rhodesian Agricultural Journal* 27 (1930): 1032–34.

"Senex". "Treatment of Native Servants." *Native Affairs Department Annual* 2 (1924): 49–51.

Sibanda, Arnold. "Theoretical Problems on the Development of Capitalism in Zimbabwe (Towards a Critique of Giovanni Arrighi)." *Zimbabwe Journal of Economics* 1, no. 2 (January 1985): 11–20.

Swai, Bonaventure. "The Labour Shortage in 1930s Kilimanjaro and the Subsequent Employment of Child Labour." *Utafiti* 4, no. 2 (1979): 111–32.

Taylor, C. T. C. "Lomagundi." *Rhodesiana* 10 (1964): 17–44.

Thompson, E. P. "Time, Work-Discipline, and Industrial Capitalism." *Past and Present* 38 (1967): 56–97.

———. "The Moral Economy of the English Crowd in the Eighteenth Century." *Past and Present* 50 (1971): 76–136.

Thornton, S. "The Land Bank, Its Functions and How It Operates." *Rhodesia Agricultural Journal* 25 (1928): 411–34.

"Tobacco Production Cost." *Rhodesia Agricultural Journal* 25 (1928).

"Tobacco Sale; Some Hints and Suggestions." *Rhodesia Agricultural Journal* 9 (1911/12): 507–11.

Turrell, Rob. "Kimberley's Model Compounds." *Journal of African History* 25 (1984): 59–75.

Vail, Leroy. "The State and the Creation of Colonial Malawi's Agricultural Economy." In *Imperialism, Colonialism and Hunger: East and Central Africa*, ed. Robert I. Rotberg. Lexington: Lexington Books, 1983.

Van Onselen, Charles. "The Role of Collaborators in the Rhodesian Mining Industry, 1900–1935." *African Affairs* 72, no. 289 (1973): 401–18.

————. "Worker Consciousness in Black Miners: Southern Rhodesia, 1900–1920." In *Studies in the History of African Mine Labour in Colonial Zimbabwe,* edited by Charles van Onselen and I. R. Phimister. Salisbury: Mambo Press, 1978.

————. "Sex and Social Control in the Rhodesian Mine Compounds, 1900–1933." *South African Labour Bulletin* 1, no. 7 (November 1974): 17–31.

————. "Black Workers in Central African Industry: A Critical Essay on the Historiography and Sociology of Rhodesia." *Journal of Southern African Studies* 1, no. 2 (1975): 228–46.

Wadsworth, V. M. "Native Labour in Agriculture (part 1—Tobacco)." *Rhodesia Agricultural Journal* 47, no. 3 (1950): 234–53.

————. "Native Labour in Agriculture (part 2—Maize)." *Rhodesia Agricultural Journal* 47, no. 6 (1950): 486–93.

Newspapers and Periodicals

Government Tobacco Research Station Magazine, 1926.

Rhodesia Herald, 1907–45.

The Countryside: The Official Organ of the Rhodesia Agricultural Union, 1928–43.

Unpublished Sources

National Archives of Zimbabwe (NAZ)

Banket, Magistrate's Court, Criminal Cases, 1933–40
Bindura, Farmers' Association Minute Books, 1910–29
Bindura, Magistrate's Court, Criminal Cases, 1935–37
British South Africa Police, Inquests, 1928–33
Compound Inspectors Monthly Reports, 1940–44
Concession, Magistrate's Court, Criminal Cases, 1929–50
Darwendale, Magistrate's Court, Criminal Cases, 1927–38
Gwebi Experimental Farm, Experiments, Crops, 1912–23
High Commissioner for Southern Rhodesia, Correspondence
Land Bank, Correspondence 1912–45
Lomagundi, Census, Natives Employed, 1936–46
Lomagundi, Magistrate's Court, Criminal Cases, 1942

Lomagundi, Corrspondence, 1894–1939

Mazoe, Census, Natives Employed, 1936

Mazoe, Correspondence, 1897–1940

Mazoe, Farmers' Association Minute Books, 1904–15

Medical Treatment to Natives, 1925–31

Motor Lorry Service for Migrant Native Labour

Native Affairs Department, Records, 1899–1945.

Native Juveniles Employment Act, 1926–28

Native Labour Board, Correspondence

Public Health, 1924–36

Recruitment of Native Labor, 1925–51

Rhodesia Agricultural Union, Reports, 1925–27

Rhodesia Native Labour Bureau, Unpaid Wages, 1929

Rhodesia Tobacco Association, Correspondence

Scurvy, 1937–39

Sinoia, District Court, Civil Cases, 1924–39

Sinoia, Magistrate's Court, Criminal Cases, 1933–37

Sipolilo, Magistrate's Court, Criminal Cases, 1924–30

Tobacco Experiment Station Annual Reports, 1926–27

Tobacco, General Correspondence, 1928–47

Umvukwes Farmers and Tobacco Growers Association Minute Books, 1913–52

Public Records Office, London (PRO)

COLONIAL OFFICE [C.O.]
Recruitment of Native Labour for Southern Rhodesia
Report of Committee on Native Labour [Nyasaland]
Transport of Nyasaland Labour to and from Southern Rhodesia—Proposed Road Transport Service

DOMINION OFFICE [D.O.]
Industries: Southern Rhodesia—Growth and development of the Tobacco Industry in Southern Rhodesia
Native Affairs: Southern Rhodesia Wages for Natives

Theses and Dissertations

Boeder, Robert Benson. "Malawians Abroad. The History of Labor Emigration From Malawi To Its Neighbors, 1890 to the Present." Ph.D. diss., Michigan State University, 1974.

England, Kersten. "A Political Economy of Black Female Labour in Zimbabwe 1900–1980." B.A. Honours Thesis, University of Manchester, 1982.

Machingaidze, Victor Evan Mathia. "The Development of Settler Capitalist Agriculture in Southern Rhodesia, with Particular Reference to the Role of the State, 1908–1939." Ph.D. diss., University of London, 1980.

Makambe, Elioth Petros. "The African Immigrant Factor in Southern Rhodesia, 1890–1930: The Origin and Influence of External Elements In a Colonial Setting." Ph.D. diss., York University, 1979.

Margolis, W. "The Position of the Native Population in the Economic Life of Southern Rhodesia." M.A. Thesis, University of South Africa, 1938.

Seminar and Conference Papers

Masocha, Shepard. "The Tobacco Research Board, 1935–1965: A History with Special Reference to the Flue-Cured Virginia Tobacco Industry of Southern Rhodesia." Department of Economic History Seminar Paper, University of Zimbabwe, 1991.

Steele, Murray C. "The African Agricultural Labour Supply Crisis, 1924–26." Paper presented at Department of Economics, University of Rhodesia, October 4, 1973.

Interviews

Binali, Sani, Gabaza Farm, Beatrice. Interview by the author. September 5, 1996. NAZ.

Burton, Ian, Gabaza Farm, Beatrice. Interview by the author. September 5, 1996. NAZ.

Chidemo, Senesai, Choto Homestead, Hwedza. Interview by the author. August 31, 1996. NAZ.

Chimombe, Adam, Chishawasha. Interview by Elizabeth Schmidt. November 23, 1986. Copies in possession of the interviewer.

Chindawi, Chakanyuka, Chiweshe. Interview by L. L. Bessant and Elvis Muringai. December 12, 1984. NAZ.

Chivandire, Ganda, Shopo, Chiweshe. Interview by L. L. Bessant and Elvis Muringai. December 19, 1984. NAZ.

Chiwocha, Chari, Mukondzongi, Chiweshe. Interview by L. L. Bessant and Elvis Muringai. December 17, 1984. NAZ.

Choto, Dake, Mushangane Farm, Marondera. Interview by the author. August 22, 1996. NAZ.

Colbourne, Richard, Woodleigh Farm, Banket. Interview by the author. May 13, 1985. NAZ.

Gatsi, Philemon, Shopo, Chiweshe. Interview by L. L. Bessant and Elvis Muringai. December 7, 1984. NAZ.

Gordon, Trevor, Audley End Farm, Darwendale. Interview by the author. May 11, 1985. NAZ.

Howell, Michael, Harare. Interview by the author. December 12, 1984 and February 25, 1985. NAZ.

Jarata, Misheck, Katena, Chiweshe. Interview by L. L. Bessant and Elvis Muringai. December 6, 1984. NAZ.

Kandiero, Bonifasio, Gabaza Farm, Beatrice. Interview by the author. September 5, 1996. NAZ.

Kaviya, Gweshe, Chiweshe. Interview by L. L. Bessant and Elvis Muringai. December 11, 1984. NAZ.

Keevil, Bruce, Dodhill Farm, Chegutu. Interview by the author. March 30, 1985. NAZ.

Khamiso, Kachepa, Grove Farm, Acturas. Interview by the author. January 23, 1985. NAZ.

Liwakwa, Erina, Gabaza Farm, Beatrice. Interview by the author. September 5, 1996. NAZ.

Makina, Lyman, Grove Farm, Acturas. Interview by the author. January 23, 1985. NAZ.

Makonyonga, Handina, Chihota, Chishawasha. Interview by Elizabeth Schmidt. February 15, 1986. Copies in possession of the interviewer.

Makumbira, Jana, Munemo Farm, Marondera. Interview by the author. August 22, 1996. NAZ.

Mandaza, Mugari, Nyakudya Village, Chiweshe. Interview by L. L. Bessant and Elvis Muringai. December 13, 1984. NAZ.

Marangwanda, Z. C., Katena, Chiweshe. Interview by L. L. Bessant and Elvis Muringai. December 6, 1984. NAZ.

Mhindurwa, Hamundidi, Chaitezyi, Chishawasha. Interview by Elizabeth Schmidt. January 26, 1986. Copies in possession of the interviewer.

Mkondwa, Eddison, Munemo Farm, Marondera. Interview by the author. August 22, 1996. NAZ.

Monanji, Emidres, Gabaza Farm, Beatrice. Interview by the author. September 5, 1996. NAZ.

Mtikira, Wilson, Grove Farm, Acturas. Interview by the author. January 23, 1985. NAZ.

Murambwa, Grove Farm, Arcturus. Interview by the author. January 23, 1985. NAZ.

Muvra, Grove Farm, Acturas. Interview by the author. January 23, 1985. NAZ.

Mwandenga, Chibaiso, Choto Homestead, Hwedza. Interview by the author. August 31, 1996. NAZ.

Mwandela, Namazo, Gabaza Farm, Beatrice. Interview by the author. September 5, 1996. NAZ.

Mwicha, Magombo, Gabaza Farm, Beatrice. Interview by the author. September 5, 1996. NAZ.

Nazombe, Divarson, Gabaza Farm, Beatrice. Interview by the author. September 5, 1996. NAZ.

Palmer, Eric D., Harare. Interview by the author. December 12, 1984 and February 25, 1985. NAZ.

Purchase, G. T., Harare. Interview by the author. February 4, 1985. NAZ.

Quinton, H. J., Harare. Interview by the author. October 2, 1984 and December 17, 1984. NAZ.

Rali, Fraser, Gabaza Farm, Beatrice. Interview by the author. September 5, 1996. NAZ.

Saidi, Grove Farm, Arcturus. Interview by the author. January 23, 1985. NAZ.

Scott, John, Rainbow Nursery Farm, Banket. Interview by the author. May 11, 1985. NAZ.

Sinclair, David, Solario Farm, Banket. Interview by the author. May 13, 1985. NAZ.

Sinoia, Grove Farm, Acturas. Interview by the author. January 23, 1985. NAZ.

Smith, Lance, Pindi Park Farm, Banket. Interview by the author. May 8, 1985. NAZ.

Staunton, Ashley, Grove Farm, Acturas. Interview by the author. January 23, 1985. NAZ.

Thurburn, Duda, Stround Farm, Trelawney. Interview by the author. May 9, 1985. NAZ.

Visani, Fillimon, Gabaza Farm, Beatrice. Interview by the author. September 5, 1996. NAZ.

Wise, Nina, Rainbow Nursery Farm, Banket. Interview by the author. May 11, 1985. NAZ.

Index

Monographs in International Studies

Titles Available from Ohio University Press

Southeast Asia Series

No. 56   Duiker, William J. Vietnam Since the Fall of Saigon. 1989. Updated ed. 401 pp. Paper 0-89680-162-4 $20.00.

No. 64   Dardjowidjojo, Soenjono. Vocabulary Building in Indonesian: An Advanced Reader. 1984. 664 pp. Paper 0-89680-118-7 $30.00.

No. 65   Errington, J. Joseph. Language and Social Change in Java: Linguistic Reflexes of Modernization in a Traditional Royal Polity. 1985. 210 pp. Paper 0-89680-120-9 $25.00.

No. 66   Binh, Tran Tu. The Red Earth: A Vietnamese Memoir of Life on a Colonial Rubber Plantation. Tr. by John Spragens. 1984. 102 pp. (SEAT*, V. 5) Paper 0-89680-119-5 $11.00.

No. 68   Syukri, Ibrahim. History of the Malay Kingdom of Patani. 1985. 135 pp. Paper 0-89680-123-3 $15.00.

No. 69   Keeler, Ward. Javanese: A Cultural Approach. 1984. 559 pp. Paper 0-89680-121-7 $25.00.

No. 70   Wilson, Constance M. and Lucien M. Hanks. Burma-Thailand Frontier Over Sixteen Decades: Three Descriptive Documents. 1985. 128 pp. Paper 0-89680-124-1 $11.00.

No. 71   Thomas, Lynn L. and Franz von Benda-Beckmann, eds. Change and Continuity in Minangkabau: Local, Regional, and Historical Perspectives on West Sumatra. 1985. 353 pp. Paper 0-89680-127-6 $16.00.

No. 72   Reid, Anthony and Oki Akira, eds. The Japanese Experience in Indonesia: Selected Memoirs of 1942–1945. 1986. 424 pp., 20 illus. (SEAT, V. 6) Paper 0-89680-132-2 $20.00.

* Southeast Asia Translation Project Group

249

No. 74   McArthur M. S. H. Report on Brunei in 1904. Introduced and Annotated by A. V. M. Horton. 1987. 297 pp. Paper 0-89680-135-7 $15.00.

No. 75   Lockard, Craig A. From Kampung to City: A Social History of Kuching, Malaysia, 1820–1970. 1987. 325 pp. Paper 0-89680-136-5 $20.00.

No. 76   McGinn, Richard, ed. Studies in Austronesian Linguistics. 1986. 516 pp. Paper 0-89680-137-3 $20.00.

No. 77   Muego, Benjamin N. Spectator Society: The Philippines Under Martial Rule. 1986. 232 pp. Paper 0-89680-138-1 $17.00.

No 79   Walton, Susan Pratt. Mode in Javanese Music. 1987. 278 pp. Paper 0-89680-144-6 $15.00.

No. 80   Nguyen Anh Tuan. South Vietnam: Trial and Experience. 1987. 477 pp., tables. Paper 0-89680-141-1 $18.00.

No. 82   Spores, John C. Running Amok: An Historical Inquiry. 1988. 190 pp. paper 0-89680-140-3 $13.00.

No. 83   Malaka, Tan. From Jail to Jail. Tr. by Helen Jarvis. 1911. 1209 pp., three volumes. (SEAT V. 8) Paper 0-89680-150-0 $55.00.

No. 84   Devas, Nick, with Brian Binder, Anne Booth, Kenneth Davey, and Roy Kelly. Financing Local Government in Indonesia. 1989. 360 pp. Paper 0-89680-153-5 $20.00.

No. 85   Suryadinata, Leo. Military Ascendancy and Political Culture: A Study of Indonesia's Golkar. 1989. 235 pp., illus., glossary, append., index, bibliog. Paper 0-89680-154-3 $18.00.

No. 86   Williams, Michael. Communism, Religion, and Revolt in Banten in the Early Twentieth Century. 1990. 390 pp. Paper 0-89680-155-1 $14.00.

No. 87   Hudak, Thomas. The Indigenization of Pali Meters in Thai Poetry. 1990. 247 pp. Paper 0-89680-159-4 $15.00.

No. 88   Lay, Ma Ma. Not Out of Hate: A Novel of Burma. Tr. by Margaret Aung-Thwin. Ed. by William Frederick. 1991. 260 pp. (SEAT V. 9) Paper 0-89680-167-5 $20.00.

No. 89   Anwar, Chairil. The Voice of the Night: Complete Poetry and Prose of Chairil Anwar. 1992. Revised Edition. Tr. by Burton Raffel. 196 pp. Paper 0-89680-170-5 $20.00.

No. 90   Hudak, Thomas John, tr., The Tale of Prince Samuttakote: A Buddhist Epic from Thailand. 1993. 230 pp. Paper 0-89680-174-8 $20.00.

No. 91 Roskies, D. M., ed. Text/Politics in Island Southeast Asia: Essays in Interpretation. 1993. 330 pp. Paper 0-89680-175-6 $25.00.

No. 92 Schenkhuizen, Marguérite, translated by Lizelot Stout van Balgooy. Memoirs of an Indo Woman: Twentieth-Century Life in the East Indies and Abroad. 1993. 312 pp. Paper 0-89680-178-0 $25.00.

No. 93 Salleh, Muhammad Haji. Beyond the Archipelago: Selected Poems. 1995. 247 pp. Paper 0-89680-181-0 $20.00.

No. 94 Federspiel, Howard M. A Dictionary of Indonesian Islam. 1995. 327 pp. Bibliog. Paper 0-89680-182-9 $25.00.

No. 95 Leary, John. Violence and the Dream People: The Orang Asli in the Malayan Emergency 1948–1960. 1995. 275 pp. Maps, illus., tables, appendices, bibliog., index. Paper 0-89680-186-1 $22.00.

No. 96 Lewis, Dianne. *Jan Compagnie* in the Straits of Malacca 1641–1795. 1995. 176 pp. Map, appendices, bibliog., index. Paper 0-89680-187-x. $18.00.

No. 97 Schiller, Jim and Martin-Schiller, Barbara. Imagining Indonesia: Cultural Politics and Political Culture. 1996. 384 pp., notes, glossary, bibliog. Paper 0-89680-190-x. $30.00.

No. 98 Bonga, Dieuwke Wendelaar. Eight Prison Camps: A Dutch Family in Japanese Java. 1996. 233 pp., illus., map, glossary. Paper 0-89680-191-8. $18.00.

No. 99 Gunn, Geoffrey C. Language, Ideology, and Power in Brunei Darussalam. 1996. 328 pp., glossary, notes, bibliog., index. Paper 0-86980-192-6 $24.00.

No. 100 Martin, Peter W., Conrad Ozog, and Gloria R. Poedjosoedarmo, eds. Language Use and Language Change in Brunei Darussalam. 1996. 390 pp., maps, notes, bibliog. Paper 0-89680-193-4 $26.00.

No. 101 Ooi, Keat Gin. Japanese Empire in the Tropics: Selected Documents and Reports of the Japanese Period in Sarawak, Northwest Borneo, 1941–1945. 1998. 740 pp., two volumes. Illus., maps, notes, index. Paper 0-89680-199-3 $50.00.

No. 102 Aung-Thwin, Michael A. Myth and History in the Historiography of Early Burma: Paradigms, Primary Sources, and Prejudices. 1998. 210 pp., maps, notes, bibliography, index. Paper 0-89680-201-9 $21.00.

No. 103 Pauka, Kirstin. Theater and Martial Arts in West Sumatra:

Randai and Silek of the Minang Kabou. 1999. 288 pp., illus.,
map, appendices, notes, bibliography, index. Paper 0-89680-
205-1 $26.00.

Africa Series

No. 43   Harik, Elsa M. and Donald G. Schilling. The Politics of Education in Colonial Algeria and Kenya. 1984. 102 pp. Paper 0-
89680-117-9 $12.50.

No. 45   Keto, C. Tsehloane. American-South African Relations
1784–1980: Review and Select Bibliography. 1985. 169 pp.
Paper 0-89680-128-4 $11.00.

No. 46   Burness, Don, ed. Wanasema: Conversations with African
Writers. 1985. 103 pp. paper 0-89680-129-2 $11.00.

No. 47   Switzer, Les. Media and Dependency in South Africa: A Case
Study of the Press and the Ciskei "Homeland." 1985. 97 pp.
Paper 0-89680-130-6 $10.00.

No. 51   Clayton, Anthony and David Killingray. Khaki and Blue: Military and Police in British Colonial Africa. 1989. 347 pp. Paper
0-89680-147-0 $20.00.

No. 52   Northrup, David. Beyond the Bend in the River: African
Labor in Eastern Zaire, 1865–1940. 1988. 282 pp. Paper 0-
89680-151-9 $15.00.

No. 53   Makinde, M. Akin. African Philosophy, Culture, and Traditional Medicine. 1988. 172 pp. Paper 0-89680-152-7 $16.00.

No. 54   Parson, Jack, ed. Succession to High Office in Botswana:
Three Case Studies. 1990. 455 pp. Paper 0-89680-157-8
$20.00.

No. 56   Staudinger, Paul. In the Heart of the Hausa States. Tr. by Jo-
hanna E. Moody. Foreword by Paul Lovejoy. 1990. In two volumes., 469 + 224 pp., maps, apps. Paper 0-89680-160-8 (2
vols.) $35.00.

No. 57   Sikainga, Ahmad Alawad. The Western Bahr Al-Ghazal
under British Rule, 1898–1956. 1991. 195 pp. Paper 0-89680-
161-6 $15.00.

No. 58   Wilson, Louis E. The Krobo People of Ghana to 1892: A Political and Social History. 1991. 285 pp. Paper 0-89680-164-0
$20.00.

No. 59   du Toit, Brian M. Cannabis, Alcohol, and the South African

Student: Adolescent Drug Use, 1974–1985. 1991. 176 pp., notes, tables. Paper 0-89680-166-7 $17.00.

No. 60   **Falola, Toyin and Dennis Itavyar, eds.** The Political Economy of Health in Africa. 1992. 258 pp., notes, tables. Paper 0-89680-166-7 $20.00.

No. 61   **Kiros, Tedros.** Moral Philosophy and Development: The Human Condition in Africa. 1992. 199 pp., notes. Paper 0-89680-171-3 $20.00.

No. 62   **Burness, Don.** Echoes of the Sunbird: An Anthology of Contemporary African Poetry. 1993. 198 pp. Paper 0-89680-173-x $17.00.

No. 64   **Nelson, Samuel H.** Colonialism in the Congo Basin 1880–1940. 1994. 290 pp. Index. Paper 0-89680-180-2 $23.00.

No. 66   **Ilesanmi, Simeon Olusegun.** Religious Pluralism and the Nigerian State. 1996. 336 pp., maps, notes, bibliog., index. Paper 0-89680-194-2 $23.00.

No. 67   **Steeves, H. Leslie.** Gender Violence and the Press: The St. Kizito Story. 1997. 176 pp., illus., notes, bibliog., index. Paper 0-89680195-0 $17.95.

No. 68   **Munro, William A.** The Moral Economy of the State: Conservation, Community Development, and State-Making in Zimbabwe. 1998. 510 pp., maps, notes, bibliog., index. Paper 0-89680-202-7 $26.00.

No. 69   **Rubert, Steven C.** A Most Promising Weed: A History of Tobacco Farming and Labor in Colonial Zimbabwe, 1890–1945. 1998. 264 pp., illus., maps, notes, bibliog., index. Paper 0-89680-203-5 $26.00.

Latin America Series

No. 9   **Tata, Robert J.** Structural Changes in Puerto Rico's Economy: 1947–1976. 1981. 118 pp. Paper 0-89680-107-1 $12.00.

No. 13   **Henderson, James D.** Conservative Thought in Latin America: The Ideas of Laureano Gomez. 1988. 229 pp. Paper 0-89680-148-9 $16.00.

No. 17   **Mijeski, Kenneth J., ed.** The Nicaraguan Constitution of 1987: English Translation and Commentary. 1991. 355 pp. Paper 0-89680-165-9 $25.00.

No. 18   **Finnegan, Pamela.** The Tension of Paradox: José Donoso's

The Obscene Bird of Night as Spiritual Exercises. 1992. 204 pp. Paper 0-89680-169-1 $15.00.

No. 19   **Kim, Sung Ho and Thomas W. Walker, eds.** Perspectives on War and Peace in Central America. 1992. 155 pp., notes, bibliog. Paper 0-89680-172-1 $17.00.

No. 20   **Becker, Marc.** Mariátegui and Latin American Marxist Theory. 1993. 239 pp. Paper 0-89680-177-2 $20.00.

No. 21   **Boschetto-Sandoval, Sandra M. and Marcia Phillips McGowan, eds.** Claribel Alegría and Central American Literature. 1994. 233 pp., illus. Paper 0-89680-179-9 $20.00.

No. 22   **Zimmerman, Marc.** Literature and Resistance in Guatemala: Textual Modes and Cultural Politics from El Señor Presidente to Rigoberta Menchú. 1995. 2 volume set 320 + 370 pp., notes, bibliog. Paper 0-89680-183-7 $50.00.

No. 23   **Hey, Jeanne A. K.** Theories of Dependent Foreign Policy: The Case of Ecuador in the 1980s. 1995. 280 pp., map, tables, notes, bibliog., index. Paper 0-89680-184-5 $22.00.

No. 24   **Wright, Bruce E.** Theory in the Practice of the Nicaraguan Revolution. 1995. 320 pp., notes, illus., bibliog., index. Paper 0-89680-185-3. $23.00.

No. 25   **Mann, Carlos Guevara.** Panamanian Militarism: A Historical Interpretation. 1996. 243 pp., illus., map, notes, bibliog., index. Paper 0-89680-189-6 $23.00.

No. 26   **Armony, Ariel.** Argentina, the United States, and the Anti-Communist Crusade in Central America. 1997. 305 pp. (est.) illus., maps, notes, bibliog., index. Paper 0-89680-196-9 $26.00.

No. 27   **Sandoval, Ciro A. and Sandra M. Boschetto-Sandoval, eds.** José María Arguedas: Reconsiderations for Latin American Studies. 1998. 350 pp., notes, bibliog. Paper 0-89680-200-0 $23.00.

No. 28   **Zimmerman, Marc and Raúl Rojas, eds.** Voices From the Silence: Guatemalan Literature of Resistance. 1998. 572 pp., bibliog., index. Paper 0-89680-198-5 $23.00.

Ordering Information

Individuals are encouraged to patronize local bookstores wherever possible. Orders for titles in the Monographs in International Studies may be placed directly through the Ohio University Press, Scott Quadrangle, Athens, Ohio 45701-2979. Individuals should remit payment by check,

VISA, or MasterCard.* Those ordering from the United Kingdom, Continental Europe, the Middle East, and Africa should order through Academic and University Publishers Group, 1 Gower Street, London WC1E, England. Orders from the Pacific Region, Asia, Australia, and New Zealand should be sent to East-West Export Books, c/o the University of Hawaii Press, 2840 Kolowalu Street, Honolulu, Hawaii 96822, USA.

Individuals ordering from outside of the U.S. should remit in U.S. funds to Ohio University Press either by International Money Order or by a check drawn on a U.S. bank.** Most out-of-print titles may be ordered from University Microfilms, Inc., 300 North Zeeb Road, Ann Arbor, Michigan 48106, USA.

Prices are subject to change.

* Please add $3.50 for the first book and $.75 for each additional book for shipping and handling.

** Outside the U.S. please add $4.50 for the first book and $.75 for each additional book

Ohio University
Center for International Studies

The Ohio University Center for International Studies was established to help create within the university and local communities a greater awareness of the world beyond the United States. Comprising programs in African, Latin American, Southeast Asian, Development and Administrative studies, the Center supports scholarly research, sponsors lectures and colloquia, encourages course development within the university curriculum, and publishes the Monographs in International Studies series with the Ohio University Press. The Center and its programs also offer an interdisciplinary Master of Arts degree in which students may focus on one of the regional or topical concentrations, and may also combine academics with training in career fields such as journalism, business, and language teaching. For undergraduates, major and certificate programs are also available.

For more information, contact the Vice Provost for International Studies, Burson House, Ohio University, Athens, Ohio 45701.